# A New Approach to Teacher and Education in the Emerging Indian Society

**Published by**
**Saurabh Publishing House**

# A New Approach to Teacher and Education in the Emerging Indian Society

Pradeep Aggarwal

Publishing House
4735/22, Prakash Deep Building,
Ansari Road, Daryaganj,
New Delhi-110002

**Published by :**
**SAURABH PUBLISHING HOUSE**

**Distributed by :**
**LOTUS PRESS PUBLISHERS & DISTRIBUTORS**
Unit No. 220, Second Floor, 4735/22, Prakash Deep Building,
Ansari Road, Daryaganj, New Delhi - 110002
Ph : 011-23280047, 32903912, 098118-38000
E-mail : lotus_press@sify.com

Saurabh Publishing is an imprint of
**Lotus Press Publishers & Distributors**

**A New Approach to Teacher and Education in the Emerging Indian Society**



**ISBN** : 978-93-83045-07-5 (P/B)



Printed at : Bharat Offset Works, Delhi

# Preface

In the ancient Indian society the teacher always enjoyed a dignified place. During the Vedic and Post-Vedic periods the teacher's place was second to that of God only. He was more respected than the king in society. The Guru-Ashrama was known as the Gurukul (the family of the teacher) and the Guru was regarded as a rishi (sage) or Acharya (the one who practises what he professes). The Guru was given this significant place, because without him it was impossible to attain knowledge. The Guru was the guide and could help anyone to carve out his course of action. He used to bring light wherever there was darkness. Thus, the people always felt his necessity whenever there was a difficulty in solving any issue or problem. During the Upanishadic period as well, when self-study was considered as dignified the place of Guru in society remained intact. It was believed that no knowledge could come without the assistance from the Guru. In other words, it was believed that the attainment of salvation was not possible without the help of the Guru.

The teacher was expected to lead a life of penance free of worldly things. He, too, was required to follow all the rules of strict discipline, thinking and meditation which were prescribed for the students. We find many references to such a position in the Maitrayan Upanishad. After the demise of the Guru even one of his disciples could succeed him if his son was not considered worthy of the same.

This book deals with the topics of—*Philosophy and Education; Aims of Education in Indian Society; History of Indian*

*Education : Ancient to Medieval; Growth of Modern Education System; Education in Contemporary India; Education Under Constitution; Women Education in Society; Education to Disabled; Equalization of Educational Opportunities under New Education Policy; Teacher Training Programme in Education; National Integration and Education;* etc.

I hope that students and those in the education field will find it useful for academic and competitive examinations. I owe a deep sense of gratitude to my publisher for materializing my present endeavour.

**Pradeep Aggarwal**

# Contents

# 1

# Philosophy and Education

The highest aim according to Indian philosophy is the attainment of liberation and since liberation cannot be achieved without the true knowledge of self, the ultimate aim of all educational endeavour is self-realization. From the legendry gurus of Rigvedic and Upanish adic ages down to modern philosopher—educators—Tagore, Vivekananda, Gandhi, Dayananda, Aurobindo—the highest aim has been accepted in most distinctive terms. The attainment of self-realization is the most difficult work which a human being has to perform before he can hope to realize that much longed for eternal peace for which he is struggling consciously or unconsciously.

It is believed that Indian education reached its climax and achieved the highest degree to efficiency and success in this period. The Upanishads were produced during this period. The Upanishads are universally admitted to contain the utmost possibilities of human speculation regarding some of the ultimate problems of life and metaphysical mysteries. Vedic schools were schools of both law and learning. There was no divorce between theory and practice, thought and life, speculation and action. The seats of learning were also the centres of life and influenced the community life also. These ancient schools were colonies in which were centred the piety, talent and the culture of the community, from which they radiated in all directions. They represented the highest level of life, making the high water-markes of the nation's progress. The vedic schools were the chief agents in the spread of culture and social system resulting from the Vedas.

Education in ancient times in India, though always looking to the spirit did not neglect the other aspects of temporal life. I was clearly understood that self-realization could be achieved only by following certain values. Accordingly these values were reflected in the curriculum. The curriculum was divided into two parts higher knowledge (*para vidya*) and the lower knowledge (*apara vidya*) and the two parts were not contradictory to each other. In fact the lower knowledge (*apara vidya*) or the study of secular subjects formed the basis for the higher knowledge (*para vidya*) or spiritual realization or self-realization. Knowledge was to be gained not merely for the sake of knowledge but to make man moral and practical.

One of the best accounts of the curriculum construction is to be found in the Upanishads. The Upanishads conceive of the human being as consisting of five elements which envelope one another in succession. That is why these are named as 'Kosa'—sheaths or coverings.

**(1) 'Adandamaya Kosa'.** This last one is the self which consists of pure bliss.

**(2) 'Anoamaya Kosa'.** This is the gross physical sheath which is the first and the outermost.

**(3) 'Manomaya Kosa'.** This consists of feeling and imagination.

**(4) 'Pranamaya Kosa'.** The second one is that of vital breath *i.e.,* the physiological.

**(5) 'Vajnanamana Kosa'.** This comprises intellectual and rational pursuits.

A balanced curriculum must meet the needs of all these aspects of the human being. The curriculum, therefore, must include physical sciences and technology to meet the first two needs, social sciences and humanities dealing with the next two and religious pursuits with the last one.

These are two paths following any of which man can reach, the highest goal—the 'Pravirithi Marg' and the 'Nirvithi Marg.' The second path is extremely difficult. Hence, it is adopted by rare personalities who directly embark upon the last stage of life that it *Sanyasa* after finishing their first period of life, namely *Brahmacharya* The common man must follow the four stages in order to attain self realization. So in its broader sense, the whole life to an ancient philosopher was education. The ancient system of education enabled the students to live as responsible citizens of the real world. In view of this, the charge of other worldliness does not stand against Indian idealistic philosophy of life.

**Modern Indian Educational Philosophers Swami Vivekanand and Economic uplift.** To Swami Vivekananda, education had no meaning if it did not uplift the common mass of people. "So long as the millions live in hunger and ignorance, I hold every man a traitor who, having been educated at their expense, pays not the least heed to them. I consider that the great national sin is the neglect of the masses and that is one of the causes of our downfall." He reminded that the nation lived in the cottages and therefore it was the duty of every educated youngman to go from village to village and make the people understand their real condition, awake them from their long slumber and advise them how to improve their own miserable lot. The sunken vitality of the helpless victims of social injustice was to be restored physically, intellectually as well as spiritually. I call him a Mahatma who feels for the poor. Let these people be your God—think of them, work for them, pray for them incessantly—the lord will show you the way". In social education he had visualized effectiveness of audio-visual aids as he advised youngman to "go to a village in the evening with a camera, a globe, some maps etc."

**Education Must Reach Every Home.** Swami Vivekanand observed, "If the poor boy cannot come to education education, must go to him. There are thousands of single-minded, self-sacrificing 'synthesis' in our own country, going from village to village, teaching religion. If some of them can be organised as teachers of secular things also they will go from place to place, from door to door not only preaching but teaching also. Suppose two of these men go to a village in the evening with a camera, a globe, some maps etc, they can teach a great deal of Astronomy and Geography to the ignorant. By telling stories about different nations, they can give the poor a hundred time more information through the ear than they can get in a lifetime, through books".

**Rabindranath Tagore on Education Realism in Education.** Tagore thinks, "the last point is that our education should be in full touch with our complete life, economical, intellectual, aesthetic, social and spiritual; and our educational institutions should be in the very heart of society, connected with it by the living bonds of varied co-operations. For, true education is to realise at every step how training and knowledge have organic collection with our surroundings."

**Education and Physical Strength.** Again Swami Vivekanand has stated, "Be strong, my young friends that is my advice to you. You will be nearer to Heaven through football than through the study of the Gita. You will understand Gita better with your biceps, your muscles, a little stronger. You will understand the mighty genius and the mighty strength of Krishna better with a little strong blood in you. You will understand the Upanishads better and the glory of the Atma, when your body stands firm on your feet and you feel yourself as men."

**Gandhiji as an Educational Philosopher.** What was the Social Order that Gandhiji visualized? A society that would help each man realize the highest aim of his life in a co-operative endeavour to search after truth—is the answer. A co-operative approach implies love and fellow feeling and excludes all thought of hatred and exploitation. Thus, the social order has to be based on truth and non-violence, the other name of love. Exploitation in any form social, political, economic or religious must have to disappear, for it devastates the divine dignity of man. The economic and social structure of the society must depend on decentralised industry and agriculture. Everyone has to be independent for one's vital needs; for dependence brings helplessness and helplessness engenders exploitation. And yet, one has to be inter-dependent since a co-operative living demands it. To materialize this vision of a society, Gandhiji evolved a scheme of education after many trials and experiments over a period of 40 years. His ideas revolutionised the current thinking about education. In 1937 the All India National Educational Conference was held at Wardha which unanimously approved of his idea and appointed a committee of the leading educationists with Dr. Zakir Hussain as its chairman to give shape to Gandhiji's plan.

**Sriniketan as a Centre of Rural Re-construction.** The object of Sriniketan is to bring back life in its completeness into the village making them self-reliant and self-respectful acquainted with the cultural traditions of their own country and competent to make an efficient use of the modern resources for the improvement of their physical, intellectual and economic condition.

## PHILOSOPHIES OF EDUCATION AND CURRICULUM

The curriculum is the sum total of the school's efforts to influence learning, whether in the classroom, on the playground, or out of school. In the words of K.G. Saiyidain,

"The Curriculum is primarily an aid in the process adjusting the child to the environment in which he functions from day to day and in the environment in which he will have to organise his activities later".

Burbacher writes that the word curriculum has Latin origin "It is a runway, a course which one runs to reach a goal, a course of study."

Curriculum is a means by which the aims of the philosophy of education are attained.

## Philosophies and Curriculum

We have three philosophies of education *i.e.* Naturalism, Idealism and Pragmatism. All these three agree that desirable experiences should be provided to children. But they differ as to what type of experience should be provided and what should be the basis of the experience to be provided.

## Naturalism and the Curriculum

Naturalism has been defined by Joyce as "a system whose salient characteristic is the exclusion of whatever is spiritual, or indeed whatever is transcendental of experience from our philosophy of nature and man". James Ward writes that naturalism is the "doctrine that separates nature from God, sub-ordinates spirit to matter and sets-up unchangeable laws as supreme." Rousseau has been the outstanding exponent of naturalism in education.

Naturalism believes in negative education. Therefore, the child is not to be taught the traditional subject. The curriculum is conceived as a natural phenomena presented in the natural order before the child. No place is given in the curriculum to the conventional habits, ideas, knowledge and information built by sophisticated society. The primary place is given to the budding activities and interests of the child's own nature. The curriculum is to unfold the natural powers to the child in order to meet his natural needs. Hence, the curriculum will include those activities which spring naturally from the needs of the child's life.

Naturalism believes in the theory of 'self-teaching'. Rousseau says, "I like not explanations given in long discourses. Young people pay little attention to them and retain little from them. The things themselves! The things themselves! I shall never repeat offer, enough that we attach too much importance to words. With our chattering education we make nothing but chatteres." Again he writes, "I hate books" because they are a 'curse to children, they teach us to talk only that which we do not know.' "One who reads does not think." "By relieving school children of their course books I take away the chief cause of their misery."

**Rousseau has divided education into four stages.**

In the *first stage* he recommends purely physical education "All wickedness comes from weakness, a child is bad only because he is weak, make him strong and he will be good." Running; jumping and playing with simple objects of nature such as branches with fruits and flowers are the various activities recommended by him.

The *second stage* of childhood (five to twelve) is "the most critical period of human life." Organs are to be developed freely and senses should be given ample exercise. There should be no verbal lessons. No moral education or positive education is to be given. Education at this stage is non-intellectual and non-social and therefore, it is called Negative Education.

**Adolescence.** (Twelve to fifteen) is, the *third stage*, Rousseau recommends that child is to be taught physical sciences, language, mathematics, manual work, social relations, trade, music and drawing. The knowledge of these subjects is to be acquired through child's own experiences.

Geography is not to be taught through maps, globes and rather such aids. The child is to be encouraged to observe the rising and setting sun and the moon during different seasons and draw the inferences himself therefrom. Rousseau has recommended only one book and that is Robinson Crusoe.

The *fourth stage* is the youth. Regarding the education at this stage, he writes, "we have formed his body, his senses and his intelligence, it remains to give him a heart." In order to give a heart to Emile, Rousseau brings him back from isolation, to mix, not with aristocratic classes, but with the poor and the miserable in prison houses, to feel pity on them, to sympathies with them and thus, to have a love for them.

**Education of the Girls**

Rousseau thinks that women do not possess any individuality of their own. They should be regarded only as subordinate to the nature of man. He says, "The whole education of women ought to be relative to men. To please them, to be useful to them, to make themselves loved and honoured by them, to educate them when young...", "Every daughter should have the religion of her mother and to very wife that of her husband." Thus, Saphia, the wife of Emile gets training in Domestic Science, needle work, cooking etc., and in the art or pleasing her husband.

**Curriculum and the Idealism**

The chief representatives of the idealism are, Socrates, Plato, Fitcbe, Hegel, Hume, Kant, T.P. Nunn and Ross.

Plato believed that the highest ideal of life was the attainment of the highest good or God and for this he has suggested that the curriculum should aim at the inculcation of the three spiritual values, *i.e.* Truth, Beauty and Goodness. These three values determine three types of activities—intellectual, aesthetic and moral. Subjects represent these activities. Languages, Literature, Mathematics, Science, History and Geography represent intellectual activities Aesthetic activities are represented by Art and Poetry, Religion, Ethics and Metaphysics represent moral activities.

Nunn says that the schools should give place to those human activities, "that are of greatest and most permanent significance in the wider world, the grandest expressions of the human spirit." Thus, Nunn has given the idealist standpoint about the curriculum.

What are those human activities of greatest significance? These may be grouped under two heads:

*(i)* Activities that are essential for maintaining the standard for individual and social life. Care of health, manners, religion and social organization etc., are included in this group.

*(ii)* Activities those represent the worthy attainments of civilization. Under this group we may include literature, science mathematics, history, geography, art, etc.

**Pragmatism and Curriculum**

John Dewey is the chief exponent of the pragmatic philosophy.

Pragmatism is a middle way between naturalism and idealism. According to the pragmatic philosophy, whatever fulfills one's purposes and develops his life, is true. Pragmatism has no absolute values.

Pragmatism protests against the formality in instruction and considers learning as an active process rather than a passive acceptance of facts.

Dewey analyses the interests of the child into four groups.

*(i)* The interest in conversation or communication.

*(ii)* Interest in enquiry, or finding out things.

*(iii)* In making things or construction.

*(iv)* In artistic expression

The different activities of the real life will determine the contents of the curriculum.

Curriculum in pragmatism is based on four facts:

*(i)* Utility is the first consideration in curriculum construction. Useful experiences are to be provided in the school to the child. The curriculum is to include those subjects which impart knowledge and various types of skills which the child requires for his present as well as future life.

*(ii)* The child's own experiences, his occupations and activities should form the basis of curriculum construction.

*(iii)* The curriculum should be constructed according to the natural interests of the child at the successive stages of his development.

*(iv)* Curriculum should be guided by the principles of integration. It should not be divided into independent subjects.

The pragmatist thinks that the ideal student is lost in a self-projected obscurity and on the other hand the idealist thinks that the pragmatist student is a 'short-sight success-seeker' and untouched by spiritual consciousness.

## TEACHING AND PHILOSOPHIES OF EDUCATION

In the process of teaching all the three items of philosophies are to be considered together. The one is inseparable from the other. Each represents one point of view.

## Naturalism and Teaching

Naturalists start from the point of view of the goodness of the human nature. "Everything is good as it comes from the hand of the Author of nature. God made all things good; man meddle with them and they become evil" said Rousseau. Accordingly the teacher has to proceed on the assumption that in no child there is anything evil and has to work with the child in such a way that he acts according to the laws of nature with respect to the child mind and does not violate the design of God. Naturalism thus, tells us where and how to start. It points to the starting point.

## Idealism and Teaching

Idealism makes the spirit all important. It asks the educator to realize the divinity in the child and let the child unfold himself to make that Divinity patent which at present is latent. The teacher's job is to take care of him so that "the young mind should be saturated with the idea that it has been born in a human world which is in harmony with the world around it. Idealism makes the spirit all important, leading us to things as they ought to be. All the plants in this garden should be properly looked after and should be so looked after that they develop the quality of adaptation and acclimatization, without losing their individuality. The heritage is not only possessed, it should be preserved and improved, so that they proceed steadily towards their goal, their purpose in life, each individual attaining to what is collect self-realisation.

The teacher in this scheme of things, is the gardener. If naturalism marks the starting point, idealism points to the destination to be achieved in the future.

## Pragmatism and Teaching

Pragmatism refers to the activities in the living present. It takes nothing for granted, whether from the past or for the future. It believes in values, which are ever-changing. The data are two interacting entities: The child and the environment. The child is ever active, doing, doing, doing, While doing he is learning. While learning he is doing better. The discipline, with regard to the child, is of the child, not on the child, *i.e.*, self-discipline. Nothing eternal, nothing is binding from the past. The child is in the real situation. He must take the limitations of the situation which constitute indiscipline, acting spontaneously, pursuing his purposes, allowing other such purposes of others and thus, his activities are:

*(a)* Spontaneous activities.

*(b)* Purposeful activities.

*(c)* Socialised activities.

The teacher's job is to keep him alive to:

*(a)* His purposes.

*(b)* His capacities.

*(c)* His limitations.

so that he evolves his own discipline:

*(a)* Developes his own values.

*(b)* Makes his own adjustment.

and thus, releases himself.

**Pragmatism Points Out**

Face the child with real situations. Help him to adjust himself, not by a passive surrender but by a constant, dynamic interaction between himself and the changing situations, himself also changing all the while, for the improvement involves a change in his self. Doing and learning; learning by doing, let him have a perception of "self". Let him project himself into a self which he would like to be. Let him strive, struggle, change the situation, change his self and achieve, thus, realising his "self". All knowledge, all experiences are to be coordinated in human terms. All principles are just pointers. They are not to be taken as such. A perception of each has to be developed which is relative and related to the individual of the striving self. This self-conscious self is the architect of his dentiny.

Every classroom situation is a struggle between the self of the student and a problem. The teacher must take into account the existing physical and mental state of every, child and give each a vision of his infinite power to solve the problem in his own way. Let not the teacher think that the whole class should go together. As Rousseau said, "Human institutions are one mass of folly and contradiction". Teaching is individualization, Socialization and universalization all combined.

## AIMS OF EDUCATION

Educational aims in any country have varied with its political, social and economic conditions. The educational system of Greece and Rome raised an issue that is still very important in education today. Should education train good individuals or good citizens? Are the social needs in education more important than the needs of the individual? An individual is born with certain potentialities and natural endowments. It is the task of the educator to develop into a distinct individual. But personality development does not take place in a vacuum. Thus, we have to decide whether the individual or the society would occupy the first place in education.

### Educators who Emphasis Individual Aim of Education

To enable men to release, to mature, to discipline the human mind and spirit,.... this most influential of all the varieties of energy has always been the task of education. *(John H. Fischer.*

*"The Energies of Education" Education Age, November-December, 1965. P.42 Visual products Division, 3M Company St. Paul Minn).*

Schools exist to help children succeed. *(Gordon Mc. Ctoskey. Education and Public Understanding. New York: Harper & Row. Publishers, Inc. 1958 p. 297).*

Therefore, we would ask education to give us men with taste, respect for intelligence and independence of judgment that will give them confidence to approach the public for what it is a group of distinct individuals, not a lump of reflexes waiting to be conditioned. *(Monroe E. Spaght. The Bright Key. New York: Appleton-Century Crofts, 1965 p. 10).*

In Rigveda, education has been defined as something, which makes a man self-reliant and selfless.

The University Education Commission (1948) speaks about education in these words. "Education according to Indian tradition is initiation into the life of spirit, a training of human soul in the pursuit of truth and the practice of virtue."

According to Sir Percy Nunn, "Nothing good enters into the human world except in and through the free activities of individual men and women and that educational practice must be shaped to accord with that truth."

Aristotre thinks that "Education is the creation of a sound mind in a sound body".

Mahatma Gandhi, the father of Basic Education considers education as a means to develop man. He said "By education we mean an all round drawing out of the best in child and man body, mind and spirit".

Froebel regards education "As the process through which the child markes internal external".

In the words of Kant "Education is the development in the individual of all the perfection of which he is capable."

**Why Stress on Individual Aim**

**1. The Naturalists Support to the Individual Aim of Education.** The naturalists like Nunn and Rousseau are, of the view that the central aim of education is the autonomous development of the individual. According to Rousseau, "Everything is good as it comes from the hands of Author of Nature, but everything degenerates in the hand of man. God makes all things good. Man meddles with them and they become evil." It is, therefore, that education should be in accordance with the nature of the individual.

**2. The Biologist's Support to Individual Aim of Education.** According to Prof. G. Thompson, "Education is for the individual : Its function being to enable the individual to survive and live out its complete life. Education is improved to preserve the individual life." Education is given for the sake of the individual save him from destruction. Community exists for the individual, not the individual for the community. Community being the means and individual being the end, education should not set mean over the end. Individual and not society, therefore, should be the centre of all educational efforts and activities.

**3. The Psychologists Support to Individual Aim of Education.** The psychologists regard each individual a unique one. According to them no two children are identical. The function of education should be to develop the innate powers of the individual so that his maximum development may take place.

**4. The Spiritualists Support to Education.** The spiritualists are of the view that every individual is a separate entity and responsible for his own actions. Therefore, the main function of education should be to lead the individual to self-realisation. Swami Vivekanand states, "Man is potentially divine. The goal is to manifest this potentiality from within, by controlling nature—external and internal through education."

**5. The Progressivists Support to the Individual Aim of Education.** The progressivists hold the view that the progress and advancement of the world is due to great individuals born in different periods of history. It is, therefore, stated by them that the education process should secure condition for the complete development of individuality so that each individual may make his original contribution to the human life.

**Criticism of the Individual Aim of Education**

1. According to Raymont, an individual is only a figment of imagination. An individual cannot be conceived in isolation from society.
2. The exaggerated claim of the individual may have an adverse effect in the politics and economy of a country. The policy of 'Laissezfaire' is not conducive to national interests in the modern times.
3. The critics of individual aim believe that the individual left to himself is an animal, selfish and indisciplined. The animal instinct of man, if given, a loose reign is sure to lead him to the state of primitive barbarism where the law of jungle prevailed.
4. Absolute freedom to the individual should not be given. The individual may begin to assert that I must have what I want.

**Social Aim of Education.** The individual is regarded as endowed with a social nature, he is social by instinct. An individual seems everywhere and always to be caught up in an intricate web of social relations. Without them the newborn baby would almost perish. The social process and the educational process are essentially one and the same.

Curriculum is the social stuff out of which the individual realises itself.

**Narrow Interpretation of Social Aim of Education.** The protagonists of this view think that State is an idealized metaphysical entity over and above the individual citizen, superior in every way. Hence, the individual exists for the society. It is, therefore the State that should decide the aim, mode and type of education or training which an individual should receive for its welfare. The Spartan system of education in ancient times and the Nazi system of the recent past reflect this tendency. Undoubtedly such notions played a major role in world conflicts which led to the Two World Wars in 1914 and 1939.

**Broader Interpretation of the Social Aim of Education.** The Social aim of education finds expression in such concepts as 'education for social service', 'education for citizenship' and education for social efficiency'.

## Social Aim in Education

Social aim has been stressed as the supporters of this aim believe that an individual cannot live and develop in isolation from Society. Raymont says that the isolated individual is a figment of the imagination. The individual being a social animal, will be moulded to the needs of the society. The individual will develop through social contacts.

According to John Dewey, social aim in education is stressed as education should make each individual specially efficient and this social efficiency must be achieved by the positive use of individual powers and capacities in social occupations. A socially efficient individual is able to earn his livelihood. He also conforms to moral and social standards of conduct.

Gandhiji formulated the basic scheme with the objective of making public realise that education was not merely for the benefit of the individual but for needs of a predominantly rural and agrarian population.

**Limitation of Social Aim in Education**

1. Social aim of education envisages the individual as a non-entity and leaves little scope for his personality and unique characteristics to flourish.
2. Aggression and violence against neighbouring countries have resulted in educational aims of this type. Militant nationalism "my country, right or wrong", are attitudes which may develop in tender minds.
3. In recent years there has been a tendency in Western countries among the young people to rebel against the cult of social efficiency. Many students prefer the development and growth of individuality and would want to give up the struggle for social efficiency.

Definitions which Stress Individual and Social Objective of Education:

1. The main objectives of general education should be two-fold: First to help the student develop those qualities and abilities that will serve him and the community well, no matter what his calling or status in life: And second to foster in him those interests and abilities that will enable him to continue to grow to leant by himself and in whatever joint activity he may be engaged.
2. Education is that which increases our ability to enjoy more things more, to live more richly, more creatively and in greater harmany with ourselves, our environment and our fellowmen. (*Theodore O. Yntema. The Enrichment of Man. The Benjamin Fitirless Memorial*

*Lecture, given, at Carnegie Institute of Technology 65 p. 47).*

3. The goals are to enable each child to play a constructive, respected role in society and to lead a life which to him will be satisfying. *(Educational Policies Commission, American Education and the Search, for Equal Opportunity, Washington, D.C. National Education Association, 1965, p. 17).*

**Social and Individual Purposes of Education not Incompatible.** 'Social purpose' of education and 'individual purpose' of education are not incompatible terms. The Education Commission 1964-66 has explained the position as, "One of the important principles to be emphasized in the socialistic pattern of society which the nation desires to create is that individual fulfillment will come, not through selfish and narrow loyalties to personal or group interests that through the dedication of all to the wider loyalties of national development in all its parameters."

According to Ross, "Individuality is of no value and personality is a meaningless term apart from the social environment in which they are development and made manifest. Self-realization can be achieved only through social service and social ideas of real value can come into being only through free individuals who have developed valuable individuality. The circle cannot be broken."

The individual and the society, both be regarded as realities, neither of the two being absolutely independent of the other. Instead of being regarded as isolated entities, the individual and the society should be considered as functionally related to each other. The individual acting on the society and the society reacting on the individual. The individual is the product of society which the society in its own turn finds its advancement in the development of its individual members.

In the words of John Adam, "Individuality requires a social medium to grow. Without social contacts we are not human."

**Democratic and Totalitarian Aims in Education**

Educational aims in any country have varied with its social economic and geographical conditions. In recent past political system has been the dominating factor in determining the aims and ideals of education. The two systems which are considered here in relation to aims in education will be democratic and the totalitarian.

**Aims of Education in the Totalitarian and Democratic States**

Both use educational systems as a direct means of economic development.

Both use educational systems as a conscious means of transforming their society.

Both lay great stress on vocational skills to bring about economic efficiency.

Both make all out attempts to provide schooling for all. An attack on mass illiteracy is a must.

**State Control of Education in a Totalitarian State**

The child in a totalitarian state is educated not only exclusively by the state but ultimately exclusively for the state as well. Thus, the state comes to assume ethical as well as political sovereignty in the education of its wards. The state organizes and maintains schools for its own. The teachers in a totalitarian state must propagate and indoctrinate the decisions made by higher ups. As in the army, the schools of a totalitarian state will emphasize drill and obedience at the expense of initiative and criticism.

The merits and demerits of such an educational philosophy are the same as those of the political theory after which it is patterned. Thus, the aims and ideals of education depend upon the philosophy that prevails in a society. In the mid-twentieth century, Japan and Nazi regimes stressed that education should produce patriotic citizens who would fight to expand the territories of their nation's superiority. The cultural revolution in China in the 1960's was directed towards the ideals set by the totalitarian state.

In a totalitarian state, pupils are not encouraged to look critically at the problems and evils existing in society. They may be content with the *status quo*. Passive acceptance of the country's political, economic and other policies will grow in the minds of the students. Militant nationalism, "My country, right or wrong" are attitudes which may develop in tender minds. Aggression and violence against neighbouring countries have resulted in educational aims of this type.

Aims of education in a totalitarian state may be enumerated as under:

1. Each individual must be trained to subordinate his interests to the interests of the state.
2. The student is made to realize the value and importance of obedience and conformity.
3. Every child must undergo a rigorous code of discipline.
4. Physical education and military training are given great importance.
5. Thinking along the lines approved by the authorities is stressed. Very little independent thinking is allowed.

**Education in a Democracy**

Since every individual counts in a democracy, it enjoins that every person be always treated as an end. A man is to be educated as man because of his humane nature no matter whether he is high born or low and no matter what the economic condition of his parents is. Nothing less than universal education will suffice. Education is conditioned by deep regard for civic responsibilities; emphasis on hard work, dignity of labour, initiative, enterprise reliance etc. Since all men in a democracy are free, education must be free, that is there must be no economic barriers to its acquisition. Since in a democracy all men are politically free, all should have a liberal education.

Following will be the aims of education in a democratic set-up:

1. It should develop the capacity of the pupil to sift truth from falsehood, fact from propaganda and to reject the dangerous appeal of fanaticism and prejudice.
2. It should develop ability of constructive and independent thinking.
3. It should develop a wide range of wholesome interests in each pupil by providing for learning through cooperative work.
4. It should develop social outlook.
5. It should provide for the training in dignity of labour.
6. It should cater to the individual differences of children and teach them accordingly. No attempt should be made towards uniformity.
7. It should develop a passion for social justice based upon sensitiveness to the social evils and exploitation of the weak.
8. It should develop love and respect for others. It should develop human relations.

9. It should provide equal opportunities for all.
10. It encourages originally and inventiveness.
11. Vocational choices are broad based.

**State Control of Education in a Welfare State Like India**

It is generally believed that neither a policy of complete *Laissez faire* nor of complete state control of education is suited in a Welfare State. The state must take positive as well as negative action to maintain a proper balance of social welfare for its citizens. The state must step forward and ensure not only an adequate amount of education but also education of an adequately high standard.

The degree of State control of education has varied from state to state at different times. Prof. John S. Burbacher outlines the position as, "At one time all education was under private supervision, latterly, more and more of it has come under the Government. In some places the Government merely provides the school building and teacher. In other it goes further and offers free textbooks and supplies. In still others, it furnishes such services as medical care, transportation to and from school and noon day lunches. Probably no one today would like to see the Government abandon any of these services."

❋❋❋

# 2

# Aims of Education in Indian Society

Different ideologies such as political, social, economic, religious, psychological, scientific and philosophical and present problems affect the aims of education. Aims of education are laid down keeping them in view. To know this problem it is essential to throw light on various conditions, which are as follows:

**Economic Conditions.** In India economic conditions are not good. India is a country where large number of people are under poverty line. There is no equitable distribution of wealth, which increases the gap between rich and poor. Unemployment is increasing day-by-day. We are not economically sound.

**Political Conditions.** Political environment is also becoming polluted day-by-day. India wants such leaders who can guide people in right directions. Indian electorate are not properly educated, they are unable to choose the right people for governance. To preserve freedom is becoming a great problem. The existence of freedom is in danger.

**Social Conditions.** Social conditions of India are also badly affecting the Indian society. Many social evils are prevailing in Indian society such as dowry system, illiteracy, early marriage etc. Diversity of religion, caste, culture and language is assuming the form of serious problem.

**Religious Conditions.** India is a secular state. Here, all religions have equal importance. But it is pity that people do not understand the meaning of religion, they are misusing the concept of religious freedom. There is lack of religious toleration among people due to which anarchism is increasing. It has become a great danger for national integration.

On the basis of these conditions, the aims of education have been patronised by different Commissions from time to time which are as follows:

After independence, democratic view point was adopted. At that time education made its contribution and tried to bring prosperity in country. According to Rajendra Prasad, "India has to choose for herself a culture that derives inspiration from what is noble in our ancient culture and at the same time does not ignore the demands of the present age."

### Aims of Education According to University Education Commission, 1948

**Pandit Nehru had Observed:** "Great changes have taken place in the country and the educational system must also be in keeping with them. The entire basis of education must be revolutionised."

According to University Education Commission, 1948, the aims of education are as follows:

*(a)* Development of leadership.

*(b)* Preservation and transfer of culture.

*(c)* Development of democratic qualities in school.

*(d)* Character development.

(*e*) Vocational efficiency.

(*d*) Emphasis on human and spiritual training.

**Aims of Education According to Secondary Education Commission, 1952-53**

This Commission has stated that education which is national in character must develop in its citizens habits, attitudes and qualities of character and equip them to bear the burden of life in the changing economic structure.

According to Secondary Education Commission aims of education are as follows:

(*a*) Development of democratic citizenship.

(*b*) Development of personality.

(*c*) Development of sense of patriotism.

(*d*) Development of vocational efficiency.

**(a) Development of Democratic Citizenship.** It is a challenging responsibility with education to carefully train every citizen for democratic citizenship. Such a training develops following qualities:

(*i*) ***Clear Thinking.*** A democratic citizen should have the understanding and the intellectual integrity to distinguish truth from falsehood and facts from propaganda. Education should train the child for this purpose.

(*ii*) ***Receptivity to New Ideas.*** Education must aim at broadening the intellectual horizon of young scholars to enable them to accept new ideas that can help in strengthening democratic forces.

(*iii*) ***Clearness in Speech and Writing.*** This quality is essential for successful living in democracy which is based not on force but on free discussion and persuasion.

**(b) Development of Personality.** Education should develop literary, artistic and cultural interests of the students. These are necessary for self-expression and for the full development of human personality. For this purpose subjects like art, craft, music, dance etc., should be included in the scheme of studies.

**(c) Development of Sense of Patriotism.** Another important aim which the secondary school must foster is the development of a sense of true patriotism. True patriotism involves a sense of appreciation of the social and cultural achievements, a readiness to recognise its weaknesses and an earnest desire to serve one's country.

**(d) Development of Vocational Efficiency.** Education must aim at increasing the productive or vocational efficiency of young students.

**Aims of Education According to Indian Education Commission, 1964-66**

According to Dr. Radha Krishnan, "It is my earnest desire that the Commission should survey all aspects of educational system at all levels and give suggestions that may help the educational system in progressing at all levels."

According to Kothari Commission, "One of the important social objectives of education is to equalise opportunity, enabling the backward or underprivileged classes and individuals to use education as a tool for improvement of their social and economic condition".

The most important and urgent reform needed in education is to transform it, to relate it to the life, needs and aspirations of the people and thereby make a powerful instrument of social, economic and cultural transformation, necessary for realization of the national goals. For this purpose the commission has suggested the following objectives of education:

1. Education for Increasing productivity.
2. Education for national integration.
3. Education for Modernisation.
4. Education for social, moral and spiritual values.

These objectives are discussed below.

**1. Education for Increasing Productivity.** Though India is a land of vast resources, yet it has not become self-sufficient. For this purpose, the resources must be exploited and education must be related to productivity to increase national income. In order to create a link between education and productivity the following programme has been suggested by Kothari Commission:

***Science Education.*** Science education must become an integral part of school education and ultimately some study of science should become a part of all courses in the humanities and social sciences at university level also. The quality of science teaching must also be improved considerably so as to promote a deep understanding of basic principles, to develop problem solving and analytical skills and to promote the spirit of enquiry and experimentation.

***Work Experience.*** In the programme of relating education to life and productivity, work experience must be introduced as an integral part of all education—general and vocational. To Commission work experience implies participation in productive work in school, in the home, in a workshop, on a farm, in a factory or in any productive situation. All purposeful education should include study of languages, humanities and social sciences, study of mathematics and natural sciences, work experience and social services.

Work experience is a method of integrating education with work. In the present education system work experience and social services have almost been totally neglected. Along with other elements of education work experience should be greately emphasised for the following reasons:

(*a*) It will bridge the gap between intellectual and manual work.

(*b*) It will make the entry of youth into the world of work and employment easier by enabling them to adjust themselves to it.

(*c*) It will decrease the over academic nature of formal education.

(*d*) It will relate education to productivity and also as a means of social and national integration.

***Vocationalisation.*** Every attempt should be made to give a vocational bias to secondary education and to increase the emphasis on agricultural and technological education at the university level. This will surely bring education into closer relationship with productivity. In the modern Indian society which is heading towards industrialisation, it is essential to considerably expand professional education at the university level, especially in agricultural and technological fields.

**2. Education for National Integration.** India is a land of diverse social groups. Unity and harmony among these groups is the basis of national integration. Social and national integration is an important objective of a national system of education. The Commission has suggested the following steps for strengthening the nation through education.

*The Common School System.* The present educational system in our country instead of bringing social groups and classes together is tending to increase social segregation and class distinctions. The schools for the masses (generally maintained by the Government) are of poorer quality than those run by private bodies. Good schools are not within the reach of a common man's pocket. This is one of the major weaknesses of the existing educational system. In the opinion of the Commission, "If our educational system is to become a powerful instrument of national development in general and social and national integration in particular, we must march toward the goal of a Common School System of public education." The common school must be opened to all children irrespective of caste, creed, community and economic or social status.

(*a*) It should charge no tuition fee.

(*b*) It should maintain a good standard of education in order to meet the needs of average parents so that they may not ordinarily feel the need of sending their children to other expensive schools.

***Social and National Service.*** Social and national service should be made obligatory for all students at all levels. It should form an integral part of education at secondary school and university levels. This programme will prove an effective instrument for building character improving discipline, inculcating a faith in the dignity of labour and developing a sense of social responsibility, if it is organised concurrently with academic studies in schools and colleges. The following are the main forms of organising such a programme:

(*a*) At the primary stage this programme should be developed in all schools on the lines of Basic Education.

(*b*) At the lower secondary stage social service should be made compulsory for all students for thirty days a year, at the higher secondary for twenty days and at the undergraduate stage it should be made obligatory for all students or sixty days a year, to be done in one or more stretches. Every educational institution should develop a programme of social and community service of its own in which all students must be involved for the periods as indicated above.

(c) Labour and social service camps or N.C.C. should be organised in each district as alternative forms of such service for those students for whom no other programmes of social service have been organised in their own institutions.

***Promoting National Consciousness.*** India is a land of different castes, peoples, communities, languages, religions and cultures. The main role of our schools, colleges and universities should, therefore, be to enable our students to discover 'unity in diversity' and in this way, foster a sense of national solidarity and national consciousness among them. This can be done by:

***The Promotion of Understanding and Re-evaluation of Our Cultural Heritage.*** This can be achieved by the well-organised teaching of language and literature, philosophy, religion and history of India and by introducing the students to Indian architecture, sculpture, painting, music, dance and drama. Holiday camps and summer schools on interstate basis, can also be organised fruitfully, for breaking down regional and linguistic barriers.

Creation of a strong faith in the future towards would involve an attempt to bring home to the students, the principles of the Constitution, the great human values, referred to in its preamble, the nature of the democratic and socialistic society.

***Education for International Understanding.*** There is no contradiction between national consciousness and developing international understanding. Schools should promote international outlook through the study of humanities and social sciences, simultaneously with developing national consciousness.

***Democratic Values.*** The educational programme in schools and colleges should be designed to inculcate democratic values, such as scientific temper of mind, tolerance, respect for the culture of other national groups etc. This will enable our young citizens to adopt democracy not only as a form of Government but also as a way of life.

**3. Education for Modernisation.** In a modern society stock of knowledge is far greater, the pace of its growth is infinitely quicker and social change is very rapid. This needs a radical change in the educational system. Education in a modern society is no longer concerned mainly with the imparting of knowledge or the preparation of a finished product but with the awakening of curiosity, the development of proper interests, attitudes and values and the building up of such essential skills as independent study and capacity to think and judge for oneself, without which it is not possible to become a responsible member of a democratic society. Therefore, the process of modernisation will be directly related to the pace of educational advance. Education brings modernisation in following ways:

*(a)* The way to modernise quickly is to spread education.

*(b)* By producing educated and skilled citizens.

*(c)* By training an adequate and competent intelligentsia.

*(d)* By bringing a radical change in the method of teaching and in the training of teachers.

**4. Education for Social, Moral and Spiritual Values.** The expanding knowledge and the growing power which it places at the disposal of modern society must be combined with the strengthening and deepening of the sense of social responsibility and a keener appreciation of moral and spiritual values. For this purpose, active measures should be adpoted to give a value-orientation to education. These measures are:

*(a)* The Central and State Governments should introduce education in moral, social and spiritual values in all institutions.

(*b*) University department should undertake preparation of special literature for this purpose by students and teachers.

(*c*) For this purpose, a syllabus giving well chosen information about each of the major religions, should be included as a part of the course in citizenship or general education to be introduced in schools and colleges.

(*d*) The privately managed institutions should also follow the same steps.

(*e*) Some periods should be set apart in the time table for this purpose.

We may say that education is the most vital force which can help in the realisation of national objectives. While keeping in view the best features of the modern European culture and civilisation, the Commission did not ignore the essential characteristics of our ancient culture and civilisation as well as the needs and aspirations of our present day society. It is for the first time that we have been given an integrated picture of Indian education in all its wide and diverse dimensions.

## EDUCATIONAL THOUGHT OF ROUSSEAU'S

In modern times, we make use of a number of progressive methods of teaching and a variety of audio-visual aids, to make classroom teaching effective and attractive. But upto the seventeenth century, there was no systematic organization or arrangement for imparting education to children. Schools in those days were very few and those that existed, were the terror of pupils and the slaughter-houses of mind. They followed no methods and used no aids. Every teacher had his own methods to follow. Severe punishments were given to pupils and all types of rods, canes and sticks were used for this purpose. The early educators, if any, "had confined their education to the training of the governing classes of the community and until the time of Comenius, it was only idealistic. There were many who could hazard the suggestion that all in their childhood be instructed in learning, in their own native tongue." During the seventeenth, eighteenth and the nineteenth centuries a number of educationists were born who, in fact, revolutionised education, Rousseau, Froebel, Montessori and Dewey are the most prominent among these.

Rousseau (1712-1778), was the great educator of the 18$^{th}$ century and one who belonged to the new school of education. Rousseau's life was greatly influenced by the prevailing atmosphere of society in France, his native country. In the beginning of the 18$^{th}$ century, the privileged classes in France, flourished at the cost of the poor and the helpless. Hypocrisy, artificiality, cruelty and despotism of the privileged classes, led to discontentment among the common people. However, in the later half of the 18$^{th}$ century a new era of 'Equality, Liberty and Fraternity,' began in France which revolutionised the entire French society. Rousseau and Voltaire were the pioneers of this new era. It was a result of these new ideas that in the sphere of education also many new changes found their way. Children began to be treated well, properly understood and humanly educated.

**1. Rousseau's Philosophy and Concept of Education.** Rousseau's philosophy goes by the name of "Naturalism". The keynote of his philosophy was to have a "Natural State, a Natural Man and a Natural Civilisation". He felt that all ills and miseries in the Modern world were due to a departure from the previous "State of Nature". He declared, "Everything is good as it comes from the hands of the Author of Nature (the Creator), but everything degenerates in the hands of man." He believed that child was essentially good but was made bad when he came in contact with society and its environment. He contended that "man in society is born, lives and dies in a state of slavery. He is fettered by our institution, which drags him away from his good nature." So Rousseau pleaded, "Leave the child alone. Let him be a natural man rather than a civilised man. Let him have a state of nature rather than artificial surroundings that stunt his proper growth and arrest his natural development." Thus, Rousseau preached for a life according to nature—which was simple and real and free from all customs, traditions and conventions. He, in fact, wanted to educate the child for manhood and not for citizenship.

It should, however, be clearly understood that by Natural State and Natural Man, Rousseau did not mean the primitive social order and the savage man. He believed that human institutions were one mass of folly and contradictions. To regain the old vitality and happiness, human society should give up the present artificial modes of life and revert to the natural state. He favoured natural civilisation, free from all artificial and rigid barriers that pollute the goodness of our nature. The Natural Man of Rousseau's conception was a fully developed Man enjoying social life, without being carried away by the passions and prejudices of society. Reason was the only guiding force in producing natural Civilisation and Natural Man by Natural State also he meant 'a simple farming community or state, without the evils of large cities, corrupt rulers, social classes and luxury. His Natural Man is a true man, who is 'governed and directed by the laws of his own nature rather than those of social institutions. Natural powers, emotions and reactions are most trustworthy as basis for action, rather than reflections or experiences that come from association with society.' The catch-words of Rousseau's 'Naturalism' were freedom, growth, interest and activity. And all these words are the life and soul of modern progressive education.

**2. Three-fold Meaning of Nature.** Rousseau made use of the word 'Nature' in a very wide sense. He gave three-fold meaning to it, namely:

(a) ***Isolation from Society.*** Rousseau advocated that children should be saved from the evil influence of society. They should be isolated from society and brought up in contact with the beauties and wonders of nature. This, however, does not mean no-education. It simply signifies a non-social education *i.e.,* an education which is not based on meaningless traditions and formalities of society. For Rousseau, society was not natural, but an artificial product, the outcome of a contract and evil. Nature and society, thus, become opposed to each other. Nature is accordingly, defined 'negatively to society'. It is a preventive education saving the child from the evil influences of society.

(b) ***Contact with Natural Phenomena.*** Education according to child's nature, must be provided in natural environment. Rousseau himself was a great lover of nature, mountains, streams, sunrise, sun-set, solitude and country life. He, therefore, recommends contact with hills, streams, plants, trees, animals, birds and physical forces of all kinds. One who is brought up and taught in natural environments automatically becomes a 'natural man' He follows nature and obeys, the voice of his own conscience.

(c) ***Instinctive Make-up of the Child.*** Instinctive make-up means the native instincts, tendencies and capacities of the child. Rousseau believed that learning takes place when the child is free to develop and grow according to his natural impulses. So education must start from the child's instinctive tendencies and should be based on the same because these tendencies are more reliable bases of education than experiences, gained from society. According to Rousseau, "Education is no longer a procedure, artificial, harsh, dull, unsympathetic and repressive of all natural inclinations. It is, on the other hand, an organic growth. It is a development from withim."

**3. Three Source of Education.** At the outset of his book "*Emile*" Rousseau states that education comes from nature, from men and from things. In other words, the problem of education is the relationship of man to his physical and social environment. Explaining these sources of education, he says, "The internal development of our organs and faculties is the education of nature; the use we are taught to make of that development, is the education given by men; and the acquisition made by our own experience on the objects that surround us, is our education from things." In other words, by education from nature, he meant development according to the child's natural endowments and capacities. By education from men, he emphasised the importance of social environment, teaching how to make use of that development. By education from things, he understood physical environment, helping to gain experience by ourselves. He says that the harmonious development of these three factors constituted an ideal scheme of education.

Such harmony in education is possible by subordinating the education of men and things to that of nature because we have no control over nature. We must, therefore, direct the other two, to ensure cooperation of these three factors for imparting ideal education.

**4. Rousseau's Aims of Education.** Before Rousseau's time, the aim of education was either spiritual or social or vocational, Efforts were made to mould the child into the artificial forms of conduct, satisfactory to the judegment of adults in society. The child was trained to speak, think, act as a miniature adult without any consideration of his natural instincts and interests. Rousseau revolted against this wrong concept of education. He believed that education was a life-long process, which began from birth and ended only with the end of life. It was development from within and not an imposition from without.

So Rousseau's aim of education was the attainment of fullest natural growth of the individual leading to balanced, harmonious, useful and natural life. The real aim of education is to help the child to live his life. He says, "To live is not merely to breathe. It is to act, to make us of our organs, senses, our faculties and of all those parts of ourselves, which give us the feeling of our existence."

This general aim of education was split up by Rousseau, according to the nature, at different stages of human development.

(*a*) In infancy *i.e.*, from birth to the age of five years, the aim of education is to develop a well-regulated freedom. For realisation of this aim, he recommends purely physical education in an atmosphere of perfect liberty.

(*b*) In boyhood or pre-adolescent period *i.e.*, from twelve years to fifteen years, the aim of education is "to acquire such knowledge which may satisfy the wants of the child and must be functionally useful". This is the period for intellectual education—the period of instruction, labour and study.

(*c*) In adolescent period *i.e.*, from 15 to 20 years, the aim of education is the training of heart, to make the child loving and tender-hearted so that he may live peacefully in social relationship. In this period religious, moral and social education is recommended. In the previous periods, the child has already developed physically and intellectually. He must now grow emotionally, aesthetically, socially and morally. The sex instinct, which is suficiently developed by this time, is to be sublimated by re-directing it to the love of some noble idea and by keeping the young person occupied in work and activity.

(*d*) In childhood *i.e.,* between the age of five and twelve, the main aim of education is to provide the child with the strength which he needs for the attainment of well-regualated freedom. So at this stage also no formal education is recommended, but the continuance of the same physical care and natural education, Rousseau's advice for this period is, "Exercise the body, the organs, the senses and powers and keep the soul lying fallow, as long as you can."

**5. Role of the Teacher.** Rousseau assigns a very minor place to the teacher in the educative process. He is not called an instructor but only a guide. His main responsibility is to motivate the child to learn. This he can achieve by exploiting the innate tendencies of the child. He must possess a profound understanding of the child's nature and be able to control his emotional reactions. He is not to impose any rules of control upon the child. He is to allow him perfect feedom and guide him properly.

**6. Rousseau's Theory of Negative Education.** As we have already stated, Rousseau believed that everything is good as it comes from the Author of Nature. Everything degenerates in the hands of man. By saying so, he meant that child is good; but it is society that makes him bad. So he advocated that first education should be purely negative. The child should not be taught the principles of truth and virtue but guarded against vice and error. In his own words, "I call a positive education one that tends to form the mind pre-maturely and to instruct the child in the duties that belong to man. I call a negative education on that tends to perfect the organs that are the instruments of knowledge and endeavours to protect the way for reason, by the proper exercise of the senses."

The following are the chief characteristics of his theory of Negative Education:

(a) ***No Time Saving.*** According to Rousseau, in childhood no time should be saved. It should rather be lost. Let the child run, jump and play all day long. In all these activities he will have a continuous re-construction of experience which is nothing but education, pure and simple. Time lost on play and recreational activities in childhood, is not lost but profitably gained. Childhood is not the time for intellectual pursuits.

(b) ***No Social Education.*** In Rousseau's time, society was corrupt to the core. So he wanted children to be isolated from such a society and to educate them in the midst of nature till their power of reasoning and judgement is perfected, with which they are in a position to protect themselves from the evils of society.

(c) ***No Book Learning.*** Rousseau says, "I hate books because they are a curse to children. They teach us to talk only that which we do not know. Instead of making the child stick to his books, I keep him busy in the workshop; his hands will work to the profit of his mind." Rousseau felt that readymade material found in books, was of little advantage. Let children gain knowledge by their own efforts and through different types of experience.

(d) ***No Formal Discipline.*** Rousseau is in favour of free and positive discipline for children. Let the children suffer natural consequences of their own actions without the intervention of humam beings to protect or punish and in this way they will set themselves right. If a child breaks a window pane, let him sit in the cold wind that gushes in, as a result of his folly.

If he climbs a tree, let him fall down and learn not to do so again.

(e) ***No Habit Formation.*** In his own words, "The only habit which the child should be allowed to form is to contract no habit at all." Young children should not be made slaves of rigid habits. They should be left free in all their activities. If any habits are to be formed in childhood, let them form natural habits.

(f) ***No Direct Moral Education.*** Rousseau is not in favour of direct teaching of morals. Let the child be left free to act and learn what is right and wrong, by the consequences of his own actions. He says, "Much more harm than good is done by your ceaseless preaching and moralising." He further says, "Inflict on the child no sort of punishment and never make him ask your pardon. As there is no moral quality in his actions, he can do nothing wrong.

(g) ***No Sticking to Traditional Precedure of Education.*** Rousseau was greatly disgusted with the prevailing social, political, economic, religious and educational conditions in his country. So he said, "Follow the reverse of the current practice and you will almost do right." He challenged the traditional procedure of education saying, "Give me a child of twelve who knows nothing at all. At fifteen I will restore him to you, knowing as much as those who have been under instruction from infancy, with the difference that your scholar only knows things by hearts, while mine knows how to use his knowledge.

It will, thus, be clear from his theory of Negative Education that many of its principles have been accepted by the modern educators. No doubt, at times, Rousseau went to the extreme. But it was natural and he had to eradicate wrong social practices like a reformer by focusing public attention to those practices. His play-and-activity principles in a child's education, his free and positive discipline, his advice against formal book-learning and his principle of no direct moral instructions of children, have all been incorporated in modern educational theory and practice. However, it is his theory of natural consequences which is not acceptable and dependable at all times.

## JOHN DEWEY'S VIEWS OF AN IDEAL SCHOOL

John Dewey (1819-1952) was a famous American philosopher, psychologist and educator. Being brought up in rural environments, he realised from the very beginning that traditional methods of instruction were not at all effective and that social contacts of everyday life provided effective, dynamic and unlimited learning situations. These very ideas formed the foundation of the educational theory, formulated later by him. His outlook on education reflected the Industrial Revolution and the Development of Democracy. He believed in the dynamic nature of things and values. So he changed with the change in ideas, as a result of experience and experimentation and finally emerged out as a Pragmatist. Today, he stands in the front rank of the world educators. His works on education are a great source of inspiration and hope and help in developing our experimental and scientific attitude of mind. Perhaps no other educator has written so much on educational problems as John Dewey.

**1. Dewey's Philosophy—Pragmatism.** Dewey's philosophy represents a happy blend of naturalism and idealism because it is based on the evolutionary concept soft Darwin and Pragmatism of William James. Like Darwin he believes that world is still in the process of making and that life in this world is an every-changing and self-renewing process. Like William James, he believes that whatever useful is good and whatever good, is useful. Truth is also that which works, which fulfils our purposes and satisfies our desires.

For John Dewey there are no eternal and absolute values. All values change with time and space. Man is the creator of his own values. What is true today may cease to be true tommorrow. Man's life is a series of experiments and purposeful action. "Everything is provisional, nothing ultimate. Knowledge is always a means, never an end itself." It is purely instrumental. Hence, the title of Dewey's philosophy is "Instrumentalism".

Then Dewey believes that knowledge and thinking are closely associated with action. They are tentative plans of action. They have to be tested by action and by knowing the result of their being acted upon. He affirms, "The essence of pragmatic instrumentalism is to conceive of both knowledge and practice as means of making good. It does not imply that action is higher and better than knowledge and practice inherently superior to thought. Constant and effective interaction of knowledge and practice is something quite different from an exaltation of activity, for its own sake. Action, when directed by knowledge, is method and means, not an end. The aim and end is the securer, freerer end more widely shared embodiment of values in experience, by means of that active control of objects which knowledge alone makes possible."

Further more, he is convinced of the organic relationship between the individual and the society, to which he belongs. He is conscious of both the physical and the social environment. Self can neither grow in solitude nor in natural surroundings. For his proper growth an individual must live both in natural (or physical) environment and (human or social) environment. Man is not a solitary self but an individual, who lives with the rest of mankind. "He is a citizen, growing and thinking in a vast complex of interactions and relationships."

Lastly, Dewey holds that barriers of creed, religion, language, nationality and colour have divided humanity and separated man from man. These barriers must be broken to establish harmony between individuals and groups and ensure the process of human growth. To him, growth stands for the "being process" and not for the "done product". Not perfection as a final goal, but the ever enduring process of perfecting, maturing and refining, is the aim of living. He further declares, "The bad man is one, who is beginning to deteriorate, to grow less good. And the good man is one, who is moving to become better." This is the function of education to break the barriers of separation and bring men and nations together for establishing a happier and nobler world.

**2. Dewey's Ideal School.** Dewey was dissatisfied with the existing system of education. In his opinion, the Industrial Revolution, the development means of communication and transport, various discoveries and inventions of science and ideals of democracy, had brought about extraordinary changes in social life. As such, an ordinary school had not been able to keep pace with these changes. It could not give the present day child an exact idea of the social, political and economic life of the community around him. It is, therefore, that social education is not connected with his daily life. John Dewey wanted to bridge this gulf between school life and home or social life, outside the school.

**3. Dewey's Educational Theory and Aims.** About the importance of education, John Dewey writes, "What nutrition and reproduction are to physiological life, education is to social life. Education is a social necessity. It is a means of social continuity of life. It is a means by which a person is helped to have useful and helpful experience." All this he said in the light of the rapid changes in social and economic life of his own time.

Defining education, Dewey says, "Education is development of all those capacities in the individual which will enable him to control his environment and fulfil his responsibilities." It means that education extends the limits of human possibilities. It is progressive both for the individual and the society. Thus, education, to John Dewey, is a bipolar process. It has two sides, the psychological and the sociological; neither of the two can be sub-ordinated or neglected. The psychological side is the study of the child, with all his inclinations, instincts, endowments and interests. It forms the very basis of education. The sociological side is the social environment in which the child is born, lives and grows for society. On a further analysis of his educational theory, we find the following four fundamentals:

(a) ***Education as Growth.*** Growth is the real function of education. It, therefore, must lead to growth. But growth is not directed towards any pre-determined goal or end. The end of growth is more growth and so the end of education, more education. An individual is a changing and growing personality and education is to facilitate that growth. It is, therefore, the duty of the teacher to provide opportunities for proper growth by arousing the instincts and capacities of children and by providing to them the solution of those problems which make the children think.

(b) ***Education as Social Efficiency.*** Man is a social animal who continuously draws energy, strength, knowledge, experience and attitudes in a social medium. As a social being, he is a citizen, growing and thinking in a vast complex of interactions and relations." He owns character and mind, habits and manners, language and vocabulary, good taste and aesthetic appreciation, to his interaction with the social consciousness of his community. When as an individual he shares such rich resources of a good society, he should also be ready to give back to that society and thus, help other members to develop. It is the function of education to teach him this give-and-take process and make him aware of his social obligations. Education must transform the immature child into a social human being. It is in this sense that education becomes a social process and social efficiency becomes the aim of all education.

(c) ***Education as Life.*** Dewey believes that education is not a preparation for life. It is life itself. "Life is a by-product of activities and education is born out of these activities." School is now taken as a miniature society which faces problems, similar to those faced in life outside. For education, pupils should be made active participants in the social and community life of the school and thus, trained in co-operative and mutually helpful living. They should be encouraged to face actual life problems in the school and gain varied experiences. As our children are required to live in a democratic society when adults, they must experience same life in the school.

(d) ***No Fixed Aims of Education.*** However, being a pragmatic education, John Dewey has no fixed aims of education. He believes that since physical and social environments are always changing, aims of education must also change. They cannot be fixed for all times to come. Thus, he revolted against the traditional aims of education—namely: The moral aim, the disciplinary aim and the knowledge aim etc. of the nineteenth century. He rejected the very idea of education as preparation for future life and said that education must cater to the present needs of the child rather than the future because the child is not interested in the unknown future. He therefore, said that educational aims must be restated and re-formulated in the light of the rapid social and economic changes in present day life.

(e) ***Education as Reconstruction of Experiences.*** According to John Dewey, experience is the only source of true knowledge. One experience leads to further experiences and each new experience calls for the revision, modification or rejection of the previous experiences. In this way the old pattern yields place to a new pattern. Dewey says, "We should so regulate the learning and experiencing activities of the young, that a newer and better society will arise in the end." Therefore, there is a need of continuity of experiences, helping man to grow physically, mentally, socially and morally. Education must create environments for the promotion of continuity of experiences. Dewey, therefore, conceived of education as a process, involving continuous reconstruction and reorganization of experience. He says that education is by experience, for experience and of experience.

**4. Scheme of Education.** Dewey outlined a definite scheme of education, according to the stages of mental development of the child. These stages were:

*(a)* Play period from 4 to 8 years of age.

*(b)* Period of spontaneous attention from 8 to 12.

*(c)* Period of reflective attention from 12 onwards.

In the Play period, the child studies the life and occupations of the home. Then he studies larger social and community activities on which his home-life depends. Finally, he learns about the development and significance of other occupations and inventions. In the last year of this period, he also learns reading, writing and geography.

In the period of spontaneous attention, the child understands the difference between means and ends. He is able to act for the solution of practical problems of life. At this stage he is also taught social studies with a view to make him understand how man achieved his purposes under various conditions in different periods of history.

In the period of reflective attention, the child is grown-up enough to raise new problems and find out their solutions. At this stage he acquires definite skills and arts so that after leaving the school, he should adjust himself as a useful and efficient member of society.

**5. His Concept of an Ideal School.** Dewey considered ideal school as an enlarged ideal home. In this home, the child learns to subordinate his interests to the general interest of the household. Here, he learns the habits of obedience, regularity, hardwork, cooperation, sacrifice, fellow-feeling, patience and discipline. In the ideal school, teachers play the same part as parents at home. Being better equipped than home, the school must provide ideals, high and noble and worthy of being pursued and lived upon. These ideals are quite in conformity with the ideals of society which the school is required to serve.

Then the ideal school of Dewey's concept, is a society in miniature in which real life experiences of the community are provided on smaller scale. It is an activity school, wherein ample opportunities are provided to the child to construct his experiences, under the scientific guidance of teachers. In this ideal school, the child learns by doing and by actual participation in purposeful and intelligent activities. These activities include cooking, sewing, wood-work, weaving as well as other occupations and violations. Thus, the schools provide various types of social, economic and moral experiences of practical utility.

**6. Curriculum.** Dewey's curriculum is not a mere scheme of studies. Nor is it a list of subjects. It is an entire range of activities and experiences, because to him subjects are only summaries and recapitulation of human activities. Dewey does not recommend any ready made curriculum. He rather wants the curriculum to grow out of the pupils own impulses, interest and experiences. It consists of activities and projects, leading to reconstruction and re-organization of experience.

Thus, he makes occupational activities or crafts, the core of school curriculum. He also includes moral, aesthetic and religious education in the curriculum. But this education is also imparted through parctical experiences and not through "chalk and talk lessons," in the classroom. In his opinion, "Purposeful activity and a curriculum comprising standard factors of social life, would give the children more interest and insight, through the functioning of intelligence and will, in the achievement of self-control and the appreciation of social values."

**7. Dewey's Contributions and Influence.** John Dewey is, by far the most original thinker in the field of educational philosophy. He stands in the front rank of the educators of the world. It is under his influence that today we find freedom, happiness and friendliness in schools. Dewey is a philosopher of the present dynamic age, which is dominated by the forces of science, technology, industrialism and democracy. He has made an original approach to the problems, confronting man to-day and has offered sound solutions for them. To educators, he has given a new progressive outlook and called it life itself. He has also given new aim of education, new curricula, new methods of teaching, new role of the teacher and new concept of discipline. In fact, he glorified every aspect of education that he touched. His watch-word, "Progress more and more progress; growth, unlimited and illimitable," has given a new impetus of education.

Rousseau glorified the individual at the cost of society. This was not a balanced approach. Dewey fused both the psychological and the psychological aspects of education. He said that education is impossible without social medium Education must proceed by the participation of the individual in social relationship, with other persons. Children should, therefore, be acquainted with social institutions and industrial processes by creating the same environment in the school and by actual living and working.

Another great contribution of John Dewey is democracy in education. Democracy stands for providing equal educational opportunities to all. It thus, stands for free universal education. It emphasises education through cooperative and shared efforts, in a social medium, to secure the best for the individual and the society. It also emphasises the breaking down of social, national, religious and economic barriers between man and man, group and group and nation and nation. So John Dewey says that it is the school which can contribute a lot in this direction by training young children in experimental thinking and democratic cooperation.

Then, his Project Method is the practical outcome of his philosophy. It is based on "learning by doing and experiencing". This method encourages pupils to learn through self-effort and creative activity in real life situations. It is based on the fact that different branches of knowledge are not separate. They are studied separately for the sake of convenience alone. It incorporates integration and correlation of activities and subjects. It upholds the dignity of labour, favours social discipline and stresses problem solving, in place of cramming and memorisation.

Let us conculde with the words of R.R. Rusk:

"In education we cannot but be grateful to John Dewey for his great services in challenging the old static cold-storage ideal of knowledge and in bringing education more into accord with the actualities of present day life. The general principle, underlying the developments in his philosophy and his application of these in education. Appears to be that both philosophy and education should reflect the main currents of contemporary thought and incorporate the techniques that have so signally contributed to modern material and social progress."

❋❋❋

3

# History of Indian Education : Ancient to Medieval

The ancient education, system has been a source of inspiration and guidance to all educational systems of the world. Dr. F. E. Kay holds that not only did the Brahmin educators develop a system of education which survived the crumbling of empires and the changes of society, but they also, through all these thousands of years, kept aglow the torch of higher learning. Some of the features of the education system of ancient India which other systems have borrowed are given as below. The ingredients, which our present system lacks and which were the pre-dominant facets of our ancient system relate to admission policies (*upnayan*), monitorial system, low teacher-pupil ratio, healthy teaching surroundings, free schooling and college education, sympathetic treatment, role of punishment in discipline, regulations governing student life.

**(1) Developing the Wholesome Personality.** The primary aim of any system of education should be the development of a whole some personality. The Brahmanic system of education stood on firmer grounds of lofty ideals because its primary aim was development of personality and character. Moral strength and moral excellence were developed to the fullest extent, which we lack so utterly. The moral stature of our educated people is deplorably low.

Moral values are at stake. "The old values, which held society together are disappearing and as there is no effective programme to replace them by a new sense of responsibility. Innumerable signs of social disorganization are evident everywhere and are continually on the increase. These include strikes increasing lawlessness and a disregard for public property, corruption in public life." The social, moral and spiritual values which our ancient system developed in the educand have been totally lost sight of.

**(2) Starting Academic Session Solemnly.** In most cases the boy went to a teacher for studentship. The maximum age of entrance into school was different for different castes. The period of schooling was long: At least 12 years for one Veda. The academic session started with a special ceremony 'upkarman' on the Guru Purnima (Full moon month of Shravana) and as solemnly closed on Rohini (Full moon month of Pausha) with 'utsarjan'. The whole session was punctuated with holidays especially on new moon and full moon days to the month. Here, is a lesson for us to learn. Neither do we start our academic session solemnly nor do we close it well.

**(3) Making Formal and Informal Education Responsible.** Imparting and receiving of education was as sacred as anything can be. *For example,* education started and ended with certain prescribed religious rituals like upanayan and samvartan. The disciple was to devote himself whole heartedly to the cause of learning while the remained with his teacher. Not every boy was required to enter studentship. It was still a custom to receive education at the hands of his father. How many of the parents look after their children now in this respect! The ancient system gave an equal importance to informal education as it did to the formal one.

**(4) Adjusting School Hours.** The school in the Ancient Education system lasted for 7 to 8 hours a day: 7 A. M. to 11 A. M in the morning and 2 P. M. to 6 P. M. in the evening. The morning and evening shifts which run nearly for four to five hours are but half of the old school-day. The day-schools are not also of the same duration.

In fair weather classes were held in the open under shady groves. In the rainy season schools ran in a set of apartments. Temple Colleges of the past had been of great renown for having spacious buildings for classrooms, hostels and residential quarters for teachers. Gurukuls and Ashrams were generally situated on the river banks or on the lakes. The whole atmosphere was quiet; calm and peaceful. It must be noted that schools and colleges were not kept far away from human habitation.

**(5) Emphasising Discipline.** The student had to observe strict regulations. Instruction was important, but what was even more significant than teaching was discipline—discipline inculcated through strict obedience to laws and regulations of student life, discipline that was rooted in morality and religion. Every Brahmachari was required to get up early in the morning, take a regular bath, worship Sun as the universal deity, pray in a holy place thrice a day (at morning, mid-day and evening), have yajnopavita on, be dressed habitually in clothes assigned to him according to his caste and carry on the work of studying Veda. Moral disipline was stressed. A student was required to give up lust anger, greed, vanity, conceit and overjoy. It was ordered to him not to gamble, gossip, lie, backbite, hurt feelings of others, dance, sing, look at or talk to or touch the other sex and kill animals. It was demanded of every student whether rich or poor, that he should lead a simple life in the Gurukul or in the Ashram. No one was allowed to indulge in sexual pleasures.

**(6) Close Contact.** Never in the history of education you will find such a close contact between the teacher and the taught. The teacher was the spiritual father: He was to nurse when the pupil fell sick: He was to feed, clothe and teach his student as he fed, clothed and taught his son. The student also regarded the teacher as he regarded his parents, King and God. Both were united by communion of life. In fact, they communed together.

**(7) Low Teacher Pupil Ratio.** In all schools and colleges, the pupil-teacher ratio was too low, a lessen to be learnt by the school administrators who tolerate 60 to 70 students in a class those days. Individual attention was maximum. The number of students in a school was kept very small. But when, under certain conditions the enrolment increased, the teachers sought the co-operation of more advanced and senior boys who were appointed as monitors (Pittiacharya). In the absence of the teacher the entire work was entrusted to them. The monitorial systems of Bill and Lancaster were but caricatures of the ancient Indian educational model. The British systems were mimetic in grotesqueness because they were evolved simply to keep school boys in order.

**(8) Respecting Child's Personality.** Punishment had practically no place in a school system. Pupils received very sympathetic treatment from their teachers. Their personality was respected. Teachers were required to use sweet and gentle speech in dealing with pupils. If an offence was to be corrected and corporal punishment was deemed desirable, the teacher was advised not to beat the pupil on the weaker parts of the body. Gautam the great Shastrakar said, "He who strikes them will incur the same guilt as a thief." Striking the student with an instrument like a rod was forbidden.

**(9) Providing Free Education.** Education was free. It was free because no student was required to pay any fees. It was free also because no outside agency could interfere in the matters education. There was perfect autonomy. The Shastrakars forbade a teacher to accept a fee. They forbade the teacher to punish a student corporally. Such impositions were of an internal nature. No external authority, no external beneficiary, no politics was permitted to enter the school or college system.

A student had to pay nothing in return for education he received in a Gurukul or Ashram. Access to good education depended not on wealth, nor on class but on talent. The student was expected to offer a present to his teacher according to his financial position in the society. He could offer a field, a cow, a horse and even vegetables but he was never compelled to do so. Education could not be bought. One could go up the ladder as his abilities permitted.

## FEATURES OF ANCIENT INDIAN EDUCATION

Ancient Indian education was primarily the education of the Vedas. It meant the perfect acquirement of the text through oral repetition from a teacher. The source springs of education were Brahmans, Upnishads and Dharma Sutras. Amar Kosha, the writings of Aryabhatta, Panini, Katyayana, Kautilya, Patanjali and medical treatises of Charaka and Susruta were other elements of Brahminic literature.

The Brahminic education has been a source of inspiration of determining educational aims and objectives to future generations. Dr. A. S. Altekar says that the Brahminic education aimed at 'infusion of a spirit of piety and religiousness, formation of character, development of personality, inculcation of civic and social sense, promotion of social efficiency and preservation and spread of national culture.'

**(1) Infusion of Spiritual and Religious Values.** The primary aim of ancient education was instilling into the minds of pupils a spirit of being pious and religious for glory of God and good of man. The pursuit of knowledge was a pursuit of religious values. Studies commenced and ended with religious rituals. The life of the pupil was full of ritual acts. Mornings started with religious prayers and the nights ended with the same. Prayers were common. Every pupil was required to perform religious ceremonies duly. He had to participate in all religious festivals. Education without religious instruction was not education at all. It was believed that a keener appreciation of spiritual values could be fostered only through a strict observance of religious rites.

**(2) Development of Civic Responsibilities and Social Values.** The inculcation of civic virtues and social values was an equally important objective of education in India. The Brahmachari after his education in the Gurukuls went back to the society to serve the rich and the poor, to relieve the diseased and the distressed. He was required to be hospitable to the guests and charitable to the needy. After a certain period of studies he was required to become a householder and to perpetuate his race and transmit his culture to his own offsprings.

**(3) Preserving and Diffusing National Culture.** Vedic culture was kept intact and transmitted through word of mouth to succeeding generations. Every individual was required to commit to memory at least a portion of the sacred scriptures. Everyone was required to serve as a medium of transmission. The members of the priestly class learnt the whole of Vedic literature by heart and passed it on.

**(4) Character Development.** In no period of the History of India, was so much stress laid on character building as in the Vedic period. Vyas Samhita states, "The result of education is good character and good behaviour. A conquest does not make a hero, nor studies, a wise-woman. He who has conquered his senses is the real hero. He who practises virtues is really wise." Wisdom consisted in the practice of moral values: Heroism in the control of sensual pleasures. Self-discipline which is being talked about so much now was regarded as the chief concern of education then. Control of senses and practice of virtues made one a man of character. Moral excellence could come only through practising moral values. Example, was better than precept. The teacher and the taught were ideals of morality, for both practised it all through their lives. Lack of moral values was thought to be dangerous. The Guru was the torch bearer in the search for the knowledge of self, of the meaning of life, of the relations of man to other human beings and of ultimate reality.

**(5) Personality Development.** The Guru in the ancient times realised that the development of personality is the sole aim of education. Human Personality was regarded as the supreme work of God. The qualities of self-esteem, self-confidence, self-restraint and self-respect were the personality traits that the educator tried to inculcate in his pupils through example.

## Ideals of Brahminic Education

Above-mentioned ideals of Ancient Education in India can be understood well if we analyse the meaning attached to education. Three terms are used in Vedic literature synonymous to 'education'. They are 'shiksha', which meant learning to recite, 'adhyayana' which meant going near the teacher for education and 'vinaya' an activity in which inborn faculties are led out or trained in a particular way. Just as education is a process and product we had in ancient terminology vinaya as a process and prabodh (awakening) as a product of education.

The Rig Veda states that a man is superior to another not because he has an extra hand or eye but because his mind and intellect are sharpened and rendered more efficient by education. Education not only transformed man. Through education one could attain Brahmanism. It sharpens the intellect, improves the grasping power and develops the faculty of discrimination and thus, protects us from falling into errors. It includes physical development. Mere book learning is not education. Really educated is he who shows himself as a man of action.

The Ancient Education system achieved its aims to the fullest extent. Greeks who were bitter opponents of Hindus were highly impressed by Hindu character. 'Indians have never been convicted of lying, Truth and Virtue they hold in high esteem', says Megasthenes. Again, "They are not litigious. Witnesses and seals are not necessary when a man makes a deposit, he acts in trust. Their houses are usually unguarded. Yuan Chwang wrote in the 7th century that Hindus were of pure moral principles and that they did not practise deceit and they kept the sworn obligations. Ali Idrisi said that the Indians were naturally inclined to justice and never departed from it in their actions. The morality of that trading class was very high. Marco Polo said of the Brahman merchants that they were the most truthful and never told a lie for anything in the world. All these are evidences enough that the ancient Indian education system succeded remarkably in raising the national character.

The educational system infused a sense of responsibility with the help of caste discipline and religious tenor. 'The average man in ancient India was always loyal to the interests of his guild, village and caste, says Dr. A. S. Altekar. He was socially efficient and happy.

The ancient Indian education system was also successful in preserving and spreading its culture and literature even without the help of the art of writing. It was only because of the destruction of temples and monasteries by invaders that literature was lost. The cultural unity that exists even today in the vast sub-continent is due to the successful preservation and spread of culture and the credit goes to the education system.

**Vedic Education**

What are the Vedas? What have been their objectives? Why were they written? These questions are being debated since long. Many commentators have expressed their views on these issues. But the commentary written by *Sayan* is accepted as most authentic. He has explained the meaning of Veda in his book entitled Krishna Yajurveda. According to *Sayan* Veda in his book entitied Krishna Yajurveda. According to

*Sayan* Veda is a symbol of that thing through which one attains his objective and protects oneself against bad traits, undesirable things and behaviours.

Vedas have their own characteristic features. Through them we are able to know about the culture, civilization, life and philosophy of people in ancient India. Vedas symbolise the chief objective of human life which has been deliberance from this world of births and deaths. This objective has always been unchangeable. The Indian philosophy of life has never accepted life as purposeless. The deliberance of soul has been the chief objective of this philosophy of life from time immemorial. This fact is very clear from the study of the Rigveda.

Yajna (Sacred offering or religious sacrifice to Fire) occupied a very important place in human life during the Vedic period. In each and every sacred work some Yajna was performed. It will be wrong to regard Yajna as a tradition of ancient Indians. In fact, they were purposeful as experimental laboratories of great thinkers, teachers, philosophers, Rishis and Munis of the period. Through these Yajnas the learned saints used to realise the truth of human life. The great saints like Vashistha, Vishwamitra, Kanva, Narad, Atri and Gautam etc., realised the truth through their penances of which Yajnas were essential parts. The Rigveda, the chief of all the Vedas is the essence of their basic teachings and realizations.

Yajnas were not only experimental laboratories. They may be compared with those successful experiments through which man may obtain knowledge of even many practical spheres of life. The Yajnas were performed under the headship of Brahma.

**Curriculum of Vedic Education**

Various subjects were incorporated in the curriculum of Vedic education. Grammar, rhetoric, astrology, logic, Nirukti (etymological interpretation of words) Manan the meanings of Vedic Mantras were developed and preserved were the main subjects. Vedang was the synonym of all these subjects taken together. The study of logic occupied a special place, because knowledge of any other subject was tested on its basis. Debates and discussions were organised for training in logic. Logic was regarded as the criterion for finding out truth and untruth. Logical discussion was usually organised between two scholars or two groups of learned persons. The main purpose of this discussion was to find out the truth and untruth and to make as assessment of the same.

**Method of Teaching.** Two methods of teaching were being practised during the Vedic period. The first method was Muakhik (*Oral*) and the second was based on Chintan (*Thinking or reflection*). In the oral method the students were to memories the Mantras (*Vedic hymns*) and Richayas (*Verses of Rigveda*) in order that they might not be changed wrongly and they might not be changed wrongly and they might remain preserved in their original forms. Under the oral methods those prosodies were thoroughly taught on which Richayas happened to be based. Special emphasis was laid on the various lines of a particular verse, their pronunciations and meanings. In the oral method correct pronunciation was specially emphasised. For this instruction in grammar and pronunciation was compulsory for all. The success of the oral method of the Vedic age lies in the fact that it could preserve the Richayas (*Vedic verses*) in their original forms down the ages.

Thinking method was another part of the teaching method. Through this an attempt was made to preserve the Veda Mantras (*Vedic hymns*) and Richayas (*Vedic verses*).

Manan was a higher method of teaching than thinking. Through Manan the meanings of Vedic Mantras were developed and preserved in one's own mind. This method was used to encourage the highly intelligent students. Just as in modern days teachers encourage intelligent students by guiding them to make research, similarly in ancient days 'Manan' (*Reflection*) was a method specially for highly intelligent students.

During the Vedic age the oral education was started in the family. The Rishis (*Sage or ascetic*) used to educate their children in the family through the oral method. They used to emphasise the learning of correct pronunciation. No new word was taught unless it was ascertained that the previously taught word was correctly learnt with correct pronunciation. The teachers were very particular about the correct learning of all vowels, consonants, rules of Sandhis (*i.e.,* joining of words) and compound word (*Samasas*). Through the oral method one had to learn through hearing and the Veda Mantras (*hymns*) were learnt through hearing. Therefore, the Vedas were also called Shruti (that which is heard). It was after learning the correct pronunciation through hearing that the student was advised to follow the method (*Chintan-Manan*). From the above it is clear that there were two methods of teaching. The oral method meant for students of average intelligence and the thinking (*Chintan-Manan*) method was for those who were highly endowed.

**Equal Right for Education to All.** During the Vedic period educational right was given to all without any distinction of class and colour. There was no caste system then. According to one's capacity each one was free to receive education.

**Women Education.** During the Vedic age women were given full status with men. They were honoured and respected in society. Therefore, women education was at its peak at the time. Women were regarded as a great source of power, peace and knowledge for men. It was thought that without women, men could not progress. Therefore, girls during the Vedic period were taught like boys. No distinction was made between the two. The importance of women has been explained in the Vedas days 'Manan' (Reflection) was a method specially for highly intelligent who due to their deep scholarship and penance were regarded as Women-sages. Lopamudra, Apala, Ghosh and Vishwavara were some of the great women-sages who were held in high esteem.

**Characteristics of Education**

Such terms as knowledge, awakening, humility, modesty, etc., are often used to characterise education in the Vedic period. Ancient texts refer to the uneducated person as an ignorant beast. Education is regarded as the source of light. The main features of Vedic education can be briefly enumerated as follows:

**1. Knowledge.** Education is knowledge. It is man's third eye. This aphorism means that knowledge opens man's inner eye, flooding him with spiritual and divine light, which forms the provision for man's journey through life. Through education, the development of every aspect of human life becomes possible. Knowledge protects an individual like a mother, inspires him to follow the path of good conduct as a father does and gives the pleasure that one's wife provides.

Education leads to the development of personality. The word 'Veda' originates from the root 'vid' which bears the meaning of knowledge. Sayana declares that the Veda is a means to the obtaining of the adorced that which is worthy of worship, as well as a means to the banishment of the underised, the evil. Knowledge of the four Vedas (*Rigveda, Yajurveda, Samaveda* and *Atharvaveda*), along with the knowledge of Shruti, Smriti, etc., provided an individual, with new knowledge which broadened his inteclletual horizon.

**2. Aims of Education.** In the Vedic period, education had an idealistic form, in which the teachers (acharyas) laid stress upon worship of God, religiousness, spirituality, formation of character, development of personality, creation of an aptitude for the development of culture, nation and society. It is in this context that Dr. Altekar said that the objectives of education in ancient India were worship of God, a feeling for religion, formation of character, fulfilment of public and civic duties, an increase in social efficiency or skill and the protection the propagation of national culture. These objectives and ideals took an individual along the path of spiritual development. In their fundamental form, these objectives and ideals were:

(a) ***Emphasis upon Knowledge and Experience.*** The Gurukuls laid emphasis upon knowledge and obtaining of experience. During the Vedic period, the practice of distributing degrees did not exist. Students exhibited the knowledge obtained through discourses and discussions conducted in a concourse of scholars.

(b) ***Fulfilment of Duty.*** Great importance was attached to developing such qualities as discipline, obedience, performance of hostly duties, rendering help to others, fulfilment of social responsibilities, etc. Through such education social skills were developed in the students. In addition, education was also provided for earning a livelihood and for this, one or more skills were taught. Dr. Mukerjee says that this education was not exclusively theortical or literary. It was related to one or the other manual skill.

(c) ***Spirituality.*** In the Vedic period, nature was regarded as divine and worshipped. During this period, many hypotheses concerning spirituality took birth. Knowledge came to be seen as the instrument of salvation. Fire sacrifices, fasting and taking of vows became a part of life. Education was given the objective of inculcating control over these aspects and learning right conduct based on them.

(d) ***Growth of Character and Personality.*** The objective of education was the formation of character and personality of children. It was achieved through an appropriate environment, lessons on right conduct and teachings based on the life, character and ideals of great persons. Education aimed at developing the virtues of self-control, self-respect, love, co-operation, sympathy, etc., in the students.

(e) ***Sublimation of Instincts.*** Man is the virtual slave of the instinctive drives embedded in his psyche and when he is obsessed by his senses, he often adopts the wrong path. The objective of education was to sublimate these instinctive tendencies, to turn the mind away from material knowledge and centre it upon the spiritual world, thus, establishing control over materialistic and base tendencies.

**3. The 'Upnayana' Ritual.** The word 'Upnayana' means to take close to, or to bring in touch with. A ceremony called the Upnayana ceremony was performed before the child was taken to his teacher. This ceremony was performed at the ages of 8, 11 and 12 for the brahmins, kshatriyas and vaishyas, respectively. The ceremony signalled the childs's transition from infancy to childhood and his initiation into educational life. In this context, the term 'Upnayana' means putting the student in touch with his teacher. With the passage of time, the ceremony came to be confined to the brahmin class only.

**4. The Method of Education.** During the Vedic period, the Gurukul method prevailed, in which the student lived in the house of the Guru, instead of living with his parents. Along with his colleagues, he led a celibate life and obtained education in the house of the Guru. Initially, in the Vedic period, it was the teacher who occupied the primary place, but in the later period, it was the student who occupied the central place in education, the process of education passed through the three stages of comprehension, meditation, memory and nidhi-dhyaasana. The Gurukuls were the centres of education, in which education was imparted only by individuals of character and ability. The student remained with his Guru for 12 years. There were parishads or committees to satisfy the student's thirst for knowledge.

**5. Service of the Teacher.** Every student was required, while residing in the Gurukul, to serve his teacher compulsorily. Any violation of the Guru's instructions was regarded as a sin and subject to stern punishment. The student's duties included obtaining such daily necessities as water, a twig for brushing the teeth, etc., for his guru. The teachers also ensured that the students should not be distracted from their studies while performing such duties.

**6. Celibacy or Brahmacharya.** Every student was required to observe celibacy in his specific path of life. Purity of conduct was regarded as of supreme importance. Only the unmarried could become students in a Gurukul. On entering student life, the student was made to wear a special girdle called a 'makhla'. Its quality depended on the caste of the student. Brahmins wore a girdle of moonj grass, the kshatriyas of string gut-taanta—and the vaishyas a girdle made of wool. The clothes worn by them were also accordingly of silk, wool, etc. The students were not allowed to make use of fragrant, cosometic or intoxicating things.

**7. Alms System.** The student had to bear the responsibility of feeding both himself and his teacher, this was done through begging for alms, which was not considered bad, since every domestic knew that his own son must be begging for alms in the same way at some other place. The reason behind the introduction of such a practice was that accepting alms induces humility. The student realised that both education and subsequent earning of livelihood were made possible for him only through society's service and its sympathy. For the poor students, begging for alms was compulsory and unavoidable, but even among the prosperous, it was a generally accepted practice.

The work of teaching began early in the morning. After performing their ablutions, students participated in some religious rituals, such as havans. Subsequently, they were put to the task of studying. In the afternoon, after partaking of lunch, the students returned to their studies. At sunset, some more religious rituals were performed. They denoted the end of the day's routine.

**8. Duration of Education.** In the house of the teacher, the student was required to obtain education upto the age of 24, after which he was expected to enter domestic life. Students were divided into three categories:

*(a)* Those obtaining education upto the age of 24—Vasu.

*(b)* Those obtaining education upto the age of 36—Rudra.

*(c)* Those obtaining education upto the age of 48—Aaditya.

**9. Practicality.** The education of that period encompassed the necessary activities of life. Students were given education about animal-husbandry, agriculture and other professions. In addition education in medicine was also imparted. According to Dr. Alteker, the purpose of education was not to provide general knowledge about a variety of subjects, but to produce specialists of the best kind in various spheres.

**10. Curriculum.** Although the education of this period was dominated by the study of Vedic literature, historical study, stories of heroic lives and discourses on the Puranas also formed a part of the syllabus. Students had necessarily to obtain knowledge of metrics. Arithmetic was supplemented by a knowledge of geometry. Students were given knowledge of the four Vedas—Rigveda, Yajurveda, Samaveda and

Atharvaveda. The syllabus took with in its compass such subjects as spiritual as well as materialistic knowledge, Vedas, Vedic grammar, arithmetic, knowledge of gods, knowledge of the absolute, knowledge of ghosts, astronomy, logic, philosophy, ethics, conduct, etc. The richness of the syllabus was responsible for the creation of Brahman literature in this period.

**11. Education for the Individual.** In the Vedic period, every teacher devoted himself to the integral development of each student. He aimed at the physical and intellectual development of his wards. The maximum attention was devoted to the individual development of every student, but there was no provision for the education of the incapable and the handicapped, especially those who were lacking in mental and moral qualities or were known for moral turpitude.

## POST-VEDIC EDUCATION

To attain salvation by realising the truth has been the aim of education, during this period. Only that education was regarded true which helped one to realise this supreme truth. According to the Upanishads 'truth' alone is the knowledge and the other worldly knowledge is untruth. The worldly knowledge was regarded as ignorance. Upanishads maintain that one cannot attain salvation through worldly knowledge because through this one becomes involved in illusion (*Maya*).

**Upanayan Sanskar.** Upanayan Sanskar was considered important both in the Vedic and Post-Vedic periods. This is evident at several piaces in the Rigveda. But different values were adhered to in the two periods. It was not necessary during the Vedic period to have the Upanayan ceremony before starting education. But during the Post-Vedic period Upanayan ceremony was considered necessary for starting education.

The word 'Upanayan' means to come near. In the context of education this word signifies that the student should come near the teacher for receiving education. The Upanayan ceremony became so important during the Post-Vedic period that it was usually regarded as second birth of the individual. For the Brahmans this became very important. Brahmans began to be called as Dvij (the twice born or born again). It was after the Upanayan that a Brahman boy could be called a Dvij.

Two births signify the worldly and the spiritual births. On the Upanayan occasion the Guru (preceptor) used to give him his Mantra (Advice). His spiritual life used to begin from this point. That is, from this day his education was started which ultimately led to his spiritual development in due course of time. The Upanayan ceremony is still in vogue in certain religious groups in the world, though in different forms.

**The Important Place of the Teacher.** During this period the teacher (Guru) enjoyed a pre-dominant place not only in his Gurukul (seat of learning) but in the entire society. He was regarded as a great guide for all. To his pupils he showered all love and affection and used to teach them whatever he knew, but before doing this he always tested the deservingness of a particular pupil. The pupils were free to discuss points freely with the Guru. We find many examples of free discussion between the teacher and his taught. We may cite here an example from Brahma and his son Bhrigu. Brahma gave the Brahma-gyan, *i.e.,* the knowledge of the ultimate or God in an outline form and advised him to perceive the same through thinking (*Manan*) and meditation. Bhrigu accepted this advice and realised God (*Brahma*) on the basis of the same.

## Curriculum during the Post-Vedic Period

During this period the curriculum included more subjects than during the Vedic age. Veda mantras (Vedic hymns and verses) were principally taught in the Vedic period. During the Post-Vedic period various types of literatures were produced pertaining to the different Vedas. In addition to religious subjects many worldly subjects were also included in the curriculum. This may be verified in the conversation between Narrad and Sanat Kuman which is incorporated in the Chhandogya Upanishad. During the Post-Vedic period the curriculum consisted of Vedas, History, Puranas, Grammar, Mathematics, Brahma-Vidya, Nirukti (etymological interpretation of words), astronomy, dance, music, etc., etc.

In addition to the above three methods we find a mention of another method—Question-Answer System in the Upanishad literature. In fact, the entire Upanished literature is on the question answer system. We do not find its practice in the Rigvedic period. Through this system difficult and abstract ideas were made simple. The terse-spiritual elements were explained through this system. Examples, strories and help of certain biographies were also taken in the system for elucidating certain points. This question answer method was also successfully used by Socrates in Greece to explain abstract ideas.

**Daily Routine of Students.** During the Post-Vedic period the Ashramas (Schools) were generally organised and run by Guru (preceptors). It was compulsory to adhere to laid down rules of discipline and conduct. No distinction was made between students in this respect. Everyone was required to observe celibacy. Rules of conduct were enforced keeping in view the physical, mental and moral development of students. Strict adherence to rules of conduct and discipline was an inseparable aspect of education in those days.

(*a*) ***Practical Education.*** Practical education consisted of three parts : 1. to beg alms, 2. to prepare fire for the Yajna-kund and 3. to look after the animals and other fellow-beings of the Ashrama (School). Besides, the students were also expected to do some agricultural work.

There were varying aims of all these three aspects of practical education. Begging of alms was meant to teach politeness. Preparing of fire for the Yajna-kund signified mental development of students. Rearing up Ashrama animals and doing agricultural work were meant to make the students self-dependent.

(b) ***Moral Education.*** Leading a disciplined and controlled life is the real basis of moral education. Moral education affects the conduct of the individual. Only oral instruction cannot improve one's conduct. Therefore, observance of celibacy was considered necessary for good conduct.

(c) ***Mental Development.*** Hearing, thinking and meditation were the three parts of mental education. For full mental development all these three aspects were considered necessary. Thinking over the heard things and perception through meditation were the accepted methods of mental development. This is true even today.

**Duration of Education.** Duration of education during the Post-Vedic period was almost the same as in the Vedic age. This duration was of about twelve years, although the number of subjects of study were increased. However, there was no uniform rule for the duration of education. We find examples in which students continued to stay longer than twelve years for keeping the fire of the Yajna or looking after the animals and inmates of the Ashrama. Satyakam Jawal may be cited as an example in this respect.

## Teacher's Place in the Ancient Indian Society

In the ancient Indian society the teacher always enjoyed a dignified place. During the Vedic and Post-Vedic periods the teacher's place was second to that of God only. He was more respected than the king in society. The Guru-Ashrama was known as the Gurukul (the family of the teacher) and the Guru was regarded as a Rishi (Sage) or Acharya (the one who practises what he professes). The Guru was given this significant place, because without him it was impossible to attain knowledge. The Guru was the guide and could help anyone to carve out his course of action. He used to bring light wherever there was darkness. Thus, the people always felt his necessity whenever there was a difficulty in solving any issue or problem.

During the Upanishadic period as well, when self-study was considered as dignified the place of Guru in society remained intact. It was believed that no knowledge could come without the assistance from the Guru. In other words, it was believed that the attainment of salvation was not possible without the help of the Guru.

**Restriction on Teachers.** The teacher was expected to lead a life of penance free of worldly things. He, too, was required to follow all the rules of strict discipline, thinking and meditation which were prescribed for the students. We find many references to such a position in the Maitrayan Upanishad. After the demise of the Guru even one of his disciples could succeed him if his son was not considered worthy of the same.

**Convocation Address.** After receiving education for twelve years students used to assemble near their teacher (*Acharya*) for blessings before going home. The Acharya on this occasion used to give some places of advice for happy and smooth running of their future life. The teacher used to tell them how to lead a life of householder (*Grihastha*), how to take care of the society and the nation and how to serve the humanity as a whole. The teacher used to tell all these in a ceremony which was known as Samavartan Samaroha like the modern convocation address.

**Supreme Knowledge.** It was compulsory for the students to have full faith in the teacher. Only students were considered as deserving of attaining real knowledge of supreme truth who had full faith in the teacher. So the student was always in search of a real Guru for attaining real knowledge and the Guru wanted to find out a really deserving student who he could give all that he knew.

**Women's Education.** Many changes were introduced in women education during the Post-Vedic period. This led to the fall of women education. During the Vedic age the women enjoyed equal educational rights. During the Post-Vedic period they were deprived of the social and religious rights. They were not allowed to participate in social functions. Now they did not enjoy the same status as before. Thus, the path of their social and mental development was blocked. Ultimately the position of women in society fell down so low that the birth of a girl was regarded as a curse on the family.

But an upward trend again appeared in the status of women during the Upanishadic period. Now they were given social and educational rights again. Once again they were given equal status with men and many women bacame as learned as men. Many women became Acharya (Principal teacher-Guru) in Ashramas. The name of Gargi may be cited as an example.

**Varna System and Education in Society.** The Varna system in the Vedic age was based on one's work or duty (*Karma*). Members of a family used to engage themselves in different types of work (profession) and their work decided their varna. During the Vedic period one could choose a particular profession as he liked and accordingly his Varna was determined. But during the Post-Vedic period Varna came to be determined by birth. Consequently, the whole society was divided into four Varnas—Brahman, Kshatriya, Vaishya and Shudra.

Out of these four Varnas, the Brahmans occupied the supreme position and enjoyed more rights. Kshatriyas resented this superiority and a clash ensued between the two. Kshatriya were the winners in the clash and the administrative powers came into their hands. Gradually they established their kingdoms and principalities. Thus, in the Varna system the Brahmans and the Kshatriyas became pre-dominant. The Vaishyas and Shudras came into the lower groups. In this hierarchy Shudras were kept at the lowest order of society. In course of time the condition of Shudras fell down further and they came to be regarded as untouchables and they were denied all social and religious rights. Vaishyas remained superior to Shudras and they divided themselves into professional groups such as—goldsmith, blacksmith, potter, fowler, milkman and sweet-seller etc., etc.

However, the position of Varnas during the Post-Vedic period had not degenerated so much as it is found today. Than, its was possible to change one's Varna. One could marry a girl from a different Varna. The Vaishyas were permitted in the Rajya Surya Yajna upto some extent. Then, Brahmans also did not control the Yajnas. The marriages of Chyavan Rishi and king Shantanu and the religious rites performed by Vishwamitra (A Kshatriya) and other Kshatriyas bear a testimony to the above.

The Post-Vedic literature does not contain much about the education of Vaishyas and Shudras. Agriculture was the main occupation of Vaishyas during this period.

Shudras were given education by Brahmans. But the number of educated Shudras fell down day-by-day. According to Shatpaths, fisherman, snake-charmers and other alike professionals were some of the other students of Brahmans. Shudras were mostly engaged in manual labour in agricultural fields, grazing cattle and pottery. Some of them knew music and dance as well as we find even today.

## BUDDHIST SYSTEM OF EDUCATION

The history of education in Buddha period is inter-related with the history of monasteries and 'Vihars' because there were no independent educational institutions or centres, other than those religious centres. Only monks and shramanas were authorised to impart education to the people. Thus, the monasteries and 'Vihars' took the place of sacrificial altars and as a result, these places became the centres of cultural life. Thus, the methods of these monasteries and 'Vihars' were the educational methods of that time. Rules and regulations of Buddhist monasteries and 'Vihars' were not framed by Lord Buddha. They had been taken from Hinduism and the various sects of Sadhus and nuns so they resembled 'vedic' systems.

**Rules of Admission.** Admissions into Buddhist monasteries were based more or less on the rules and regulations observed by Gurukula as in Vedic period. Like the students of 'Vedic' period, here also the students had to present themselves before the teacher to ask for the admission. Like the 'Upanayan', 'Pabbaja or pravrajya' is to go out. The boys went out of their families and joined the monasteries. Every one had the opportunity to undergo 'Pabbaja' and become a 'Buddhist' monk. After admission into 'Sangh' they could remain a monk. They had to change the former caste, dress, character, etc. Though theoretically, all the castes were allowed to get admitted into the monastery but practically and mostly the people of higher classes were admitted there. However, it is also true that some of the monks were derived from the lower castes. At the time of entering into the 'Sangh' the disciple must have attained the age of 8 years and during this period the new monk made his preparation for the sangh-life. Afterwards at the age of 20 years, he accepted 'Upsampada' and became full-fledged member of the 'Sangh'.

**The System of Pabbaja.** At 8 years of age, one could go to any 'Vihar' or 'Sangh' according to his own will. With head shaved and a yellow cloth in hand he went to the principal monk and requested him for admission in 'Sangh'. He thus, surrendered himself fully. The monk caused him to put the yellow clothes on and surrendered to the three words of shelter in a loud voice:

I go into the shelter of Buddha.

I seek the shelter of Dharma.

I enter the shelter of Sangh.

After taking the above three vows, one became entitled to admission. No one could get admission into the 'Sangh' without the consent of his parents. Patients of infectious diseases like Leprosy. T.B., Eczema, etc., and Government servants, slaves and soldiers were not allowed to be admitted into 'Sanghs'. However, there was no discrimination of any kind on the basis of caste or creed.

**Rules for the Students.** Now the admitted student was called "Samner". He had to follow the following rules—

1. Not to kill any living being.
2. Not to tell a lie.
3. Not to use any intoxicating thing.
4. Live free from the impurity of character.
5. Not to take food at improper time.
6. Not to accept anything given to him.
7. Not to use luxurious and scented things.
8. Not to take any interest in music, dance, playshow, etc.
9. Not to accept the gifts of gold or silver, etc.
10. Not to speak ill of any body.

The ten rules were essentially observed by the new monk. The 'Upajsata' *i.e.,* the teacher took all responsibilities up to the age of 20 years when he became mature and capable for accepting 'Upsampada'. For the teacher, he was 'Sadvi Biharak'. Lord Buddha himself taught that teacher should recognise his taught (*Sadvi Biharak*) as his son and the taught (*Sadvi Biharak*) should recognise the teacher (*Upajsaya*) as his own father.

**Upasampada.** After completing the education for twelve years, the 'Monk' had to undergo the 'Upasampada' ritual at the age of 20 years and then he became the permanent member of the 'Sangh'. There is also evidence that only such monks who had enough of spiritual knowledge were taken in sangh. They were directly given 'Upsampada'. Their 'Pabbaja' and 'Upsampada' both the rituals were performed simultaneously.

The method of performing 'Upsampada' was slightly different from 'Pabbaja'. It was similar to Vedic 'Samavartan' ritual with some difference. After 'Samavartan' the Brahamchari entered into family life but after 'Upsampada' he became a full-fledged monk, having no concern with family life. While Pabbaja was a ritual for a limited period, 'Upsampada' was permanent. It was for the whole life. Celibacy or chastity was considered essential for Brahmanic education. While among Hindus those observing celibacy for the whole life were; in 'Buddhistic' education it was a common feature. In this respect, Buddhistic education was more austere than Brahmanic education.

At the time of 'Pabbaja' the new monk of 8 years would go to the teacher and say with folded hands, "You are my teacher (*Guru*)". Thus, their relationship was established. The 'Upsampada' was performed before the entire 'Sangh'. Therefore, 'Upsampada' was given unanimously or on the decision of the majority.

**Restrictions on Admission.** In 'Buddhist' education also, like 'Vedic' education, the eligibility and the competence of the entrant was taken into account. A candidate could not be admitted into 'Sangh' in the following conditions:

1. Without the permission of his parents.
2. Under any legal responsibility and who was not free from legal bondage.
3. Patient of any infections or serious disease.
4. Convict of any serious moral sin.
5. Not found generous and laborious during the probation period, which sometimes was four or five days.

Thus, Buddhist Sanghs did not intend to destroy the family system. No one was admitted into 'Sangh' without the due permission of his parents. Similarly those who wanted to get rid of their social, moral and economic obligations were not admitted. Moreover, only those were allowed admittance who were healthy both mentally and bodily. Hence, Buddhism spread rapidly and in an organised manner, in so many countries of the world.

**The Qualifications of the Teacher.** In Buddhist educational system much stress was laid on the efficiency of the teachers. This has been described as follows:

*(a) High Moral Order.* The teacher himself, must have spent at least ten years as monk. He must have the purity of character, purity of thoughts and generosity, etc.

*(b) High Mental Order.* Essentially the teachers was expected to be of a high mental order, so that he might teach his disciple the religion and nobleness and he may also successfully combat the wrong religious notions.

**Duties of the Teacher.** In Buddhist system of education, the teacher was responsible for the proper education and up-keep of the disciple. He had to fulfil the needs of the disciple during the education period. He had to treat them affectionately. He had to supply his disciple with all the necessary materials. He was responsible for their physical and mental development. At the time of sickness he would attend to the treatment and care of his students. The teacher taught them through question answer, explanation and such other methods, so that the student might gain full knowledge and realise "Nirvan."

**Daily Routine of the Disciple.** Regular service of the 'Guru' (teacher), was essential in the Buddhist system. In morning the student would arrange for water, duetonic, etc., for the teacher. He would also look after his meal. He would cook the food, feed the teacher and clean the utensils. He would go out for alms with the teacher. After bath the students would get ready for the education. The teacher would impart education according to the system of the day.

Thus, the disciple had to serve the teacher and keep the place tidy. His daily routine depended on the orders of the teacher. He was not bound to obey anyone else except his teacher. He could not take any service from any other person. nor could he go any where without the permission of the teacher. Thus, the disciples used to live under the disciplinary control of their teacher.

## LEVELS OF EDUCATION

During the Buddhist period, education had two levels—primary and higher levels.

**1. Primary Level.** the Jatakas stories indicate that during the Buddhist period, primary education took the form of worldly or materialistic education. Fa-Hien has also mentioned the existence of a system so general education. Children of six were admitted to this level of education.

**2. Higher Level.** Dr. Altekar opines that the Buddhists raised Indian's international stature considerably by the high level of education in their monastries since students from as far as Korea, Tibet, Java and other distant countries were attracted to them.

## Centres of Education

During this period, some prominent centres of education sprang up. Their characteristics were their collective nature and their association with Buddhist Viharas or monasteries. There was no discrimination between students on any basis, some of these centres possessed an international reputation, proved by the fact that Chinese, Japanese, Tibetan and other sudents came there to receive education.

As already pointed out, there were many universities in India during the Buddhist period. It was a time when democratic feelings were evolving and hence, many famous educational centres came into existence. Wherever Buddhist monasteries or viharas were established, educational centres too emerged. Among the most notable universities to develop during this period were the universities at:

**1. Taxila.** Taxila was an important centre of education during the Buddhist period. It was then the capital of Gandhar. It had been founded by King Bharata after the name of his son Taxa. Being situated on the borders of this subcontinent, the kingdom was subject to frequent external aggressions. Because of this, the university in this kingdom developed on the basis of the family. Students started their education at the age of 16. The university provided education in numerous subjects, such as the three Vedas, Vedanta, Grammar, Ayurveda, the eighteen Sippas, military science, astrology, agriculture, commerce, treatment of snake-bite, (Sarpa-dansha chikitsa), magical charius (*Tantra Vidya*) etc.

**2. Ballabhi.** From 475 A.D. to 755 A.D., Ballabhi, in Kathiavar, was a famous centre of Buddhist education. Heun Sang visited Ballabhi also in his travels. At that time, there were a hundred Sangaramas here. This university imparted education in politics, diplomacy, medicine and various other disciplines apart from religious education. Its students obtained senior positions in the courts of kings after completing their education. This university, too became the unfortunate victim of foreign invasion in the 12th century.

**3. Nalanda.** The Nalanda university was situated in the State of Bihar, 40 miles south west of Patna and 7 miles north of Rajgraha. It was an internationally famed Buddhist centre of education. It became famous because it was the birth place of Sariputra the disciple of Lord Buddha. Emperor Ashok had a monastry constructed here. By the 4th century B.C. it had become a famous centre of education and by the 7th century it became the foremost centre of education.

Kings of the Gupta dynasty took interest in the growth of the university. Buddhist monastries were constructed here by Kumar Gupta, Narsingh Gupta, Baladitya, Buddha, Gupta, Vajra and Harsha. Because of these monastries, the university continued to grow and expand. Its land was surrounded by a rampart at the entrance to which lived a profound scholar who administered an entrance test to the students desirous of joining the university. The university had eight large assembly halls and 300 rooms for study. It had been stated in Epigraphic India that the highest point of Viharavali kissed the clouds. The buildings of the university are a fine example of the engineering skill existing in that age. The remains of these buildings are sufficient to prove that the art of construction had reached a peak during this period. In addition to the buildings, the university had beautiful lakes, numbering 10, according to It-Sing. The university also had a massive nine-storied library which was divided into three parts, called Ratna Sagar, Ratnodadhi and Ratna Ranjaka.

In Bihar, the Buddhist monks, teachers and students led a balanced, regulated and spiritualistic life, far removed from leisure and luxury. Students of this university carned great respect in many foreign countries. Students came from Java, Sumatra, Japan, China, Ceylon and other countries to receive education here. The staff of the university consisted of 1500 teachers. Huen Sang, in his travellouge, mentions the names of such renowned teachers as Chandrapal, Dharampal, Gunamati, Sthirmati, Prabhamitra, Gyanchandra, Sheelbhadra, etc.

**4. Mithila.** Mithila had been a centre of Brahman education in ancient times and when the Buddhist period came, it became an important centre of Buddhist education. It was here that a scholar named Jagdwara composed his renowned commentaries on such famous compositions as the Gita, Devi Mahatamaya, Meghdoot, Gita Govinda, Malati Madhava, etc. Vidyapati was born here. Apart from other subjects, Nyaya philosophy was also taught here. A student was deemed to have passed only after he had taken a difficult examination in Nyaya and Logic.

**5. Vikramshila.** Vikramshila was located on the banks of the Ganga in Magadha, Bihar. It was surrounded by a strong rampart. The teachers of this university were among the finest scholars of the day. Many important religious texts were translated into the Tibetan language at this university. Its administration was in the hands of a committee. Students were granted admission only after a test was administered to them at the gates. Among the famous scholars of that time who administered this test were Ratankar Shanti, Baghiswara Kirti, Naroha, Pargyakamnti, Ratna Vajra and Gyana Srimitra. The university provided education in grammar, logic, philosophy, tantra, etc. It, too, was destroyed in the 12th century by Bakhtiar Khiji.

**6. Odantpuri.** Odantpuri had evolved as an educational centre before the Pal dynasty came into existence. The kings of this dynasty further developed this university. Its library was internationally known. 1000 monks received education here.

**7. Jagdalla.** Rampal had the town of Ramvati established on the banks of the Ganges in Bengal in the 11th century. He also had a monastry named Jagdalla established here. This soon emerged as a centre of Buddhist education.

**8. Nadia.** Nadia was established at the junction of the Bhaghirathi and Jalangi rivers in the 11th century by the Sen kings of Bengal. Jayaleva's Gita Govinda and Shoolapani's Smriti-viveka were composed here. It was a centre of teaching in Nyaya and Logic. It retained its reputation even during the middle ages.

Vibhutichandra, Dansheela, Shubhkara and Mokshakara were some of the famous teachers of this university.

This period gave birth to distinctions of class and varna in the sphere of education and it was in reaction to this that the Buddhist and Jain religions came into existence. Their system of education changed from the method of teaching by gurus to an institutional method.

## EDUCATION IN BRAHMANIC AGE

The educational structure in the Brahmanic Age was, to a very great extent, only a refined and developed form of Vedic education. However, during this age, various forms began to emerge in the institutions of education. Various institutions, such as shakha, charana, parishad, kul and gotra, began to emerge at the various levels of education. Besides the Upnishads, Aaranyaka, Brahman and other classical texts were created in this period. Famous ashramas or monasteries came to be established in the forests. It was in this period that the sutra literature was created, along with the development of the six systems of Indian philosophical thought—Samkhya, Yoga, Nyaya, Vaisheshika, Karma of Purva Mimansa and Vedanta or Uttara Mimansa. A significant characteristic of this period is the determination of the syllabus according to the Caste and Ashrama system. However, the education of the Shudras and women suffered a decline.

The best mirror of any country or society is the literature, it produces. From the Vedic to the Brahman period, literature and additional literature continued to be created. Even in the Brahman period, education continued to be looked upon as the means to knowledge. It has the same objectives that Vedic education had. However, with the passage of time and a change in the needs of society, the importance attached to them underwent a change. In this period, the following objectives were ascribed to education:

1. Self-control
2. Development of character
3. Generation of sociability or social awareness
4. Propagation of purity
5. Integral development of personality
6. Preservation of knowledge and culture.

Education in this age continued to proceed on the foundations given to it during the Vedic period, but a certain rigidity and narrowness now marked its implementation. Education now aimed at equipping the student for the struggle for existence. After the upnayana or introduction ceremony, teachers imparted education to their students according to the latter's interests, tendencies and nature. Celibacy was rigidly oberved. Teachers paid full attention to the psychological make-up of their students while teaching.

Students lived in close contact with their teacher or guru in the Gurukul. But, restrictions had now been placed upon the receiving of education by Shudras. For social reasons, they were not considered fit to receive education. After

Vedic education, there was a gradual increase in ritualism. The result was that shudras and women began to lose their place in the educational sphere. But, on the other hand, education became more comprehensive in this period, as it was closely associated with every aspect of life. Some of its general characteristics are :

**1. Dominance of Religion.** As in the Vedic period, education in the Brahman period also was dominated by religion. Students were given knowledge of religious activities. Numerous religious and cultural activities were organised so as to acquaint students with them.

**2. Individualism.** Because of the absence of collective education, the emphasis was upon the individual. Teachers paid attention to the personal development of individual students.

**3. Celibacy (Brahmcharya).** Like the education in the Vedic period, education in this period also laid great emphasis upon celibacy. Students were expected to obey their teachers and indulge only in moral conduct.

**4. Worldly and Other-worldly or Spiritual and Materialistic Education.** During this period, education paid equal attention to spiritual as well as materialistic or worldly matters. Education comprehended the materialism of life.

**5. Curriculum.** In this age, too, primacy was given to the study of the Vedas. Among the subjects taught were grammar, arithmetic, geometry, astrology, economics, history, politics, agriculture, millitary science, nyaya philosophy, etc. A special feature of this period is that, as time progressed, two kinds of syllabi came to be prepared, one for the short-term and another for the long-term. In addition, clear and correct pronunciation of consonants and vowels was stressed. Students were also given knowledge of metrics and figures of speech. It was on this basis that learned commentaries on the Vedas came to be composed. The Pingal Shastra was composed for the teaching of matrics. Surgery had also developed by this time.

**6. Method of Education.** In the Vedic period, education was primarily oral. Students were made to memorise aphorisms and then elaborate them. But, by the advent of the Brahman age, the art of writing had developed and so both oral and written education came into practice, though the emphasis was upon oral education. Bhojpatra, the bark of a tree, was used for writing. Teachers gave importance to purity in pronunciation. Education was conducted through discussion, answering of questions, removal of doubts, etc. Students were given continuous practice in the art of writing and for this they were required to copy manuscripts. Practical work was emphasized in such subjects as grammar, astrology, nyaya, medicine, etc. The students as well as the teachers themselves obtained informal education through the concourse of famed scholars.

**7. Physical Punishment.** In the Brahman age, the practice of giving physical punishment to students was not prevalent. Such famous acharyas as Manu, Gautum, Vishnu opposed physical punishment because they considered it inhuman.

## Merits of Education in the Brahman Period

Indian culture has developed through its system of education. This system was especially fruitful in propagating the ideas of love, truth, non-violence, religion, peace and world brotherhood. It also pointed out the path to salvation. It was also responsible for the creation and preservation of literature. F.E. Keay has expressed wonder at the fact that though divine texts were composed such a long time age and that though it seemed impossible to preserve them intact, this was done and is still being done today. The education of this period possessed the following features :

1. It paid the greatest attention to the child's physical and mental development.

2. In the teacher's house, there was an abundance of family feeling. Students did not suffer from the lack of any familial necessity.
3. It was conscious of the development of the child's character.
4. The Gurukuls were situated at a distance from inhabited areas so as to prevent excessive contact between students and society.

**Demerits of Education in the Brahman Age**

Certain demerits stood, had crept into the educational system of the Brahman age. They were:

**1. Dominance of Religion.** Since education was dominated by religion, less importance was attached to material or worldly development. This dominance also led to an increase in an anarchic attitude towards religion among the students and prevented the growth of rational thought.

**2. Emphasis upon Philosophy.** Education during this period laid excessive stress upon the study of philosophy, since the purpose was to put the student onto the path to salvation through a study of philosophy. The result was the growth of an escapist attitude towards life.

**3. Deprivation of the Shudras('s) Right to Education.** During this period, the right to education became confined to the Brahmans, Kshatriyas and Vaishyas, because of the emergence of aristocracy. The Shudras were deprived of the right to education.

**4. Faith in the Vedas.** In this period, people came to have blined faith in the Vedas. They were convinced that only the Vedas were true. Consequently, the tendeney towards logical and rational thought was hampered.

**5. Women Education.** There is some evidence of education of women during the Vedic period, but during the

Brahman age, this was neglected. In addition, women became the victims of many restraints.

**6. Lack of Handicrafts.** During this age, the caste system became characterised by rigidity and narrowmindedness. Those engaged in handicrafts came to be regarded as inferior. The consequence to this was that handicrafts gradually vanished from educational curriculum.

**7. Absence of Synthesis.** The education of this period was taking in synthesis. Instead, it laid emphasis upon profound scholarship in any one subject.

## ANCIENT INDIAN UNIVERSITIES

Seats of Ancient Indian Universities were either holy places or capitals of great kings because the private teachers began to congregate in these place on account of facilities they received for educating pupils. To the holy places like Banaras, Kanchi, Karnataka and Gangasagar pilgrims flocked in large numbers and made huge gifts to the teachers there. In the capitals kings and princes patronised them. Hence, there rose up centres of high learning at Kailauj, Mithila, Dhara, Kalyani and Tanjore. Certain kings provided villages to a set of Brahman teachers and colonised them.

These seats of learning were simply centres of education where lived many famous teachers and to which flocked students from all parts of the country. They did not possess colleges in the modern sense of the term nor university campuses. Nor were the teachers members of anyone single institution like the professors in a modern university. Every teacher with his Pittiacharyas formed an institution. He admitted as many students as he liked. He taught them what they liked. Such was the form of the Taxila university, the most important seat of learning in Ancient India. It was founded by Bharata and named after his son Taksha.

Banaras was a seat of learning situated at a holy place. In the 7th country B.C., Banaras was the most important centre of Hindu learning. With the patronage of Ashoka, Sarnath in the outskirts of Banaras became the seat of Buddhist learning. It did not organise any public institutions like the Nalanda University. In the 17th century A.D., Bernier says, "Banaras is a kind of University, but it has no colleges or regular classes as in our Universities: but it looks like the school of the ancients, the masters being spread over the different parts of the town in private houses.

The universities and monasteries which belonged to the Buddhist order were Nalanda and Vikramshila. From the 10th century onwards, Hindu Temple colleges became prominent as seats of higher education. They were a natural reaction to the Buddhistic monastic universities. The Mathas of Acharyas continued the same tradition. Salotgi Temple College in Bijapur district in the 10th century A. D. was a centre of Vedic learning. Ennayiram Temple College in South Areot was an educational institution of the modern type with 16 teachers on its staff teaching a predetermined curriculum.

**Nalanda University.** Nalanda was the seat of Buddhist learning. It was built largely by Buddhist disciples, but Guptas, the orthodox Hindus also patronised it. The University had a plan of its own. Monastic buildings and stupas were arranged in a regular fashion round the central college which had 7 halls. It had 300 smaller rooms for lecturing work. The building were exceptionally high. The very name Nalanda has been derived from the word Na-alam-da, insatiable in giving, implying that the university education in those days did not cram the mind with knowledge but created an insatiable thirst for it.

**Rise and Fall.** The date of its foundation is not known for certain. Though as a monastic seat it was founded long ago, as a seat of learning it rose into prominence about 450 A. D. General Cunningham assigns the probable date of the founding of university from 425 to 625A. D. The University began to decline during the 11th and 12th centuries when it was suppressed by Vikramshila and was finally destroyed by Muslim rulers in the beginning of the 13th century.

**Student Body.** Throughout these seven centuries of its existence Nalanda attracted students from all parts of India as well as from abroad. Students from China, Tibet, Bokhara and Korea came to Nalanda. *For example,* Fa Hien, Yuan, Chwang, Itsing were Chinese and Hwni Lun, Hwuii Viah were Koreans. Budhdharma was from Bokhara. The standard of admission to the university was naturally very high Watters says, "Of those from abroad who wished to enter the schools of discussion, the majority beaten by the difficulty of problems, withdrew: And those who were deeply versed in old and modern learning were admitted: only two or three out of ten succeeded."

**Teachers.** The standards of scholarship among the teachers were very high. They were not only famous for their piety, but were renowned for scholarship also. They were eminent for 'conspicuous talent, solid learning, great ability and illustrious virtues.' Saraha, the tutor of Nagarjun, Nagarjuna the founder of the school of Madhya-mika Philosophy, Aryadeva the pupil of Nagarjuna, Arya Asanga and his younger brother Vasubhandu, Dharampala the famous logician and grammarian and Silbhadra were some of the illustrious pundits of the University.

**Library Facilities.** Library facilities for self-study were abundant. A monastery without a library was like a castle without an armoury. From the Tibetan accounts mentioned by S. C. Vidya-bhushan in Medieval School of Indian Logic we learn that Nalanda had a fine library situated in Dharmganj and was housed in three splendid buildings; Ratansagara, Ratnadadhi, Ratnarayaka, Ratna-dadhi was nine-storied. Such spacious libraries met the needs of hundreds of teachers and thousands of students.

**Administration.** The university was controlled and administered well. At the head was the Abbot-Principal who was assisted by two councils, one academic and the other administrative. The chief abbot was elected by the members of the Sangha on the basis of his scholarship, seniority and character. Local and provincial jealousies did not influence the election. The academic council regulated admissions, determined courses and assigned work to different teachers. The administrative council boked after general administration and finance. The officials of this council were in-charges of construction of buildings and distribution of rations, superintendents of hostels and revenue officers. The head (chancellor) in Hiuen Tsang's time was Silbhadra. In the middle of the $8^{th}$ century A. D. Kamalshila was its head. Besides the Dwarpandit and the Abbot Principal there were two other important officers. The Karmadana was the sub-director of the university and the Stavira, the presiding priest. Karmadana or Viharswami or Viharpal was the chief officer under the Chancellor and to him the utmost deference was paid.

**Subjects of Study.** The curriculum at Nalanda was catholic; *for example,* the works of Hinayana and Mahayana schools of Buddhistic philosophy both were studied. It was not sectarian because it was not confined to Buddhism alone. Subjects like Hindu religion and philosophy, were also thought there. Vedas, Vedanta and Sankhya philosophy were taught at the university with miscellaneous works. Subjects like grammar, logic, literature, astronomy and astrology, medicine which were of common interest were taught profusely.

**Teaching Methods.** The methods of teaching at the Nalanda University were tutorial as well as professional. Beal says, "They arrange every day about 100 pupils for preaching and the students attend these discourses without fail even for a minute." There was a close touch between students and professors. Itsing says, "I have always been very glad that I had the opportunity of acquiring knowledge from teacher personally." A great importance was laid on discussion and debate. "The brethren are often assembled for discussion to test intellectual capacity, to reject the worthless and to advance the intellect", says Watters, "the day is not sufficient for asking and answering profound questions. From morning till night they engage in discussion; the old and the young mutually help one another."

**Hostel Arrangements.** Hostel arrangements were adequate. Satras were free-boarding hostels where students were supplied with necessaries out of the endowments to the university. Students were so abundantly supplied with clothes, food, bedding and medicine that they engaged themselves wholeheartedly in studies. *For example* it is learnt that Hiuen Tsang received each day 120 fruits, 20 arecanuts, 20 nutmegs, an ounce of tack and peck of Mahasali rice. He was supplied with butter daily and other things that he needed.

## GURUKULS AND VIHARS

In the 6th Century B. C. and thereafter for a hundred years more, a section of people rose in revolt against the priestly class especially against their religious and social ideology. The revolt was headed by the Buddhists. The educational system was also opposed and in its place developed a system which had some elements in common and others quite different. The monastic system of education had the same spirit that prevailed in the Brahminic system. But the external forms became divergent.

The Brahminic system centred round sacrificial arrangements. The Buddhist system was born and grew up in the monasteries where the monks became the custodians of cultures and sources of learning. The Buddhist system was practically that of the Buddhist order (*Sangha*) and the Brahminic system belonged to the priestly class in the Brahmins.

The Buddhist Vihars ran counter to the Hindu Gurukuls. Whereas the Gurukuls centred round the hermitages of the saints and remained independent seats of learning throughout the Vedic period, the Vihars were organised on federal basis. The smallest link of the federation was a school—a small group of novices under a Uppajjhaya (*Acharya*). The group worked like a guild-a society for mutual aid and promotion of the common good. In a Vihar a number of such units were organised. Each units was expected to come forward to help the other. The entire Vihar was run by a body of officials with their functions well-defined.

**Admission Policies.** The Brahminic system of education was meant for the three castes the Brahmin, the Kshatriya and the Vaishya. The low-born were forbidden to study the Vedas because of a special sanctity that enveloped them. To Vihars persons of all classes of society, all castes and ranks (except the chandals) were admitted. No one was debarred entrance. Brahmins, Kshatriyas, Vaishyas, sons of merchants, tailors fishermen could get admittance. A common school system appears to have developed in the Buddhist period. The Buddhist monasteries did not however, admit a debtor, a slave, a crippled, a robber, an employee of the state, a person affected with leprosy, boils, fits and consumption.

**Religious Rites.** Both systems admitted students only after observing certain religious rites. The auspicious ceremony of Upnayan was replaced by Pabbajja, which literally meant going out of home or previous state and presenting oneself for admission into a Sangha. Upnayan also implied nearly the same thing. Literally, it meant a process of being 'taken near the teacher', but since after Upnayan the boy had to go out of his house and live with his teacher it practically meant going out. In Brahminic system the student was called a Brahmachari and in the Buddhist one he was named as Samanera. The regulations governing the life of a Brahmachari or that of a Pabbajja were ready alike. The Pabbajja had to obey the ten commandments as strictly as the Brahmachari had to abide by the ten qualities of a student. The only difference was in the manner of asking for alms. Whereas the Brahmachari could beg by words and could beg more food than was needed to feed himself the Pabbajja was not permitted to speak when he went a begging nor could he accept more than was needed for his upkeep. A Bhikshu as he was, he lived by alms. The Brahmachari also was to live by alms for begging was the first duty of a Brahmachari to be observed in Gurukul. The more dominant principles and manners of the life of Brahmacharya were adopted in the Buddhist system; *for example,* the modes of begging, eating, sitting, sleeping, cutting hair, clothing, were nearly alike.

**Teacher Pupil Relationship.** The teacher-taught relationships in the two systems were identical in nature. Every pupil had to perform domestic services for the teacher; *for example,* he was required to sweep the hermitage or the Vihar, beg for the teacher, wait upon and nurse him when he happened to be sick.

**Teacher System.** Domesticity was the prevailing note in the Gurukul system. The teacher's hermitage was the school. His personal impact was the potent factor in the education of the pupil. A striking difference became perceptible in the Buddhist monasteries. In the monasteries we had groups of novices under one Acharya. The novices were received in the religious house—the Sangha—on probation for taking a vow. The Acharya was required to work as their guardian. The fullfledged Achara or monk had a right to vote. The monks who had equal voting rights met usually and expressed their opinions. The resolutions of the Sangha were passed democratically. The Gurukul system favoured one-teacher, one-school whereas the Buddhist system had a large federation controlled by a collective assembly of teachers. The one-teacher-one-school system worked quite independently of other schools. The federated system of schools in the Buddhist period did not work in isolation.

The teacher in the latter system did not and could not wield supreme power over his pupil because there are evidences of the novices having been punished by the Vihar without any consultation with their Uppajjhaya.

The caste of teachers in the Brahminic system was only the priestly one. Instructions could be given only by Brahmans. There was a sort of Brahminic monopoly. But the teachers in Vihars were not necessarily Brahmans unless those who had become converted to Buddhistic order. The exclusive monopoly of the Brahmans was destroyed once for all. Different categories of teachers emerged. The main categories were those of the Dahara (Small Teacher), the sthara (settled teacher) and the Acharya.

In the Brahminic system the succession of teachers was not broken and individual schools were controlled by individual teachers only. But in the Buddhist system we have confederations of school. In the larger monastic institutions a number of teachers and students took a share of a wider, collective, academic life.

**Discipline.** The Brahmachari was not permitted to walk over ploughed land or through fields where corn was growing up. Every care had to be taken not to destroy life in any form. The prevailing note of Ahimsa in the Bundhist system of education was perhaps borrowed from there. The Brahmachari and the Bhikshu both had to abandon society, disclaim relationship with home and renounce homely pleasures if they wanted to seek education and acquire learning. Physical as well as mental purity was aimed at. Fasting was necessary. The eighth, the fourteenth and the fifteenth days of each fortnight were fasting days for students in Vihars.

**Nature of Curriculum.** The subjects of study in the Brahminic system were spiritual as well as worldly (Para and

Apart Vidyas). The para Vidyas included the study of the Vedas, Chhandas, Kalp, Pitryas, Upanishads, Shiksha. The Apara Vidyas consisted of Sutras, Medicine, Surgery, Mathematics, Economics, Logic, Ethics, Physics, Chemistry, Astronomy, Biology, Bhu Vidya, Dharm Vidya, Sarp Vidya, dancing, sining, fine arts. The subjects of study in the Buddhist Vihars were Theology, Philosophy, Logic, Metaphysics, Sanskrit, Pali, Astrology, Medicine, Law, Politics, Administration but no technical subjects were taught.

The Buddhist system attached little significance to vocational training. Professional education was utterly neglected. In the Brahminic system importance was given not only to the cultivation of the mind and the spirit but also to the preparation for worldly life. It was the education for life. It was on the basis of professional education that ancient Indians could build up prosperity and fame in the comity of nations. Dr. R. K. Mukerjee holds that the professional education led to India's supremacy in export trade. Ancient India was the chief exporting country of the world, which supplied foreign lands with articles turned out by her cottage industries and handicrafts.

## MUSLIM EDUCATION (MEDIEVAL PERIOD)

Muslim education system was essentially religious in character. It was patronised by the Muslim rulers who held orthodox views regarding perpetuating Muslim faith in lands they invaded and settled.

With the emergence of Islam, the attention of Muslim kings turned towards India. Time was kind to them. It allowed them to settle themselves firmly in this country. After the Gulam, Khilji, Tuglak, Sayyed and Lodhi dynasties, Mogul kings established many educational institutions in India. This education, too, had its roots in religion. During this period, Indian art and culture came under the influence of Arab culture and civilization. It was only natural that the same political influence should also have made itself felt. In consequence, education too came under this influence. Islam had its origin between 570 A.D. and 632 A.D. Hazrat Mohammed collected his messages in the Holy Kuran and this text came to be an instrument of social direction for the Muslim kings. During this period, these kings made arrangements for education in order to serve their own interests. Mohammed Gauri started his aggressions on India, but at the same time, he also had mosques and schools constructed in Ajmer to make arrangements for education in Islam and Muslim law. His successor Kutubuddin also followed in his footsteps. The other rulers of his dynasty, Altamesh, Razia Begum, Nasiruddin, Balban and others also had mosques, maktabs and schools established with Government aid.

Ferozshah Tuglak of the Tuglak dynasty made efforts for the propagation of education. One of the schools established by him in Delhi has been described as follows. The school was located in a large ground and a big building with massive towers. It was situated in a garden in which human skill harmonized with nature, thus, creating an environment most suitable for contemplation and thought. Near the school was a lake, whose water shone like silver. The grand building of the school was reflected in its waters. It was an enchanting sight to see hundreds of students crossing the polished and soomth floors and congregating round their teachers. According to N.N. Law there were provisions for Governmental aid and scholarships in these schools.

During the reign of Sikander Lodi (1489-1519), Indians, too, had begun to learn Persian (*Pharsi*). After obtaining knowledge of this laguage, they began to work in Government departments. The Muslim rulers themselves felt the need for Hindu workers in the administrative sphere and hence, they made arrangements for the study of Indian languages. And, as a result of the contact between the Hindus and Muslims,

Urdu, which was the spoken form of Persian mixed with Hindi, was evolved. The Mughal rulers who followed the earlier Muslim rulers had relatively greater interest in education and hence, it was in this later period that education developed more adequately. Akbar authorised the translation of many important Indian texts, including the Mahabharata, the Ramayana, Atharvaveda and Lilawati, into Persian. Akbar's deep interest in education is high-lighted by Abul Fazal's comments in his famous work 'Aaiyene Akbari' to the effect that in every country and especially in India, boys were kept in school for years where they were taught about consonants and vowels. Since they had to read numberous books, a large part of the boys' time was wasted. Emperor Akbar declared that each student should be taught to write the alphabet in various ways. Each student was required to learn the name of every letter (*varna*) within two days. Emphasis was laid upon imparting education in moral values, arithmetic, political arithmetic, agriculture, medicine, logic and physical, mathematical and divine philosophy to every student.

Jehangir went so far as to enact a law that the property and wealth of any person dying without an heir would be utilized for the repair of schools and religious buildings. Shahjahan had a university established near the Jama Masjid. Auraugzeb did propagate Muslim education, but at the same time he destroyed Hindu schools and temples. He granted excessive facilities for Muslim students, but he accorded a low status to teachers.

After the collapse of the Mughal Empire, schools suffered a severe blow. Many such institutions closed down due to anarchy and lack of finances. According to Vakil and Natrajan—"It must be noted that while mosques, maktabs and madrassas sprang up with the spread of Mohammadan power and provided facilities for Islamic learning in different parts of the country, the Hindu system of education continued to prevail in pathashalas, maths and temples except where their work was disturbed or dislocated by Mohammadan inroads or invasions." One finds a lack of organization in Muslim education. In the Muslim period, education was founded on community basis. Hence, it is illogical to claim that the Muslim ruler sought to propagate education liberally. Whatever the extent to which they propagated education, it was motivated by their own objectives, selfish interests and ambitions.

Bernier, the famous French traveller who visited India during this period, observed that during the period which he had described, it was only natural to find deep and universal ignorance. Was it possible to establish suitably financially aided schools and colleges or other centres of education in India? Where would the organisers be found? And, even if they were found, from where would the students be obtained? He also observed the absence of individuals whose wealth was adequate for providing suitable aid to colleges. And, even if such individuals existed, he felt that no one had the courage to compel them to bring out their wealth for such an investment. He felt that even some individual did venture on such a foolish act, there was an absence of religious places, enterprises and offices with employment potential which could utilize the ability and science imparted to students and thus, serve as an inspiration for youth to be hopeful and to compete for future success.

## Characteristics of Muslim Education

During the Muslim period, education developed so slowly that no notable characteristic of it ever emerged. Minor rulers had educational institutions established for the satisfaction of their interests. However, the following features can be noted:

**1. Encouragement by the State.** Muslim rulers took an interest in education and so they provided aid to maktabs and madrassas. There were granted jagirs or landed property. Scholars were given places of eminence in the courts of kings.

The rulers started giving aid to madrassas and maktabs being run in or alongwith mospues. Hence, their propagation of education was communal.

**2. Religious Influence.** The education of this period was profoundly influenced by Islam. Every Muslim sought education for the purpose of searching for knowledge and for religious purposes. There is direct evidence of the influence of Islam on the education of this period. Students were required to memorise the Koran. Importance was attached to study of Islam. This religious influence upon education was positive proof of the communal attitude of Muslim rulers.

**3. Arabic and Persian.** During this period, special stress was laid on the teaching of Arabic and Persian, which were made the media of education by Muslim rulers. Knowledge of these two languages was essential for securing employment in Government offices. Consequently, Hindus too began to learn Arabic and Persian.

**4. Development of History-Writing.** By initiating the writing of the history of their period, Muslim rulers helped to develop the art of writing history. Both Mughal and Muslim rulers commissioned the writing of the histories of their period or reigns. Among the most famous of these are Babar Nama, Akbar Nama, etc.

**5. Emergence of Urdu.** The evolution of the new language 'Urdu' which emerged from the inter-mixing of Arabic and Persian, is the greatest contribution of the Mughal period. The importance that this language enjoys today is due entirely to the Muslim period.

**6. Materialism.** Muslim education sought the spread of education only from the practical and materialistic viewpoints. Education in manual skills, sculpture, agriculture, medicine, etc., is proof of this. In addition to religious education, teachers tried to ensure that after receiving education, the child should become capable of earning his livelihood.

Consequently, knowledge of military science, painting, sculpture, housing construction, manufacture of weapons, etc., was also imparted. Knowledge of such subjects was given to students directly and individually by experts through a system of apprenticeship.

**Centres of Education**

The political organization of the Muslim rulers was decentralised. The Mansabdars, kings, zamindars or landlords, etc., became dependent rulers of their individual areas after paying the requisite tax to royal treasury. These rulers had mosques constructed and soon the mosques changed into maktabs and madrassas. During the Muslim period, Agra, Delhi, Jaunpur, Lahore, Ajmer, Bidar, Lucknow, Ferozabad, Jullundur, Multan, Bijapur, etc., became important centres of education.

**1. Agra.** Agra was founded by Sikandar Lodi. He had the town established as a centre of Islamic education and it soon took the form of a university. Hundreds of madrassas in this town provided education in literature, mathematics, philosophy, medicine, etc. Later on, Akbar, Jehangir and Shahjahan also contributed to the development of education in this town.

**2. Delhi.** Delhi was renowned far and wide as a centre of Muslim education. Nasiruddin established the Nasaria Madrassas here. The Gulam dynasty also helped the spread of education in Delhi. During the reign of Alauddin Khilji, 34 famous scholars of Islam lived in Delhi. Feroz Tuglak had 30 madrassas established. Humayun opened madrassas for imparting knowledge of astrology and geography. Akbar, Jehangir, Shahjahan and Aurangazeb also established various madrassas for imparting knowledge of various specific fields.

**3. Bidar.** Bidar, too, was an important educational centre. Mahmood Gawan had a huge madrassas and a library established here. Later, Alauddin Ahmed contributed to the development of education.

**4. Jaunpur.** During the reign of Feroz, Jaunpur was a prominent centre of Muslim education. It had many schools imparting education in the arts, literature and other spheres of knowledge. The Sharkias made valuable contributions to the development of education. Sher Shah Suri himself was a student here.

In addition to the above centres, there were at least one maktab and one madrash in every village of Bijapur, Golkunda, Malwa, Khandesh, Multan, Gujarat, Lucknow, Sialkot and Bengal.

## Organization and System of Education

During the Muslim period, the system of education was organised in the following manner:

**1. Bismillah.** Education began with the performance of the ritual known as 'Bismillah', which was performed at the age of 4 years, 4 months and 4 days. It was similar to the Upnayan ceremony of the Vedic period and the Pabbaja ritual of the Buddhist period. On this day, the child was adorned with a new crown and sent to his teacher, the Maulvi, where the latter inaugurated the child's education with a recitation from the Koran. Affluent people had this ritual performed at home.

**2. Madrassa.** Madrassas provided higher education to the students. They were aided by the Government. Here, higher education was imparted through lectures. There were arrangements for hostels in the madrassas. They were owned privately as well as by the state.

**3. Syllabus.** The syllabus of education in the Muslim period included such subjects as the holy Koran, the biography of Hazrat Mohammed Sahib, the history and the laws of Islam, Arabic and Persian, grammar, literature, logic, philosophy, law, astrology, history, geography, agriculture, Unani system of medicine, etc. There were provisions for teaching Sanskrit to Hindu children. Madrassas provided both religious and material or worldly education. Subjects of religious education included Koran, Islamic laws, history and Sufi philosophy, while worldly or material education consisted of grammar, language, literature, etc. There were some specialized centres for education in particular subjects.

**4. Maktab.** Education began in the maktab, *i.e.*, a primary school. The teachers called Maulvis taught the alphabet along with verses from the Koran. The child's primary education took place in these schools. Generally, most such maktabs were appendages of mosques. The child was taught writing, the Koran, namaz or prayer, azaan, arithmetic, drafting, conversation, letter-writing, etc.

**5. Method of Teaching.** Emphasis was placed on memorisation in addition to reading, writing and arithmetic. The most prevalent method was the oral. Individual attention was paid to students. The monitor system had been used in maktabs and madrassas.

**6. Student-Teacher Relationship.** During this period, relations between students and teachers were not marked by intimacy, but there were no doubts about sincerity and purity. Though teachers received a low salary, they had an important place in society. People respected them and bestowed faith on them. The teacher had a paternal attitude towards his wards. It was believed that the students who served their teachers made God happy. Despite this, there was nothing notable in this relationship. Aurangzeb is known to have insulted his teacher Mulla Shah Saleh.

**7. Medium of Education.** During the Muslim period, Arabic and Persian were the media of education. However, after the growth of Urdu, education began to be imparted though this language.

**8. Reward and Punishment.** There was a system of severe punishment to maintain order and discipline, but brilliant scholars were also rewarded.

**Merits of Muslim Education**

**1. Compulsory.** Education was compulsory, specially for boys.

**2. Character.** Great stress was laid on character building.

**3. Co-ordination.** There was proper co-ordination between religious values and material or worldly needs and well-being.

**4. Literature.** Under Muslim rulers, through educational system, a good deal of development of literature took place.

**5. Personal Touch.** There was a personal touch between the teacher and the taught.

**6. Incentives.** There was arrangement for rewards and scholarships for meritorious and intelligent students. This provided an incentive to learning and education.

**7. Writing of History.** During this period, the tendency to write history was developed. This tendency was different from the tendency of the ancient India. It helped preservation of record.

**8. Special Centres.** There were centres of specialized education.

**9. Free.** The education during the Muslim rule was mostly free.

**10. Institutions.** During this period, great attention was paid towards establishment of educational institutions. Prospersous people were encouraged to establish institutions.

**11. Curriculum.** Curriculum included arrangement for the teaching of various subjects.

**12. Practical.** Great stress was laid on practical utility.

**Demerits of Muslim Education**

**1. Unsuitable.** Unsuitability was characteristic of the institution of education.

**2. Disbalance.** Education of the Hindus was neglected. This brought about a disbalanced development of education.

**3. Material.** There was predominance of material considerations.

**4. One-sided Curricula.** There was too much emphasis on teaching Arabic and Persian. This led to neglect of other subjects.

**5. Lack of Psychological Basis.** Muslim education lacked psychological incentives.

**6. No Universal Education.** There was no provision for universal education.

**7. Lack of Co-ordination.** There was no co-ordination between reading and writing.

**8. Defective Curriculum.** Curriculum was defective.

**9. Wrong Methods of Teachings.** Oral or verbal method of teaching did not help the consolidation of the knowledge.

**10. Indifference Towards Women Education.**

**11. No Development of Reasoning.** No encouragement to students to develop their power of reasoning.

**12. Low Status of Teachers.** The teacher-taught relationship was not ideal. The teacher did not occupy that position that he occupied during the Vedic period.

❋❋❋

# 4

# Growth of Modern Education System

"The beginnings of the present system of education in India can be traced to efforts of the Christian missionaries who came to India in the wake of European traders", remarked A. N. Basu. The missionaries that came to our country were the Portuguese, the French, the Danes, the English. Their main aim was to disseminate Christian religion among Indians. To achieve this purpose they first educated the Indian people so that they could understand and appreciate the principles of Christianity. They established educational institutions. Thus, they got an opportunity to preach principles of Christianity to them. The institutions that they built were all on the Western model. The Portuguese missionaries may be regarded as the originators of the modem system of education in India. They started colleges of higher learning at Goa, Bassein, Bombay and other places, where they taught Latin, Logic, Theology, Music and Rudiments of Portuguese Grammar. They started four types of schools; *(a)* parochial schools for imparting elementary education, *(b)* orphanages, *(c)* agricultural and *(d)* industrial training schools. They also set-up Jesuit colleges for higher education and Theological seminars for training missionaries.

The Danish missionaries, who started their institutions in Tanjore, Madras, Cuddalore, Tinnevelly, Trichinopoly, may be regarded as the torch-bearers of modern education in India. They started charity schools and taught English language to Indian children and did not teach Christianity openly. They translated Bible into Tamil and Telgu.

Why are these missionaries regarded as the originators or torch-bearers of modern education system in India? The schools established by these missionaries were different from those that existed in our country. The schools were organised on a new pattern and had more than one teacher on their staff. They had a clear-cut class system. Regular school hours were introduced with Sundays as holidays. They aimed at teaching English language. The subjects of study were Grammar, History, Geography and religious instruction. For the first time textbooks for schools were written and published.

The missionaries rendered valuable service to the cause of Indian education because for the first time the masses were imparted elementary education through the medium of their own vernacular languages. "It was due to their efforts that the early years of the nineteenth century witnessed the emergence of a new system of education in this country, a system which was different from the old and indigenous system in many respects says, A. N. Basu. The missionaries used education not as an end in itself but as a means of evangelisation. The schools were regarded as fruitful media for preaching the principles of Christianity.

**English Missionaries.** Along with the educational activities of the East India Company the English missionaries opened a number of charity schools—Calcutta Charitable School (1729), Free School (1789), Benevolent Institution at Serampore. By 1817 115 such schools were opened at Calcutta. Serampore and other places. Bible was translated in 32 Indian languages and books were published for schools and colleges. The missionaries came into conflict with the Company when they published a pamphlet "Addresses to Hindus and Mohammedans" wherein they denounced Mohammed as a false Prophet and regarded Hindusm as a religion of idolatry superstition and ignorance. Lord Minto, the then Governor-General ordered the removal of the missionaries from the field of education as they were found going against the interest of the country.

The missionaries were so furious at the order that they regarded it as an anti-missionary policy of the Company. So they began an intense agitation in England to get freedom and necessary help from the Parliament.

Charles Grant published a book to impress upon the British Government the use of English as a medium of instruction and as the language of the Government and also the conversion of the Indian masses to Christianity. Willberforce, a member of the House of Commons was so much impressed by Grant's ideas that he moved a resolution to adopt measures as may gradually advance useful knowledge and religious and moral improvement among Indians. However, the Court of Directors opposed this resolution and regarded it as madness to convert the Hindus to Christianity.

The missionaries were disappointed by the anti-missionary policy of the Company, yet they continued their agitation and at last, by the Charter of 1813 they got permission to enter India, reside there, preach, found churches and discharge all spiritual duties. The Charter Act of 1813 formed a turning point in the history of Indian education for after this date missionaries began to land in India in large numbers and establish schools. A large number of schools and colleges were opened during 1813-1833 in Bengal, Bombay and Madras. Though their main object was conversion, they did a yeoman's service to the cause of Indian education by imparting education through the mother-tongue and by popularising Indian languages. Another important thing to their credit lies in the pioneer work they did in the field of women's education in India.

**Charles Grant's View of Indian Education**

When Charles Grant went back to his country in 1792, he published a small pamphlet entitled, "Observations on the State of Society among the Asiatic subjects of Great Britain, particularly with respect to morals, the means of improving it." In this pamphlet he expressed his views regarding Indian education. He said that English should be adopted as medium of instruction, that Western sciences and literature should be taught to Indians, that efforts should be made to convert them to Christianity and that with this, purpose in view schools and colleges should be set-up. He advocated for the introduction of English as medium of instruction by degrees so that Hindus may be made acquainted with easy literary compositions in English in a variety of subjects. "It would be extremely easy for the Government to establish at a moderate expense, in various parts of Provinces, places of gratuitous instruction in reading and writing English: multitudes, especially of the young would flock to them." He wanted to make English not only the medium of instruction but he urged the Government to adopt English as the language of the Government. He hoped that the employment of English in public businesms would make it very general throughout the country. He requested the Government to patronise the scheme of introducing English as the medium or instruction and also' the language of the Government.

The second important point which he placed before the Government was that Hindus were a mass of ignorant people and their errors had never been fairly laid before them. "The communication of our light and knowledge to them", he said, "would prove the best remedy for their disorder." Charles thus, assumed that English education would be followed by conversion to Christianity. The suggestions made by Charles Grant were so important that he is sometimes described as the father of modern education in India. He clearly foresaw the future developments in Indian education. He suggested that English should be adopted as the language of the Government and his suggestion was accepted by Lord Bentinck. He suggested that English should be adopted as medium of instruction and this suggestion was accepted through the efforts of Macaulay. His foretelling came out to be true when he said that Indians would be eager to learn English and would flock to English schools and would in time become teachers of English themselves."

## THE CHARTER ACT OF 1813

Charter is a written grant of rights by the King. East India Company was allowed to conduct trade in India by such a Charter which was renewed after every 20 years. In 1813 the Charter was to be renewed. Previous to it Charles Grant had been vigorously trying to get freedom of proselytising for the missionaries. He and his friends succeeded in convincing the British people that the Company was following an anti-missionary policy. The opponents of this pro-missionary policy wanted a policy of exclusiveness. Warren Hastings who had a personal experience of India opposed vehemently the introduction of Western civilization or propagation of Christian faith in India. In spite of bitter opposition the missionaries got success and were allowed to enter India and reside here. They were also permitted to preach, to establish churches and discharge all spiritual duties.

The Charter Act, 1813 may be regarded as a turning point in the history of Indian education. It was for the first time that the British Parliament recognised the importance of education and set aside a definite sum of money for its encouragement. Till now the Company did not regard itself responsible for educating the Indian people. After 1813 it became its sacred duty to do so. A sufficiently large amount of sum henceforth began to be set aside annually for the propagation of education.

The Charter of 1813 is also important because the missionaries received full freedom for proselytising and conducting educational activities as they chose. It was after this date that missionaries began to rush into India and establish schools and colleges. The foundation of the modern education system was thus, laid.

But the Charter of 1813 did not specify how the sum of rupees one lac was to be spent. Consequently, controversies sprang up. The main issues were:

1. Should the elementary education of the masses or higher education of the upper classes be provided?
2. Should the State or any other agency be responsible for education?
3. Should the Oriental or Western learning be emphasised?
4. Should the oriental language or English be the medium of instruction?

## STUART ELPHINSTON'S CONTRIBUTION

Mr. Mountstuart Elphinston was appointed as Governor of Bombay Presidency in 1819. He established the Poona Sanskrit College out of Peshwa's Dakshina Fund. The Peshwa paid pensions and offered presents to learned Brahmins per year. When his rule was handed over to the Company, the Dakshina Fund was used for a more permanent work. But it must be remembered that in establishing the Poona Sanskrit College, Elphinston was not motivated by his love for Education but he wanted to gain the sympathies of the Brahmin who were hit hard by the change of Government from the Peshwa to the English.

**Elphinston's Suggestions to Improve Education.** When the Bombay Native Educational Society approached him for grants, he gave following suggestions:

1. The number of native schools should be increased and the method of teaching be improved.
2. Books on moral and physical sciences should be prepared and published in native languages.
3. Schools should be supplied with books.
4. Natives of backward classes should be encouraged to receive education.
5. Schools should be established for those who want to study English as a classical language and as a means to acquire knowledge of European discoveries.
6. European sciences should be taught in schools and colleges and the latter be improved.

It was Elphinston who for the first time proclaimed that it was the duty of the Government to control public education. The Government and private agencies both are responsible for the education of the people because the Government alone cannot bear all the expenses. The Government may pass such measures as may promote private enterprise and enlist the co-operation of the public in the education of the masses. It was Elphinston who defined a policy of state initiative and state control in education. It was he who stressed the need for co-operation between the state and private enterprise and advocated for a system of grant-in-aid. He said that the Government should take the initiative of starting schools, increasing their number and giving grants to bodies like Native Education Society for improving teaching.

The minute of Elphinston was deadly opposed by a member of his council who believed in filtration theory and did not like the improvement of native village schools. There was a difference of opinion; hence, Elphinston's recommendations could not be accepted by the Board of Directors. It will have to be remembered that through Elphinston's efforts the Native Education Society was accepted as the official organization for promoting education and a number of state vernacular schools were opened.

In 1827 Elphinston retired from Government service. The people of Bombay raised a sum of ₹ 2,26,172 for commemorating his services. Elphinston professorships were founded with this fund for diffusing western arts and sciences through the medium of English. The Directors also contributed two lacks of rupees and the Elphinston Institution was founded in 1834 as a body, separate from the school he had started in 1824. Thus, institution was expected to raise a class of persons qualified by their intelligence and morality for high employments in the civil administration of India.

**Adam's Report (1835-1838)**

Mr. Adam put forth a proposal for investigating into the actual state of education in this country and suggesting measures for its extension and improvement. The proposal was accepted. Mr. Adam was appointed to make a survey of indigenous education confining himself to a few districts only. Thereupon, he started his inquiry and submitted his report at three different times. In the first two reports he surveyed all the educational agencies involved in the elementary and higher education of the natives. He found that seven types of schools were imparting education—indigenous elementary schools, new types of elementary schools started by missionaries, domestic schools, English schools and colleges, native female schools, indigenous schools for advanced learning and adult schools. The indigenous schools were maintained by teachers themselves who gave free education and even fed the students. The expenditure was met out of the support given by the public. The teachers were mostly Brahmins. The system of education was being crippled due to the withdrawal of the support by the zamindars. Similarly, Maulvis taught as well as fed students in the Madarsas which were not so well-organised and maintained.

In the third report Adams put forth his scheme for improving and extending the prevalent educational system. Some of his suggestions were:

1. The people should be educated through their own language. English should not be used as the sole medium of instruction.
2. The future educational programme of the country should be based on the improvement and revitalisation of the indigenous education.
3. As knowledge ascends and not descends, education should be the first concern Government.
4. European knowledge should only be imparted.

The following measures he suggested for this improvement were:

1. A graded series of new textbooks (I-IV) in Bengali, Hindi and Urdu to be prepared by Indians.
2. Appointment of examiners for each district. Each examiner was expected to Survey his district, supply text books to teachers, explain to them the contents, examine them, distribute grants and rewards to teachers according to pass percentage and supervise their work.
3. Appointment of Inspectors to supervise the work of examiners.
4. Organization of experimental farms for agricultural education.

5. Award of small grants of land to village schools for their maintenance.

6. Training of teachers in normal schools for 3 months a year for 4 successive years.

**Thompson Plan**

In 1843 James Thompson was appointed as Lieutenant-Governor of the Provinces. He carried out to completion his plan to multiply and improve the village schools by supervision advice, encouragement and by the distribution of elementary books suited to their wants. Therefore, he is regarded as the father of elementary education in India.

Though Adam's work could not convince the Government and was turned down in Bengal, it had a far reaching effect in North Western Provinces. Thompson adopted his scheme only 5 years later. In 1842 the North Western Provinces were constituted and were separated from Bengal. The new province followed an educational policy quite different. It rejected the Downward Filtration theory. It advocated the use of mother-tongue and not of any foreign language as medium of instruction. It recognised the local demand for indigenous education. It regarded the education of the masses as its primary objective.

In 1845 he issued a circular and asked all district collectors to supply a detailed information about the existing condition of education in their respective districts. The enquiry revealed the depressed state of education and so he submitted a plan to the Government for organising vernacular education.

The main points of the original plan were:

*(a)* If the zamindar agrees to utilise the money for the maintenance of the teacher, this bit of land may be surrendered to him.

*(b)* A school should be set-up in every village of 200 houses.

(*c*) The teacher should be remunerated by grant of small jagirs of 5 to 10 acres of land of annual rent value from 20 to 40 rupees.

A second plan was submitted in 1849 when the Directors did not approve of jagirs to teachers. The new plan made the following recommendations:

(*a*) The Government should establish a tahsil school to function as a model for schools in the neighbouring areas.

(*b*) A comprehensive curriculum, considering the importance of reading, writing, accountancy, mensuration, History and Geography should be framed.

(*c*) Indigenous schools should be supervised by Inspectors (visitors) who were required to advise, assist and encourage indigenous school education.

(*d*) The plan to be followed first on experimental basis was to be spread later throughout the province.

Thompson not only wanted to improve indigenous education through advice and guidance, he wanted that primary education should come within reach of common people. With the help of one of his collectors of Mathura, he opened a new school in each halka of villages at a central place so that boys may come to that village school. The zamindars also co-operated. They contributed 1% of the revenue for the benefit of the school. Such an idea was caught up by neighbouring districts of Agra, Bareilly, Etawah, Etah, Mainpuri, Shahjahanpur.

## LORD MACAULAY AND THE OCCIDENTAL POLICY

Lord Macaulay was great scholar and educationist of his period. He was a writer of great repute. He was a good orator and could influence others very easily. On June 10,

1834 he became a member of the Governor-General's Council and was appointed the President of the Committee of Public Instruction. He was a staunch supporter of the occidentalism and had come to India with new educational ideas. When he reached India, the occidental-oriental controversy was at its peak.

As the President of the Committee of Public Instruction, he placed his proposal for spending the sanctioned one lac rupees. In his proposals he vehemently criticised the Indian languages and the literatures of Sanskrit, Arabic and Persian. He declared them useless before English languages. He showed injustice and partiality in his uncharitable criticisms and remarked that the Indians themselves wanted to learn English. He argued that the Indians were not so keen to receive free education in Indian languages as they are to receive education in English even on payment of fees.

In favour of English he observed that ultimately the Company would be a gainer financially. If English was made the commercial language, India would have better foreign relationships with other countries.

Macaulay further argued that Indians should be taught English even if they showed no interest in it, because their regeneration was possible only through English education.

Macaulay considered that person learned who knew English and European culture. He regarded the learned persons of Sanskrit, Arabic, Persian and other Indian languages as ignorant. The existing learned persons in India were great fools in his opinion.

Macaulay did not choose to interfere in the religious affairs of Hindus and Muslims, but he suggested a common law for both. He argued that this law should be based on the religious principle of both Hindus and Muslims.

He advised to close the Calcutta Madarsa founded by Warren Hastings. He regarded the Benares Sanskrit College as more useful than the Calcutta Madarsa. However, he did not want that Indians should be given education in Sanskrit, Arabic and Persian. He wanted that Indians should be given education in English and English alone.

H.T. Princep was requested to give his views on Macaulay's observations. Princep was an orientalist and he opposed Macaulay's views. But Lord William Bentinck accepted Macaulay's recommendations. Thus, a new chapter in the history of modern education in India began.

**Declaration of Educational Policy of Bentinck**

The Occidental-oriented controversy lasted for about twenty-two years. Ultimately on February 2, 1935, Lord Bentinck gave his approval to the policy advocated by Lord Macaulay. The substance of Lord Bentinck declaration was as below:

1. The British rule in India will propagate European science and literature in the country and the money sanctioned or to be sanctioned for education will be utilized towards this goal.
2. Whatever money is saved as a result of the above policy will be utilized for publishing and propagating European languages, literature and science.
3. The Government will not help in printing and publication of literature in Indian languages nor will publish them itself.
4. The old institutions will not be closed and the financial assistance already given to them will be continued. But neither the Government will give stipends to new students in the old institutions nor will be responsible for their education. But the teachers in them will be appointed by the Government.

The orientalists got a great set-back by Bentinck's policy. However, Bentinck's initiated a definite educational policy as the thought fit at the time.

## DOWNWARDS FILTRATION THEORY IN EDUCATION

During the British rule in India the downwards filtration theory was adopted in the country. Filtration means coming of something to the bottom from the top. Thus, the filtration theory in education meant coming down of education or knowledge from the top to the bottom, *i.e.*, from the higher class people to the lower classes or the general people.

There were many reasons for adopting this policy. Different views have been expressed about this policy. Some people think that this policy was adopted because of the narrow-mindedness and selfish attitudes of the English who intended to educate only a few for getting clerks for running their administration. They adopted this policy also because they wanted to create an elite group which would be given high posts in the administration and this group in turn would influence the general public for accepting the British rule in the country. In fact, according to some persons, the main reason for adopting this policy was the meagre financial resources with the Company for educational purposes. The Company thought that it could not provide education to entire mass. So it decided to educate only a few. But this 'few' were the people of the higher classes, because they alone could catch up the opportunity for English education. The downwards filtration theory had the following three chief characteristics:

1. To educate only the high class people in order to give them higher posts in the administration with a view to strengthening the roots of British empire in the Country.
2. When the higher class people would receive English education their culture would be improved and the

general public would accept them as their models. As a result, the lower class people would also be educated after being influenced by the higher class people.

3. To educate the higher class people who might undertake the responsibility of educating the general people.

Besides the occidental-oriental controversy, the Company had to face another problem during this period. This problem pertained to the education of the general masses. The Company was to decide whether to limit itself to the education of the higher class people alone, or to provide for education of all. The Company took no time in reaching a decision in this regard, as the Board of Director, gave-clear-cut directions in this context. Lord Macaulay explained the same by observing that "the aim of education in India was to anglicize the Indians through English education and to make black-coloured Indian English in their way of living, behaviour, thought, culture, traditions and morality", as such persons were likely to serve as the connecting link between the British Government and the general public. On July 31, 1837, Lord Macaulay again explained his point of view by stating that the purpose of the Company was only to educate the elite group which would educate the general public later—thus, fulfilling the goal of educating the masses in general. In 1839 the General Committee of Public Instruction again repeated the stand that education would be given only to the higher class people who should shoulder the responsibility of educating their countrymen.

During the Company's rule Missionaries were encouraged to work in the field of education and they opened a number of schools and colleges for educating children of the higher class family. They thought that if they succeeded in educating the higher class people and converting them to their own Christian faith, these converted persons would preach

Christianity amongst the lower class people. Evidently, the educational efforts of the Missionaries were religiously motivated and not politically. But only some lower class people could be influenced by these Missionaries and the bulk of the Indian population remained unaffected by them.

**Failure of the Downwards Filtration Theory.** The purposes of the downwards filtration theory could not be fully achieved. It could have only a partial achievement in the sense that the British Government got a few educated Indians who could help in running the administration. But these few Indians could not serve as connecting links between the British Government and the general people. The English educated Indians could improve their culture and ways of living, by they formed a class of their own and drifted away from the general people. Thus, the general public was in a way ignored by them as by and large they became more interested in making themselves richer and richer. As a result, education became concentrated only to those who had money.

The first cause of the failure of the filtration theory was that too many English educated Indians came out in the field and it was not possible for the Government to give them suitable employment according to their expectations. This situation led to unemployment. For ending their unemployment, these persons opened some schools on the Western pattern. Thus, a number of new English schools sprang up and the educational need of the people was met upto some extent.

The second cause of the failure of the filtration theory was that it created a feeling of self-respect, national honour and independence in the English educated Indians. These re-awakened persons could not be tempted by Government services and they took a vow to fight for national independence. For regenerating the people these enlightened persons began to spread education. Thus, education ultimately reached the people.

However, the filtration theory continued its impact till 1870 somehow or other. But because of the aforesaid two main causes this theory could not achieved its objectives fully. It was only a partial success.

Private enterprises engaged in the field of education did a lot towards educating the people and creating in them a love for freedom. Thus, the work for national regeneration and educational expansion began.

**Contribution of Lord Macaulay to Indian Education**

Lord Macaulay's Minutes ended the controversy going on, about the education system in India, for about 20 years. An Education policy was laid down. Following are the statements enabling the student to evaluate Macaulay's contribution to Indian Education.

**1. Ending Anglicist Orientalist Controversy.** In their book *"A Student's History of Education in India"* Nurullah and Naik say, "To call Macaulay a torch bearer in the path of progress, gives an exaggerated account of the role that he actually played." Lord Macaulay was not the first person who pleaded the cause of Western Education. He was not the sole founder of Occidentalist group, as these elements were working before his arrival in the country. These were started many years earlier by Christian Missionaries and men like Raja Ram Mohan Roy. Macaulay, however, ended the Oriental-Occidential controversy and laid the foundation-stone of modern education system in India.

**2. Cause of Political Disorder.** Some critics have called Macaulay responsible for Indian slavery. This is also not reasonable. Political disturbances could place in the absense of his education policy also, as many Indian students were studying in Mission Schools. The Indian Rulers, whose powers had been snatched away by the English Rulers had also assisted the political disorder to a great extent.

**3. Religious Motive.** Through English education Macaulay wanted to create, "a class of persons, Indian in blood and colour, but English in taste, in opinions, in morals and in the intellect." Of course, his policy succeeded to a great extent. He did create a group of WOGS (Western Oriented Gentlemen) who would always co-operate with British rulers in exploitation of Indians. In a latter to his father in 1836, Macaulay wrote "Our English schools are increasing with leaps and bounds and now the condition has reached to a position that it has become difficult to accommodate the students. Hindus are much influenced with education. There is no Hindu, who may keep real faith in his religion after studying English. I have full confidence that if our education policy succeeds then no idolator will be left in Bengal. All this will be done naturally without any religious preaching and interference." This statement clearly unravels the sinister motives of Lord Macaulay.

**4. Ignorance.** A learned scholar like Macaulay could not recall even the European scholars, who had praised Sanskrit Grammar, Philosophy and literature. He cracked jokes on it though he himself as ignorant about it. This charge of ignorance is irrefutable.

**5. Denigration of Indian Languages.** Some scholars had criticised Macaulay for denigrating Indian languages with malicious remarks, like calling them rustic, undeveloped and inefficient. Thus, he had given a great blow to the development of these languages. However, as the chairman of the Society of Public Instructions, Macaulay said in his report of 1836, "We have much interest in the development of Indian languages. We do not see any reason that the order of 7th March checks us in our efforts and we had already paid attention to its improvement... the development of Native languages is our final aim and our all the efforts should be utilised in its cause."

**Westernization of Education (1833-34)**

On June 10, 1834, Lord Macaulay, who was a great scholar of English, came to India as the Law Member of the Company. He supported the views of Charles Grant and believed that Eastern education was inferior. On his arrival in India, Lord Bentick made him the chief of the Public Instruction Committee also. His advice was sought regarding section 43 of the Charter of 1813 as well as about the expenditure of one lakh rupees. Macaulay was waiting for just such an opportunity. On February 8, 1835, he presented his historical 'Minutes' in which he made a bitter attack upon Indian literature and culture and vilified it.

**Macaulay's Views**

(1) In his elaboration of section 43, Macaulay included Engligh literature along with Sanskrit and Arabic literatures and along with the Indian scholars of Sanskrit and Arabic, he also enumerated English scholars. He also gave complete authority to the Company for spending the grant.

(2) A supporter of western literature, he had this to say for Indian literature—"A single shelf of a good European library was worth the whole native literature of India and Arabia." (Macaulay's Minutes). From the same viewpoint, he also praised the English language, arguing that it was the most flourishing and useful of all European languages. He, who knew this language, could esaily obtain that vast treasure of knowledge which had been created by the most intelligent races of the world. English was the language of India's rulers and hence, the higher classes living in the capitals also spoke it. It is perfectly possible that English may become the language of the trade on Eastern seas. (Macaulay's Minutes).

(3) Macaulay attached importance to the education of the higher classes and thus, emphasised the theory of Downward Filtration.

(4) In education, Macaulay laid stress on religious objectivity. As he put it, it was the duty of England to teach Indians what was good for their health and not what was suited to their tastes. He implemented the theory of Downward Filtration. He opined that the English rulers should create a class which could mediate between the English and the millons over whom they ruled. He wanted them to be Indians by colour and blood, but English by interest, morality and intellect. But, because of this principle, the objective of an education in consonance with Indian society could not be achieved.

Lord Macaulay was very typical, sincere to his country. He always thought about the propagation of English language and culture. His ideas for India were full of prejudices. Some of them are given here:

1. A single shelf of a good European library was worth the whole native literature of India and Arabia.
2. It is possible through English education to bring about a class of persons, Indian in blood and colour, but English in tastes, in opinions, in morals and in intellect.
3. English stands prominent even among the languages of the west. Whoever knows the English language has ready access to all the vast intellectual wealth which all the wisest nations of the earth have created.

Macaulay's resolution was put into the hands of the leader of the Orientalists in the Public Instruction Committee, Mr. Princep who was the leader of the opposition, he reduced it to shreds with his arguments. Despite this, Lord Bentick, who was prejudiced against eastern systems of thought, supported Macaulay's educational views and declared an educational policy founded on it. This policy gave primacy to the propagation of European literature and science, suspension of scholarships for students, neglect of publication of Eastern literature and the propagation of English literature.

Lord Bentick's acceptance of the educational policy enunciated by Lord Macaulay gave stability to the English educational policy. This was the first genuine educational policy adopted by the contemporary Government. Different people held different views on Macaulay's policy, but, in general, he is accepted as the inspiration behind the new educational policy. At least, he removed the element of doubt in this sphere and helped the Government overcome its uncertainty.

### Lord Auckland's Educational Policy

Lord Auckland succeeded Lord Bentick as India's Governor-General. Supporters of eastern education presented him with a representation opposing Macaulay's declaration. Lord Auckland agreed that the financial restraints upon oriental education were excessive. Consequently, he increased the educational grant for the orientalists, gave primacy to oriental studies, increased the number or scholarships for these studies and made arrangements for printing and publication of oriental works. However, he also permitted the spending of more than one lakh rupees for the spread of English education.

During Lord Auckland's reign, Adam, who had been appointed by Lord Bentick to prepare a report on Indian education, had published his report. It was a comprehensive document, containing some valuable suggestions for bringing about a Renaissance in India. Unfortunately, nothing was done to implement his ideas.

### Lord Hardinge's Declaration

In 1844, the then Governor-General, Lord Hardinge declared that priority in employment in the Company's organization would be given to those who had received English education. As a result, the demand for English education increased and education came to be directly linked with livelihood. At the same time, employment became more important than domestic crafts, which came to be neglected. Between 1833 and 1853, Bengal, Bombay, Madras, the Frontier areas, Uttar Pradesh and Punjab witnessed the kind of growth in education which had not taken place in many previous years. Professional or vocational institutions providing education in medicine, engineering, law and other professions were established. However, at the same time, dissatisfaction with the Compay's working was also being expressed. These improvements in the educational sphere were no more than a drop in the ocean. Hence, in 1954, Wood's Despatch was enunciated.

In 1853, when the Company's Charter again came up for consi-deration and renewal, the need for a permanent and comprehensive educational policy was felt. The British Parliament asked the Select Committee to consider this question. After deliberation, the Committee declared that the spread of education in India was not detrimental to the Company's interests. At that time, the President of the Company's Board of Control was Charles Wood, who published his declaration regarding education on 19th July, 1854. It is referred to as Wood's Despatch.

## WOOD'S DESPATCH

Sir Charles Wood, the President of the Board of Control in the coalition ministry of Earl of Aberdeen (1852-55), was a true product of the Palmerstonian era of English history. He was a firm believer in the superiority of Enlish race and institutions and sincerely believed that these institutions chould serve as a useful model for the world. Charles Wood showed a larger vision about education than most of the zealous educationists in India. In 1854 Wood prepared his comprehensive despatch on the scheme of future education in India. The despatch came to be considered as the Magna Carta of English education in India. The scheme envisaged a co-ordinated system of education on an all-India basis. The main reeommendations may be summarised thus:

(1) It declared that the aim of Government's educational policy was the teaching of Western education. "The education which we desire to see extended in India" wrote Wood in the despatch, "is that which has for its object the diffusion of the improved arts, science, philosophy and literature of Europe, in short of European knowledge".

(2) It recommended a system of grants-in-aid to encourage and foster private enterprise in the field of education. This grants-in-aid was conditional on the institutions employing qualified teachers and maintaining proper standards of teaching.

(3) It proposed the setting up of vernacular primary schools in the villages at the lowest stage, followed by Anglo-Vernacular high schools and an affiliated college at the district level.

(4) A department of Public Instruction under the charge of a Director in each of the five provinces of the Company's territories was to Preview the progress of education in the province and submit an annual report to the Government.

(5) As to the medium of instruction, it declared that for higher education English language was the most perfect medium of education. It also emphasised the importance of the vernacular languages, for it was through the medium of the vernacular languages, that European knowledge could infilter to the masses.

(6) Universities on the model of the London University were proposed for Calcutta, Bombay and Madras. The constitution of the University provided for a Senate, a Chancellor, a Vice-Chancellor and Fellows—all to be nominated by the Government. The universities were to hold

examinations and confer degrees. A university might set-up professorships in various branches of learning.

(7) Teachers' Training Institutions on the model then prevalent in England were recommended.

(8) The despatch gave frank and cordial support for fostering the education of women.

(9) The despatch emphasised the importance of vocational instruction and the need for establishing technical schools and colleges.

The new scheme of education was a slavish imitation of English models. Almost all the proposals in the Wood's Despatch were implemented. The Department of Public Instruction was organised in 1855 and it replaced the earlier Committee of Public Instruction and Council of Education. The three universities of Calcutta, Madras and Bombay came into existence in 1857. Mostly due to Bethune's efforts girls schools were set-up on modern footing and brought under the Government's grant-in-aid and inspection system.

The ideals and methods advocated in Wood's Despatch dominated the field for about five decades. The same period also witnessed a rapid Westernization of the educational system in India. The indigenous system gradually gave place to the Western system of education. Most of the educational institutions during this period were run by European headmasters and principals under the Education Department. The missionary enterprise played its own part and managed a number of institutions. Gradually private Indian effort appeared in the field.

**Importance of Wood's Despatch**

"Wood's Despatch is said to be the corner stone of Indian education. It is said to have laid the foundation of our present system of education." Says A.N. Basu, "The Despatch was a statesmanlike document wisely worded and wide in outlook and the suggestions contained therein were quite sound. It did lay out a plan for a comprehensive system of education for this country." The similar view has been expressed by Lord Dalhousie. It was a scheme of education for all India, far wider and more comprehensive than the local or the Supreme Government could have ever ventured to suggest.

The plan was comprehensive. It decided the structure of education in India. Previous to 1854 education was conducted on piecemeal basis. Now it had a structure: at the base of which were indigenous schools and primary schools and at the top were the universities. There was now a department in each province to look after the state of education. The system of education now started was well planned. It recommended the foundation of graded schools—Indigenous Primary Schools, Middle Schools, High Schools, Colleges, Universities—all over the country. It introduced the system of grants-in-aid and thus, sought the co-operation of private enterprise in the field of education. It laid due emphasis on the education of girls. 'Our Governor General-in-Council has declared that the Government ought to give to the native female education in India its frank and cordial support.' It laid down foundation for vocational education which had been so far uncared for. Vacational education was to be encouraged hereafter because the Government wanted to give employment facilities to the educated and also because it hoped that vocationally trained persons would be more grateful to the Government. The Despatch is important for drawing the attention of the local administration to the improvement and expansion of mass education. The filtration theory was rejected. It is also important because it made certain compromises. It said that religious education shall not be compulsory. Compulsory religious education will not be encouraged at public expense though it permitted missionaries to avail of state help if they gave their pupils a freedom of absenting themselves from religious classes.

"The Wood's Despatch may be regarded as a fitting close to the second period in the history of education in India", remarked Nurullah and Naik. The first two periods being : *(a)* from the early days till 1812 and *(b)* from 1813-1854.

What follows after the issue of the Despatch marks the three periods : *(a)* from 1855-1920, *(b)* from 1921-1947 and *(c)* from 1947.

The Wood's Despatch is then the climax in the history of Indian education. What goes before leads to it: and what follows flows from its.

According to the Wood's Despatch the Departments of Public Instruction were created in all the provinces and they were required to advise the Provincial Governments regarding educational matters, to make a proper use of money received from the Central and Provincial Governments, to inspect the institutions receiving grant-in-aid, to submit an annual report to the Government and to run and organise Government schools and colleges.

The education departments framed the rules for grant-in-aid schemes and began to give financial support to privately managed schools. The education departments now started secondary schools and encouraged the private ones by giving them sufficient grant-in-aid. More money poured into secondary education. The state established three Universities by 1857 on the lines of London university. The rapid increase in secondary education led to the starting of a number of colleges for higher education. Vocational education in medicine, law, engineering, agriculture, forestry and veterinary science was started.

**Limitations of Wood's Despatch**

H.R. James called the Wood's Despatch "the Magna Charta of Indian education". The Magna Charta was the great Charter of English personal and political liberty obtained from John in 1215. A Charter is the written grants of rights by a sovereign. The Wood's Despatch was a written document which gave forth recommendations to improve education of the country. It was thus, a sort of Charter giving Indians the rights of primary, elementary, secondary and higher education. It gave them rights for vocational education and for the education of girls. Had the recommendations offered by the Despatch been followed completely without any deficiency and had the suggestions been carried out entirely, the foundation for a national system of education would have been laid. But unfortunately this was not done. *For example,* if we examine the history of education in the period which followed (1854-1882) we find that the education departments were established in the province but they could not promote the interest of education. Similarly, the system of grant-in-aid did not operate well because of the inadequacy of grants, the irregularity of its release, step-motherly treatment towards the privately managed non-Mission Schools and complexity of rules. The Primany education also did not make much headway because the Government had little time to attend to the primary education, the funds were inadequate and the money raised through educational cess was diverted to other channels. The university education similarly could not be improved because the universities remained for a long time examining bodies. Not teaching was done; no chairs were formed.

The result was that there was a lopsided development of education even after the publication of the Despatch. To regard the Despatch as the climax of Indian education would be unfair and to accept what James says would be against propriety.

We cannot regard the Despatch as the Great Charter because:

1. The state did not provide for elementary education as was required.

2. The Government did not curb the proselytising activities of the missionaries. The policy of neutrality was not acted upon even for a long time after the Despatch.
3. The state did not stop the instruction in schools and colleges through the medium of English.

The Charter, if at all it was so, remained on paper. The expenses on secondary and higher education were not cut down : The funds for primary and elementary education could not be adequately provided. As a result, primary indigenous education suffered in comparison to secondary and higher education. The higher education also remained equally defective. There was no teaching in the universities. Indian languages could not find any place in higher education and were neglected.

The Depatch is said to have adopted the policy of religious neutrality. It declared that there would be no religious instruction and for an appointment to a Government post one's religion would not be a bar. It did not happen so. The Bible remained in the libraries of the colleges and schools and no notice of the religious instruction imparted in the schools was taken of by the inspectors in their periodical visits. Christianity was indirectly forced upon the pupils.

The medium of instruction did not change. English occupied the same place as it did before. The result was that pupils had to cram the subject-matter, or had to use cheap notes to pass the examination.

Had the Government adopted the ideal of universal literacy, we might have been justified to regard it as a great educational Charter but the Despatch itself did not regard it the duty of the state to educate every child. M.R. Paranjpe wrote in 1941, "It would be ridiculous to describe the Despatch as an Education Charter in the year 1941 whatever might have been its values in 1854." The same argument may be advanced for the present and it can be asserted that whatever has been the importance of Wood's Despatch in 1854 but to call it the Charter of Education now would be ludicrous. We have in the report of the Education Commission 1964-66 much more significant recommendations on the aims and objectives of nationalistic system of education, in the improvement of primary, secondary and higher education, on the medium of instruction, curriculum, teacher training, female education, vocational education and religious policy.

The Despatch failed to place emphasis on character, initiative and leadership among students. It tended to shake the faith of the future generations in the native culture and civilization for it wished 'to confer upon the people of India the vast moral and material blessings which flowed from the general difusion of useful knowledge'.

**Hunter Commission (1882)**

The E.I. Company did not make any effort to educate the masses. Most of the Directors believed in the Downward Filtration Theory that education would descend from the higher classes to the lower ones. According to this famous doctrine education was to permeate the masses from above. Hence, right from the start the E.I. Company educated the higher classes only and paid some attention to secondary or higher education. The education of the masses was completely ignored.

It was Adam (in 1835) who held up the cause of mass education and urged the Government to revive and improve the indigenous educational system. He put forth very sound proposals but his recommendations were turned down because Macaulay was not prepared to help the indigenous schools and was in favour of diffusing western information amongst the upper and middle classes. The Court of Directors wrote back that when the educational needs of the upper and middle classes had been provided for, Mr. Adam's proposals might be taken up on a liberal scale with some fairer prospects of success.

Adam's report revealed the decaying condition of primary education in Bengal and Bihar batch. Government showed a lip-sympathy only. Macaulay had pronounced that education is a luxury and is not meant for the masses. The state accepted his verdict. It did not cater to the actual needs of the country left the masses to themselves.

The missionaries, who were, however, doing some service to the cause of primary education, were also not encouraged. No official patronage was given to them. During Lord Hardinge's time (1844) some 100 elementary schools were opened in Bengal but by 1852 most of them persisted because the schools were purely vernacular and did not cater for the tastes of the people.

Lord Dalhousie made attempts to improve primary education and introduced in 1853 Adam's plan of popular schools with certain modifications in the light of Thompson's experience. But the progress was slow. In 1854 Bengal had 1400 and Bombay 1200 pupils in primary schools. The main reason of the slow progress was inadequacy of financial support.

The E. I. Company did very little for primary education. In 1854 there were 36,000 pupils in the whole of the country in Government primary schools. The mission schools were, however, teaching thrice the number. The Wood's Dispatch had advocated for expansion and encouragement of primary education. The Dispatch did not desire that the state should take up the education of the masses as her sole responsibility. It only hoped that the state may help the indigenous schools, give them grant-in-aid, inspect, guide and improve them.

For raising funds to meet expenditure on primary education some states imposed a monthly fee which was highly resented. The raising of subscription from the public agonised it because of their general poverty. In 1859, Lord Stanley stressed the need for levying a local educational cess. This again raised controversies. Some provinces liked to follow the instructions of the Wood's Dispatch and others followed Stanley's.

The main controversy centred round the school system and its finances. Some provinces tried to improve indigenous schools, encouraged private enterprise and opened Government schools to serve as models; others relied on departmental or board schools and entirely neglected the indigenous schools: still others followed the via media, *i.e.*, encouraged the indigenous schools and established the Government schools also. The result was that except in a few provinces indigenous schools were totally neglected and even rival institutions were set-up to compete against them. Hence, many of them were either absorbed in the new system or were closed down. Siqueira says that percentage of boys attending the indigenous school fell down from 10% in 1820 to 2.5% in 1882.

The second problem was that of finance. As a result of the recommendations of the Dispatch recourse had to be taken to local taxation. There were, prior to, 1882, two types of local bodies— municipalities in towns and cities and district or taluka local boards in rural areas. The early municipalities had nothing to do with education and could not legally incur any expenditure for educational purposes. Hence, they made no contribution to the cause of primary education. The boards in rural areas had been familiar with the idea of levying tax for educational purposes. Hence, tax could be levied in rural areas. Local cess was levied in many provinces. But money raised through cess was diverted again into other channels as the Government was little concerned with primary education.

## Recommendations of Hunter Commission and their Effect

The Hunter Commission was required to enquire into as to what should be the agency for the expansion of secondary education. It was also required to suggest measures for removing defects in the secondary education. Though there had been a remarkable progress in the period 1854-1882 so far as the growth of secondary schools in the country was concerned, yet many defects had crept in. English as a medium of instruction in secondary schools had by now acquired a place of dominance. The study of vernaculars was neglected specially after 1862 when students in High Schools were required to answer the question papers in English. Secondary education instead of becoming a preparation for life became a preparation for the university. Except Bombay, in no province there was any provision for vocational education at the secondary stage. The secondary school teachers were not adequately trained. There was an acute shortage of training institutions for them.

The first question 'what should be the agency for the expansion of secondary education' was answered with the following set of recommendations.

*(a)* "The duty of the Government was to establish one high school in every district and after that the expansion of secondary education in that district should be left to private enterprise."

*(b)* "The Government should gradually withdraw from the field of direct management of secondary schools and leave the expansion to private bodies through a system of grant-in-aid."

*(c)* "The Government may establish secondary schools in exceptional cases, in place where they may be required in the interests of people and where the people themselves may not be advanced or wealthy

enough to establish such schools for themselves even with a grant-in-aid."

(*d*) "With a view to making private institutions popular they should not be required to charge fees as high as those of a neighbouring Government institution."

The Commission's recommendations regarding the medium of instruction were frustrating. It recommended that in Middle Schools the use of vernaculars was preferable to English as medium of instruction and suggested that students should have some elementary knowledge of English also. The implications of this suggestion were that even in Middle Schools English should be taught. The Commission favoured the use of English. The most poisonous effect of the domination of English as a subject of study and as a medium of instruction continued to ruin the cause of education even after 1882. In almost all the provinces English remained the medium of instruction at the secondary stage. The dominance of English in the secondary schools continued to increse : And by 1902 the teaching of English came to be regarded as the prime object of the secondary course. "The study of Indian languages was consequently neglected", said Nurullah and Naik. It was in 1904 that Lord Curzon advocated the use of mother-tongue or vernaculars as medium of instruction upto High School stage and wished English to occupy the place of an optional subject.

The suggestions by the Commission regarding the training of secondary school teachers were rather half-heartedly given. Although the Wood's Despatch had laid a definite stress on the training of secondary school teachers in 1854, yet only two training colleges, one at Madras and the other at Lahore were by now esablished. There was an urgent need for such a training. The Commission recommended that students of training colleges should be examined in Principles and Practice of Teaching and the training period for graduates should be shorter than for others. The Commission recommended that the success in the examination should be a guarantee for permanent employment as a teacher in any secondary school, Government or aided. The Government of India accepted the recommendations of the Commission. It is difficult to understand why the Commission laid emphasis upon the use of English as the medium of instruction. The Commission's recommendations regarding the bifurcation of coures at the high school level was a step in the right direction. The emphasis on technical education as a part of general education was given by the Government of India after 1886 to meet the requirement of local industries. The main effect of the Commission's recommendations was that secondary education began to expand rapidly.

**Primary Education.** Wood's Despatch laid down that Government should provide education for those "who are utterly incapable of obtaining education worthy of the name by their own unaided efforts." It directed the Government to concentrate its energies on primary education. Is also asked the state to withdraw itself from the field of higher education and attend to the general education of the masses. But the Government neglected primary education altogether.

The Hunter Commission was appointed to enquire particularly into the manner in which effect had been given to the principles of the Despatch of 1854 and to suggest such measures as it may think desirable in orther to further carrying out of the policy therein laid down. So far as the progress of the primary education was concerned, the Commission was specially asked to enquire into whether the Government had actually neglected the primary education and what the state of primary education was and how it could be extended and improved. It was especially asked to suggest how grant-in-aid could be further extended.

The main recommendations of the Commission on the different aspects of Primary education were as follows:

**Policy.** The Commission boldly acknowledged the importance of primary education by declaring "the elementary education of the masses, its provision, extension and improvement to be that part of the educational system to which the strenuous effort of the state should now be directed in a still larger measure than heretofore." The Commission laid down in clear-cut terms the state policy in connection with the promotion of Primary Education. The state should give its fostering care to the fullest extent. The aim of primary education should be the instruction of the measses and not an instruction leading up to higher education.

**Administrations.** In England the Education Arts of 1870 and 1876 had placed the responsibility of primary education on the Country Council; so the Commission recommended that the control of primary education should be transferred to District and Municipal Boards. These boards should deal with the whole system of primary education, keep a careful watch over the educational needs of classes and communities and provide for all such needs either by creating new schools or by aiding existing ones. The Government primary schools were also to be transferred to these Boards. In a nutshell, the entire responsibility of the administration of the Primary Education was placed on one body which was too weak to discharge its duties properly. A wiser step for the Government would have been to assume the responsibility of primary education itself.

**Training of Primary School Teachers.** The Commission felt the necessity of training primary school teachers through a network of normal schools widely distributed throughout the country. In order to make the Normal Schools function well they were assigned to one Inspector or the other. Cost, direction, provision and inspection of Normal Schools was the first charge of the provincial funds and Normal Schools were to be so localised as to provide for the local requirements of all Primary Schools whether goverment or aided within the jurisdiction of an Inspector.

**Finance.** The Commission recommended "that primary education be declared to be that part of the whole system of public instruction which poses an almost exclusive claim on local funds set apart for education and a large claim on provincial revenues."

The Hunter Commission took a decisive initial step to place the responsibility of meeting expenditure on primary education on different types of funds. *For example,* the cost of direction, inspection and the provision of normal schools was made the first charge of provincial funds and the expenditure on Primary education was considered to have an almost exclusive claim on local funds (set apart for education) and a large claim on provincial revenues. Every District and Municipal Board was required to have a separate fund for Primary education and the Government was to give grants to local boards at the rate of one-third of the total expenditure or 50% of the total assets. The grants to individual schools were to be made strictly on the basis of results. Giving grants on the basis of results was a mistake, as the system of payments-by-results had failed wherever it had been tried. It might make the shirking teachers work, but it reduced the whole educational system to grind-as-dust-rule.

**Curriculum and Text Books.** The Commission felt the need for broadening school curriculum by introducing subjects like the native methods of arithmetic, accounts and mensuration, elements of natural and physical sciences and their application to agriculture, health and the individual arts. But it did not advocate rigidity in curriculum planning and construction. It neither liked unformity in curriculum nor the use of textbooks throughout India. Provinces were to be allowed full freedom in the use of textbooks.

Thus, the Commission made important recommendations on all the aspects of primary education for its speedy growth. But the progress of primary education was not satisfactory during 1886-1902 : The main reason for slow progress was the primary education continued to be neglected and sufficient money was not forthcoming for its full expansion. The Government did not give adequate financial aid to local bodies and while additional funds were spent on higher education, primary education was allowed to starve. Initially, the Government made some progress in the field of primary education but the pace of progress was checked partially because people who lived in the interior of the country were indifferent to education and also because the rules for recognition were made stricter.

**Hunter Commission and Special Education**

The Hunter Commission made the following recommendations for the growth of female education in India because it realised that famale education had been till now in the most backward condition and needed urgent fostering in every possible way.

1. More liberal grants should be given to girls' schools and the grant-in-aid rules should be easier.
2. Money from local and Municipal Boards and Provincial funds should be spend in an equitable proportion on girls and boys schools.
3. Girls schools should be transferred to the control of Local Boards but a board which is not prepared to take the responsibility should not be compelled to do so.
4. Capable girls should be awarded scholarships so that they may continue their higher education.
5. Inspectresses should be appointed to inspect and guide girls' schools.

6. Men and women who are interested in female education should be included in the management of schools.

7. School managers should provide hostels for women because girls find it difficult to attened schools far away from their homes.

8. Girls should not be charged any fee so that they may be attracted to get education. Charging of fees should be no condition for girls schools for getting a grants-in-aid.

9. Curriculum for girls should be different from what it is for boys as the instruction which is useful for a boy may not be useful for a girl.

10. Secondary schools may be opened for girls only where there is a demand for them.

11. Girls should be encouraged to get professional training and training schools for female teachers should be started.

12. For women who remain secluded in zenanas from their childhood should be provided with zanana teachers.

The results of these recommendations was that in the period of next twenty years 1882-1902 the education of women made slow but steady progress.

**Education for Muslims.** The Commission also felt that the education for Muslims in India was not adequate. Their backwardness in this respect was alarming. There were very few English speaking Muslims in the country. The Government was desirous of getting the support of Muslim community and wanted to make them rivals of Hindus and staunch supporters of their own rule. Hence, the Commission made the following suggestions:

1. Special arrangements of Muslim education should be regarded as a legitimate charge on local, municipal and provincial funds.

2. Higher education for Muslims be liberally encouraged.

3. A system of special scholarships for Muslims should be established. Scholarships given in primary schools should be tenable in middle schools. Those given in middle schools should be tenable in High Schools and those given in high schools should be tenable in colleges.

4. As far as possible, Muslim teachers should be employed in those Muslim schools where instruction is given through the medium of Hindustani.

5. The standard of teaching of Muslim primary schools should be raised.

6. In all schools a certain proportion of free studentships should be reserved for Muslim students.

7. Muslims should be given proportionate Government appointments.

8. For inspecting Muslim primary schools, Muslim Inspecting Officers only should be employed.

9. Where such endowments are under the control of individuals and bodies inducement should be given to them by liberal grants to establish English teaching schools and colleges.

10. Association for the promotion of Muslim education should be encouraged.

11. Higher English education should be given to the Muslims.

12. Educational endowments for the benefit of Muslims under Government control should be utilised for that purpose only.

## EDUCATION UNDER LORD CURZON

Lord Curzon by nature was a benevolent autocrat and by training he was a diehard imperialist. He had an implicit faith in a strong rule. As soon as he landed in India he took up the programme of administrative reconstruction in education. He called an educational conference in 1901 at Shimla and appointed the Indian Universities Commission (1902) for bringing out changes in the university education.

He saw that Indian unversities had become out-moded. Though the London University had been reorganised in 1898, but Indian universities maintained the old structure and pattern. The expansion of higher education was too great for exising universities to manage, the pressure of work on them was so great that they could not discharge their duties well and no university attached any importance to its real functions. So Curzon appointed the Indian Universities Commission to report upon any proposal that might be made for improving the Constitution and working of universities and to recommend to the Governor-General-in-Council such measures as may elevate the standard of university teaching and promote advancement of learning.

The Commission made valuable recommendations on the reorganised model of London University and wanted to improve the existing system. The main recommendations were embodied in an Act, *viz.*, Indian Universities Act (1904). The Act introduced some welcome measures of reform long overdue. *For example,* it introduced efficiency in university administration by giving statutory recognition to the Syndicate and by making the new Senate more efficient and manageable than the previous ones.

"It is true", say Nurullah and Naik, "that the act of 1904 by itself did not achieve much. But Curzon will still have the credit of having been the pioneer to start a new movement in university reform which slowly and laboriously, but nevertheless steadily has ever been progressing to its destined goal."

There was an appreciable change in the college education with a change in university education. A grant of 13.5 lacs given to colleges on the basis of their improved their teaching standards and provided better facilities in the form of well-equipped libraries and laboratories.

The reforms in secondary education were not of less significance. The Government of India Resolution, 1904 laid down the educational policy of Curzon in clear-cut terms. So far as secondary education was concerned, the G.R. said, "The Government is bound in the interests of the Community to see that the education provided in the Secondary Schools is sound." For achieving this objective Lord Curzon substituted in place of the old policy of expansion the new policy of control and supervision. Stricter rules of recognition of secondary schools were framed. No student from an unrecognised school could appear at the Matriculation Examination after 1904. No unrecognised school could get Government grant. The result was that all the secondary schools came under the control of the Government. For improving the quality of instruction the G.R. 1904 made some very good suggestions. The work of improving instruction was to be entrusted to Inspectors and the neighbouring Government high schools were to be made exact models and the teachers were to be trained.

It was Lord Curzon's Government that for the first time said that Vernacular should be the medium of instruction in Middle Schools and even in high schools pupils should not be permitted to leave the study of Vernaculars and that English should, in no case, be taught before a child attains the age of 13.

Lord Curzon's ideas about Primary education were very liberal. He said that the active expansion of primary education was the first duty of the state. The Government of India Resolution, 1904 laid down a clearcut financial policy for primary education. Primary education had a claim on provincial revenue and a still more pre-dominant claim on the local bodies' funds. Hence, the G.R. laid down clearly that Boards should spend their educational funds for primary education alone. These bodies should submit their budget to the Director of Public Instruction through their Inspector.

The Government advised the primary schools to apply simpler methods of teaching and to base instruction on rural needs. A distinction was also made as regards curricular for rural and urban primary schools.

Lord Curzon tried to reform other aspects of edcuation also. It was on account of his boundless enthusiasm for educational reforms that conferences for technical, agricultural, commercial education were organised; professional education in medicine, engineering, forestry, veterinary science and agriculture was expanded and improved; grants for professional education were initiated; and state scholarships for technological subjects were instituted.

For seven years (1899-1905) Lord Curzon went on toiling hard to reform every aspect of Indian education. He improved University, Secondary and Primary education. He fought vigorously for the cause of mass education and the vernaculars. There was no sphere in education which he did not enter, no space in which his reforming touch was not felt. "What Curzon achieved in 7 years' time would certainly have required twice or thrice as much time for any other man", said Nurullah and Naik. "Lord Curzon was the author of the great movement for educational reconstruction which started in the beginning of this century. He laid the foundation of the reform of Indian Universities which gathered momentum in later years. In primary education it was he who started a drive for expansion. Today it is these services that Indians remember."

Though the Indian opinion opposed his reforms, though his successors tried to revise his policies, yet it was his educational policy that was followed firmly. It was admitted by all that his educational reforms introduced a better system of education; proper control was exercised over private enterprise; universities were reorganised; secondary education was improved and a better organised system of primary education was evolved.

The attempts at reforming Indian education by Lord Curzon were not well-received. The Indian opinion considered his reforms sinister in intentions. People were suspicious of his motives. "He fell far short of the achievement which might have been his", says Cuningham, "had his temperament enabled him to win the sympathies of the people and enlist their co-operation in a congenial progress." The Indian public opinion wanted a free charter to private enterprise and Curzon curtailed it. His education policy was associated with his political ideas that started a violent agitation in Bengal. Swaraj in the freedom of development and unchecked expansion appeared to the people their birthright and therefore they did not co-operate even in his best efforts at reforming education.

**Recommendation of Commission**

The Commission made following recommendations:

1. The existing universities should be reorganised as teaching bodies.

2. The number of members on the Syndicate should be reduced to 9 and to 15 in exceptional cases. All members should be elected.

3. No new university should be set-up.

4. The territorial jurisdiction of a university should be defined.

5. The undergraduate work should be left to affiliated colleges and only advanced courses should be provided in the university campus.

6. The number of Senators should also be reduced and the period of their tenure should be 5 years at the most

7. Rules of affiliation should be strict and affiliation should not be granted to second grade colleges.

8. University and college teachers, renowned scholars and Government officials should get adequate representation in the senate.

The Government of India resolution on Educational Policy was published on March 11, 1904. The resolution gave a historical account of education under the British rule prior to 1902 and discussed the defects of primary, secondary and higher education. The defects that were pointed out in the field of higher education were as follows:

1. The higher education was highly examinantion ridden.

2. It was pursued exclusively for employment under the Government and not for its cultural value.

3. The courses were mostly literary and not practical.

4. Students had little thinking power and depended on memorisation of facts.

4. The thinking in Europe about purely examining universities had changed and hence, universities should be first-rate teaching centres.

The recommendations of the Indian Universities Commission (1902) were incorporated in the Indian

Universities Act, 1904 which limited the size of the senates, authorised teaching by the university and imposed more close supervision on its work. The important changes brought about by the Act were as follows:

1. The size of the Senate should be reduced. The number of fellows should be between 60 and 100 and that they should hold office for only 5 years.
2. The territorial limits of each university were defined by the Governor General-in-Council.
3. The three older Universities, Calcutta, Bombay and Madras were to have 20 members on the Syndicate and the rest 15 only.
4. Government was vested with additional powers. It was required to approve the regulations framed by the Senate. If the Senate failed to frame regulations within a specified period the Government was empowered to do so.
5. The functions of universities were enlarged. They could now appoint their new professors and lecturers, undertake research, hold and manage educational endowments maintain their own libraries, laboratories and museums and make regulations regarding the residence of their students.
6. The importance of Syndicate was enhanced. It was recognised as the executive Government of the university. University teachers were granted representation on the Syndicace.

The Indian Universities Act (1904) led to improvement in College education. Special grants were offered to colleges to improve teaching, equip libraries and laboratories and provide hostel accommodation to students. A grant of 13.5 lakhs was equitably distributed among provinces with due consideration to the number of university students and the population. The Syndicate was recognised statutorily. The new Senate became more manageable. Its efficiency increased. Affiliated colleges improved.

## GOVERNMENT RESOLUTION, 1904

The Government of India Resolution on Educational Policy was published on March 11, 1904. After presenting a historical account of education under the British rule prior to 1902, it discussed the main defects in the educational system.

The resolution acknowledged the fact that there had been a tremendous increase in the number of secondary schools after 1882. Secondary education had grown a hundred fold but it was totally inefficient. The main defects pointed out in the G. R. were as follows:

1. The standards of teaching were going down.
2. English as medium of instruction at secondary level had led to the neglect of the vernaculars on the one hand and to the fostering of the habit of memorisation on the other.
3. Education had been primarily liberal: there had been no diversification of courses at and stage in the Secondary School.
4. Teaching in the secondary schools had been technical, dull and dry.
5. There was a lack of trained teachers in Secondary Schools.
6. Inspection and supervision of secondary schools was meagre.

The G. R. proposed certain ways and means to eradicate these defects from secondary education.

Secondary Education suffered most because of the laissez-faire policy of the state. The resolution emphasised therefore, the need for stricter control and supervision of secondary schools. The policy of control and improvement was substituted for the policy of laissez-faire. Regulations for granting recognition to secondary schools were made stricter than those that existed before. The G. R. demanded that these regulations should be clearly defined imposed strictly on every private aided school.

The nation that has decided to adopt a secular democratic setup needed an educational system which may contribute to the fostering of right sort of citizenship with a broad national and secular outlook. The nation, which has just thrown off the foreign yoke simply to improve her economic condition, needed an educational system that may develop human resources with improved productive efficiency and fit for increasing national wealth. The taxation, whose members have been yet obsessed with the problem of earning a livelihood all their lives, needed an educational system oriented in such a way that a cultural renaissance could be brought about.

## EDUCATION UNDER DYARCHY

The period (1921-47) is remarkable for two events—the introduction of Government of India Acts, 1919 and 1935. The first of these introduced dyarchy in the provinces—a sort of dual Government and the second ushered in Provincial Autonomy. Some subjects were under popular control and education was one of them. These subjects were known as transferred. The rest were under the control of the governor and his executive councillors. The control was dual, because on one hand, we had ministers responsible to state legislatures and on the other, we had the governor and his executive councillors. In 1935 all the subjects come under the control of provincial ministers and legislatures. The govenors had some powers by which they could set aside the decisions of the ministries and legislatures. Under the dyarchy ministries were handicapped in a number of ways by the governors and their executive councils, yet they did their best, to expand education to the utmost. Under the provincial autonomy popular ministries affected the progress of education most favourably.

The period 1921-47 is significant in the history of Indian education also because it witnessed a number of remarkable events. Laws, which governed universal primary education, were passed. Teaching and residential universities saw the light of the day. An auxiliary committee Simoon Commission examined the defects of education in 1928. Wood and Abbott Committee on vocational education (1936-37) drew the attention of the public towards the inefficiency of literary education. Nehru Committee in 1938 demonstrated the importance of educational reconstruction. Sergeant report in 1944 devised a post-war educational development plan.

**Expansion in Primary Education.** The Compulsory Education Acts which were passed gave a great impetus to the expansion of primary education. The scope of these laws covered both boys and girls in both rural and urban areas. The responsibility of introducing compulsory primary education was placed on the shoulders of the local bodies and these bodies were permitted to levy taxes (educational cess) to meet the expenses of education. Education was made compulsory for children in age group 6-10 and guardians could be punished if they did not send their sons or daughters to primary schools. The laws were, however, permissive in nature. The provinces were required to specify the areas under which the laws could operate. The result was that the laws could not be enacted immediately after they were passed.

The progress of primary education during this period was not even throughout. During 1921-31 the expansion was very great and in 1931-37 there was a sharp fall and again in the decade 1937-47 the expansion became phenomenal. The first spurt was caused by the enactment of compulsory education Acts and the second by the beneficial influence of the provincial autonomy. The period 1931-37 was of a sharp fall because when a world wide depression came new programmes of expansion had to be abandoned. The expenditure on primary education increased from 495 lakhs in 1921 to 1848 lakhs in 1947. The enrolment grew from 61 lakhs to 146 lakhs. The direct expenditure nearly quadrupled itself. The lower primary schools being single teacher schools were closed down to reduce wastage. The pupils turned out by them either were not permanently literate or relapsed into illiteracy soon after.

The period 1921-47 may be described as the period of great educational thinking in the field of primary education. Burning problems of the day were: 'Is the type of primary education imparted good enough? Can the expansion be forced further? If so, how?' The question of quantity of education was nearly solved in the jubilee celebration of Marwari education society at Wardha in 1937, when Gandhiji suggested a scheme of Basic education. In the following year the plan was developed by Dr. Zakir Hussain. The scheme of Basic education was adopted in 1938 and progressed rapidly upto 1956 when the Ministry of Education issued an authoritative version explaining the concept of Basic education in the following words:

*(a)* The fundamental objective of Basic education is nothing less than the development of the child's personality which will include his productive efficiency.

*(b)* The basic craft should be such as may fit in the natural and social environment of the school and hold within it the maximum of educational possibilities.

(*c*) The effective teaching of a basic craft becomes an essential part of education at this stage as productive work. The sale proceeds of the productive work may be expected to be used by schools for meeting a part of expenditure in running it for students welfare.

(*d*) Knowledge must be related to activity, practical experience and observation.

(*e*) Basic education should not be regarded as meant exclusively for the rural areas.

(*f*) Education was to be given through mother-tongue.

The Post-War Plan of Education Development (1944) adopted Basic education embodying many ideas in the original Wardha Scheme. The idea of meeting costs of education through the products of the basic crafts were rejected. The three R's were not regarded as sufficient equipment for efficient citizenship.

**Expansion of Secondary Education.** In the period (1921-47) the secondary education expanded enormously. The Calcutta University Commission (1917-1919) had recommended for the separation of Intermediate classes from the university. The recommendations were being implemented in many provinces. Intermediate education become linked with school education. Secondary schools got the benefit of better teachers and standard and status of secondary schools were raised. The control of Intermediate Education was transferred to Boards of High Schools and Intermediate Education. At the middle stage senior basic and post-basic schools were opened.

The political leadership made the public educationally conscious. The broad minded people generously made liberal contributions to the cause of education. Secondary education became popular among the less advanced public as well as among women. It began to spread to remote areas and interior of the country. The factors leading to the spread and expansion of higher secondary education were: *(a)* increased political consciousness; *(b)* expansion of primary education; and *(c)* change of medium of instruction.

Besides expansion, other changes that were evidenced were improvement in the conditions of service, widening of curricular concept, provision of new courses, increase in school equipment, change in medium of instruction from English to the mother-tongue.

The recommendations of the Hartog Committee, Wood and Abbott Committee and the Post-War Educational Development Plan had a great impact on secondary education.

**Expansion of Higher Education (1921-1947).** In the field of higher education the progress was not less remarkable. The quantitative as well as qualitative improvement was exceptional. Perhaps it was because of the impact of the Calcutta University Commission (1917-19). Five new universities were created: Delhi (1922), Nagpur (1923) andhra (1926) and Agra (1927); Annamalai (1959), Travancore (1937), Utkal (1943), Saugar (1946) and Rajasthan (1947). Though there had been a slump land international turmoil during the period under review, higher education expanded because people demanded more and more education.

The quality of higher education also became better. Before 1921, most of the universities were examining bodies. The number of teaching and residential universities increased. The older six universities were reorganised and reformed. *For example,* Madras university undertook teaching and research work; Bombay university undertook the charge of the School of Chemical Technology; Allahabad University became a teaching and residential university. The enrolment figures rose up as a result of reform and reorganization. The establishment of Inter-University Board (I.U.B.) in 1925 led to the qualitative growth of Higher Education. Despite the quantitative and qualitative growth of higher education, it did not cease to have the shortcomings and defects from which it suffered previously. The liberal courses predominated. All the universities had Arts and sciences faculties. The medium of instruction continued to be English. Students who were rich and financially sound sought admissions to colleges. Education through a foreign medium led to large university failures. Hostel, library and other facilities could not be expanded due to shortage of funds.

**Expansion of Vocational Education.** During the period (1921-47) though liberal education was holding sway, vocational education began to receive attention both at the school and university level. The British policy to push through western science and culture still pre-dominated. Throughout the country we had in 1921, 6995 students in law, 3863 in Medicine, 803 in Engineering, 519 in Education, 479 in Commerce and 326 in Agriculture. The professional institutions prepared youths mainly for Government jobs; *for example*, the Roorkee Engineering College prepared Engineers for Civil and Irrigation purposes, Veterinary colleges for armed forces, the colleges of Agriculture and Forestry for state services. The demand for technical and industrial research institutes began to increase. Bose Research Institute, Calcutta, Harcourt Butler Technological Institute, Kanpur, Imperial Research Institute, New Delhi, the Indian Institute of Science, Bangalore and Indian School of Mines, Dhanbad were established during the period under review.

### Hartog Committee on Primary Education

When the political movement was at its climax, the national leadership was trying hard to evolve a system of education which could suit the needs of the country. The Government of India Act, 1919 could hardly satisfy those who were pressing the Government for more. And hence, the British Government thought of reviewing the matters by appointing another Commission under the chairmanship of Sir John

Simon. The Simon Commission appointed an Auxiliary Committee to enquire into the various aspects of Indian Education under the chairmanship of Sir Philip Hartog. The Hartog Committee focussed its attention on primary, secondary and higher education. Its recommendations about female education were also remarkable.

**Wastage in Primary Education.** The report was published in 1929. The observation of the Committee about Wastage and Stagnation in Primary Education had been spectacular. The Committee said, "Throughout the whole educational system there is a waste and ineffectiveness. In the primary education the waste is appalling. The wastage in the case of girls is even more serious than in the case of boys."

The Commission pointed out that there had been a phenomenal growth of primary education. The traditional apathy of the masses towards the education of children was losing ground. There was increased enrolment in all the states and in all the areas arural as well as urban. But the progress was not satisfactory. The difficulties in the path of progress of primary education were largely due to ignorance and backwardness of the rural society and the physical factors involved. The Commission remarked that in India primary education was a rural problem. The rural schools did not attract teachers. The conditions in the villages were deplorable, Supervision, inspection and administration of rural schools was very difficult. Women teachers did not like to serve in rural areas at all. The rural parents were ignorant of the benefits that accrue from education. The average villager was poor, illiterate and conservative and did not want to send his children to the school. He would like to send his child to the fields but will not like to have him educated in schools.

There were many backward areas which did not have any primary school. The question of having a school in bigger villages even in these areas did not arise. Children cannot move for more than 2 miles from home to get the knowledge of 3 R's. "Scantiness of means of communication, physical obstacles and unfavorable climatic conditions presented difficulties in their way."

Regular attendance at school was not possible. In sowing and reaping seasons there is a lot of work to be done in the fields; hence, children could not be sent to school. Epidemics illness at home and work in fields checked students from attending their schools regularly.

These factors lead to a great deal of stagnation and wastage in schools. The causes of wastage and stagnation their, impact on primary education and remedies will be discussed in sections 11.4, 11.5. It was Hartog Committee which for the first time drew the attention of the public and the Government to this terrifying feature of primary education.

**Some Other Defects in Primary Education.** The Committee pointed out the following defects in the primary education system which were equally appalling.

1. Many primary schools are of ephemeral character.
2. The distribution of primary schools is unsystematic and uneven. There are large areas without any school and there are areas in which there is unnecessary competition among schools for attracting children.
3. Their equipment and buildings are inadequate.
4. They are mostly one-teacher schools.
5. The compulsory education Acts are defective. They require local bodies to introduce compulsion. "Because officials lack experience, local bodies show no interest in the experiment and do not want to prosecute the guardians who do not send their children to schools."

6. The required number of teachers for primary education is not available in the country and the teachers who are working in schools are, as a general rule, untrained and not qualified.

7. The inspecting staff is insufficient and regular inspection of primary schools is not possible.

**Secondary and Wgher Education**

The Hartog Committee report not only visualised the defects of the then existing primary education system, it reviewed the field of secondary and higher education as well. The defects in the Secondary Education, as were pointed out by the Committee, were as follows:

**Defects in Secondary Education**

1. The aim of secondary education was narrow. Every student of a secondary school wanted simply to pass the High School Examination and get admission to the university. The Committee said, "The lure of Government service through matriculation still remains potent. In some provinces a School Final Examination has been set-up, entirely distinct from matriculation examination with the doubtful object of providing an alternative qualification for entry into Government service and of widening the curriculum by permitting the inclusion of vocational and provocational subjects. But this has been largely a failure."

2. The percentage of failures at the matriculation examination was increasing. It was partly because of promotion in the earlier classes and partly because of non-selective admission to the high school stage.

**Suggestions.** The Committee suggested that the aims of secondary education should be defined and that education be given accordingly. To reduce wastage at the high school stage it was suggested to train children for rural pursuits, to offer them diversified industrial and commercial courses after the middle school stage. In order to improve the quality of secondary school education, the pay scales should be revised. The training of secondary school teachers should be improved upon as the quality of training colleges in several provinces was bad. The methods of teaching were old and traditional. Modern methods of teaching were not adopted. The training colleges were producing mechanically trained teachers who did not understand the manifold problem\, or school organization and were ill-equipped to solve them. The Committee recommended that the duration of training period should be raised and refresher courses be provided to teachers in service.

The pay and service conditions of secondary school teachers were not satisfactory. The quality of secondary education could not be improved unless pay scales are revised and conditions of service improved. The Committee observed that the pay of a secondary school teacher was deplorably low in many provinces. A hungry stomach does not teach as he cannot worship. Even worse than that was the insecurity of tenure. Schools in most states were privately managed or controned by local bodies. Thus, bodies frequently sent the teachers away at short notices. In some schools teachers were recruited for 9 months and were let of in the summer vacations so that vacation salaries could be avoided.

**Defects in Higher Education.** The Hartog Committee was also equally grieved over the appalling situation in Higher education. The bad quality of education and its lowering standards were its distressing features. The universities failed to produce right type of leaders. They admitted students without selection. They produced graduates who could not take the lead in any sphere of life.

A large number of those students, who got admission to a university, failed. The contributing factor for this large percentage of failures was poor work done in the secondary schools. The lowering of standards of higher education was the result of competition among universities themselves. Some universities had lowered their standards themselves to attract a larger body of student. The Committee observed, "We admit that there are universities which have resisted the temptation to lower standards. But the great majority of undergraduates are aiming not at learning for its own sake, but at a degree for its market value: And they naturally flock to a place where a degree can be obtained most easily and cheaply".

## WOOD-ABBOTT COMMITTEE

S. H. Abbott the Ex-Chief Inspector of Technical Schools, Board of Education, England and A. Wood, the Director of Intelligence, Board of Education, England, were invited by the Government of India in 1937 to advise on the following two problems. 'Should any vocational or practical training be imparted in Primary, Secondary or Higher Secondary Schools? And if so, what should be its nature and extent? The experts were requested to advise the Government whether the technical or vocational schools already in existence could be improved and if so, in what manner. They were requested to suggest the type of institutions and the stage at which diversion of the students from the ordinary secondary schools to such institutions should be made and the way by which it was to be brought about.

The two experts visited educational institutions in the Punjab, Uttar Pradesh and Delhi and submitted their report in 1937. The Report on Vocational Education was written by S. H. Abbott and that on General Education by A. Wood.

**Proposals.** The primary aim of Vocational Education was defined as making available to the industry the services of better qualified persons so that industrial sector may expand and work efficiently. The recommendations made to improve vocational education were as follows:

1. Vocational and General education should not be regarded as two different branches of education, nor anyone of the two should be regarded as of greater significance than the other. They are essentially two phases of a continuous process. General education being the earlier phase and vocational education the later one, should follow in that direction. Each subject taught in a vocational school has its origin in a non-vocational-school. "If general education, brings about the development of the non-material culture of a country, vocational education does the same thing for material culture; hence, both are necessary for the progress of a country".

2. The Junior Vocational schools should receive their students at the end of Class VIII and provide a course for 3 years and run parallel to 3 years Higher Secondary Schools and should be of an equal status. The Senior Vocational Schools should receive their students at the end of Class XI of a Higher Secondary school giving general education, provide a 2 years' course and run parallel to an Intermediate college.

3. Vocational education must be based on general education. A. Wood gave his valuable suggestions separately. The boy who has passed Class VIII should be allowed to enter a vocational school and the one who has not passed that stage may be allowed to join Junior Vocational Schools which would provide general education plus vocational education. Those who have passed XI, the final class of a Higher Secondary may be admitted to Senior Vocational Schools.

4. Vocational education should not be regarded as being on a lower plane than literary education. Both the experts emphasised that vocational education was equally important.

5. Provinces should motivate the employers to provide facilities for vocational education to their employees. They may supply buildings, equipment, materials and funds for establishing part-time vocational schools. They may be induced to release their employees for two half-days in a week.

6. Besides these regular vocational schools, part-time vocational schools may also be established so that vocational education may be imparted to those youths who are in service somewhere and wish to get a training in some vocation. These part-time vocational schools may receive their students on two half-days in a week when released by their employers.

   A vocational training college may also be established by the Government in each province. A Junior Technical School, a part-time Technical School and a School of Arts and Crafts may also be established.

7. The expansion of vocational education should not be permitted to outstrip the needs of the industry and commerce of the province concerned. It means that the nature of vocational education and the types of vocational institutions should be decided by a province in relation to its needs. In each province an Advisory Council for Vocational. Education should be set-up. The functions of the council would be to secure a close co-operation between industry and commerce, on one hand and between industry and education on the other. With their co-operation,

each province has to decide the plan of expanding vocational education.

8. Provision should be made in every school providing general education to give vocational guidance. Guidance may be given in Primary, Secondary and Higher Secondary schools so that necessary talents may be deflected to vocational schools at appropriate stages. The main aim of guidance should be to identify interests, aptitudes, abilities and help children and youth to make vocational plans and choices.

## WARDHA SCHEME

In 1937 Congress ministries assumed office in seven major provinces of India. Their main concern was to fight for the cause of national system or education in the country. The traditional education system or had been faulty in many respects. It was highly academic. It produced a gulf between the masses and the elite, the rich and the poor, the educated and the uneducated. Education was meant for those who could buy it. It was not everybody's birthright.

**Gandhiji Contribution to the Cause of Primary Education.** The two main items involved in the programme of establishing a National system of education were mass education and temperance. Both these items ran counter to each other. If a policy of temperance was to be pleaded for and implemented, there would be a marked decline in revenue. If mass education was to be pleaded for, it required a large amount of money—a trenmedously heavy additional expenditure on primary education only. The ministries were at the horns of dilemma.

Gandhiji came to their rescue at such a critical hour. He wrote in Harijan (July 31, 1937), "As a nation we are so backward in education that we cannot hope to fulfil our obligations to the nation in this respect within a given time during this generation, if the programme is to depend on money. In have, therefore, made bold, even at the risk of losing a reputation for constructive ability, to suggest that education would be self-supporting. I would therefore begin the child's education by teaching it a useful handicraft and enabling it to produce from the moment it begins its training. Thus, every school can be made self-supporting, the condition being that the state takes over these products."

The same year in October an All India National Education Conference was organised at Wardha under the presidentship of Mahatma Gandhi and his ideas on national education were discussed and it was resolved that free and compulsory education should be provided to children for seven years (6-14) through mother-tongue and that the process of education throughout this period should centre round some form of manual and productive work and that all other abilities that were to be developed should be integrally related to the central craft chosen with due regard to the environment of the child. The conference expected that this system of education would gradually be able to cover the remuneration of teachers.

A Committee was appointed under the chairmanship of Dr. Zakir Hussain to design a scheme on the lines suggested by the above resolution. It submitted its report in 1938 which came to be known as Wardha Scheme of Education. The main aspects of this scheme of education were as follows :

*(a)* A free and compulsory education for age group 6-14.

*(b)* Craft-centred instruction.

*(c)* Mother-tongue as the medium of instruction.

*(d)* Emphasis on manual work.

*(e)* Co-education upto 5$^{th}$ class.

*(f)* Education to be closely related to social and physical environment of the child, *i.e.*, to his home, his village, crafts, industries, occupations followed in his neighbourhood.

*(g)* Teaching of craft in a way that it might enable the school to meet the cost of education.

*(h)* Course in a basic craft, mother-tongue, mathematics, social studies, general science, art work, Hindustani music—all these subjects correlated with the basic craft.

*(i)* Little importance to be attached to examinations and textbooks.

**National Scheme of Education**

The Wardha Scheme involves the basic principles of the National System of Education as perceived and conceived by Gandhiji. The scheme is known as a scheme of Basic Education because, *(a)* it is expected to form the basis of our national culture, *(b)* it provides the basic amount of knowledge which is essential for an average Indian child to have an intelligent insight into his environment, *(c)* it is related to the basic interests and needs of the child and *(d)* it is correlated with the basic occupation of the community.

Basic education is regarded as the most valuable gift which Gandhiji bestowed to India. It is one of the 14 pillars of his programme for national reconstruction. A social revolution could be made possible by such a scheme of education which was expected to create a free, classless, egalitarian society which recognised dignity of labour as the most important value of life. Basic education unlike the traditional education would be universal, free and compulsory. It should be free because it would cover all costs of expenditure and there would be no problem of finance.

The Experiements in this National System of Education were started as early as 1938 just after its being adopted in the Haripura session of the Indian National Congress. But it was only after the attainment of Independence that Basic education could be considered as the national pattern of elementary education for children of 6 to 14 years of age.

Education in a basic school began to be imparted through the medium of work and activities connected with physical and social environment but it could not be adopted universally. A common syllabus from Classes I to VIII was recommended for the country as a whole and the differences between basic and non-basic syllabi were reduced to the minimum.

**Basic Education : A Retrospect and Prospects**

The scheme of National Education, devised by the Zakir Hussain Committee, was adopted by the Haripura session of the Indian National Congress in 1938." Experiments began to be made on the scheme. At first they were isolated and had a narrow scope. They were then hampered by the toppling of ministries in the provinces in 1939. In some provinces the experiments were done away with and in others they were damped down.

After the attainment of Independence in 1947, the Wardha Scheme of education was reconsidered as the national system of education fit for adoption on a large scale. Schools began to be changed to Basic education pattern. In the two plan periods the number of Basic schools increased and side by side ran the traditional elementary schools. So far as the total number of students in the Basic schools was concerned, it was not more than the number of pupils in elementary school.

**Reasons for Slow Progress During Plan Periods**

The reasons for the slow progress of Basic education as revealed in two plan periods were: *(a)* a lack of clear-cut concept of Basic education, *(b)* impossibility in the attainment of self-sufficiency and *(c)* its expensiveness. There was no clearcut concept of Basic education. There was a confusion in the mind of the general public about the objectives and contents of basic education. The principle of education through productive work meant one thing for one man and the other for others. Some of the strict adherents of Gandhiji insisted on real production of usable goods in the school: Others said that Basic education was a play-way education.

Gandhiji regarded self sufficiency to be the integral element of Basic education. He expected that the Basic education would, under favourable conditions support the cost of running the school partially and it would be easier to control the primary education. Even in the most progressive states like Bihar in the matter of the implementation of the scheme, schools were self-supporting to the extent of 18 percent only. The Assessment Committee on Basic Education appointed by the Government of India at the end of the first Five Year Plan said that the expectation that Basic Education would become self-supporting was belied. Though Basic education was a better type of education, it was more expensive than the traditional type of elementary education. The conversion of an elementary school into a basic school needed money. The result was that many schools had their name plates changed overnight but could not develop into genuine basic schools even in years' time.

The financial stringency with the states had been so great that they could not increase the number of Basic Schools either by changing their ordinary schools to Basic pattern or by raising new Basic schools by more than 5% per year.

Gandhiji wished that the education should be given through craft right from the beginning. When this idea was worked out in practice, there was little production and much wastage at the initial stage where the number of children was large and where the immaturity led to nil production. People suggested therefore that the introduction of craft should be delayed and other activities like clay-modelling, kitchen gardening should be introduced in lower grades.

Then there was a problem of co-ordinating Basic education of 7 years with higher secondary education. For such of the scheme it was necessary that the post-Basic education should have been closely related to the present system of higher secondary education. A scheme of multipurpose schools was set on foot through the advice of Mudaliar Commission. But the idea did not gain ground.

The Orientation Programmes that were taken up in the third Five Year Plan period did not work well. It was considered necessary to introduce certain inexpensive elements of Basic education in all the existing elementary schools so that there may be a complete change-over in the shortest time possible. *For example,* if an elementary school had a good piece of land and irrigation facilities, it may take up kitchen gardening as its craft. But such orientation programmes could not be implemented due to one reason or the other.

To give proper encouragement to basic education programmes, NIBE (National Institute of Basic Education) was set-up in 1954 in Delhi (now known as the Department of Basic Education in NCERT). This institution has done valuable work in the development of Basic education in the country. It has been preparing literature on Basic education and developing new crafts suitable for adoption in urban areas.

In spite of state patronage the scheme of Basic Education is receiving a set-back in the country as a whole. The reasons are as follows:

1. The conversion and orientation programmes taken up in the first three Five Year Plans did not gain the required impetus.
2. The idea of self-sufficiency of basic education has proved to be unsound as tested by experience.

3. The state ministries remained engaged in other activities and did not give any priority to the scheme of Basic education.

4. People all over the country felt that Basic education was simply an experiment and hence, it need not be accepted as a pattern.

5. The stress on craft has been played down because it could not stand the bitterness of criticism of the opponents.

6. The Education Commission (1964-66) has dealt a blow to Basic education by side tracking the issue and by laying a greater emphasis on work experience.

7. The staff-in-charge of crafts in schools has been of low quality and could not support the movement adequately.

8. The Government of India in its national policy on education has felt the idea of improving basic education completely.

## Sergeant Committee Report

In the year 1944, Sir John Sargent, the then Educational Adviser to the Government of India, prepared a report on the post-war educational development on the request of the Central Advisory Board of Education. The report is known by various names; the scheme of Post-War Development in India, Report by the Central Advisory Board of Education and Sargent Plan or Scheme. The aim of the Plan was to reorganise the entire system of education at a total cost of ₹ 313 crores and was to be carried out in 8 stages by means of 8 five year programmes. It aimed at attaining the educational standard of contemporary England within 40 years.

**First Comprehensive Scheme of National Education.** The Sargent Scheme has been the most comprehensive scheme, so for presented by the Government for the development and expansion of Indian education. It presented a very detailed scheme of educational reconstruction from top to bottom, from primarly to universities and higher technical institutions. It touched every aspect of Indian education. It is the first comprehensive scheme of national education, worte K.G. Saiyidain, "it does to start with the assumption that India was destined to occupy a place of educational inferiority in the comity of nations: it is based on the conviction that what other countries have achieved in the field of education is well within the competence of this country."

It is said about the report that it was not an original document. It was a patchwork of different reports published from time to time by the Central Advisory Board of Education to consider the different aspects of Indian educational problems. So far as the Basic education is concerned it is the summary of the useful suggestions made by previous reports and schemes including the Wardha Scheme. The scheme was not accepted because the time of 40 years was required to implement it and the educational public leaders did not like to lengthen the period of attaining mass literacy to such an extent. Had the scheme been implemented, at least some targets would have been achieved; the percentage of illiterates would have gone down. But the scheme was not given a fair trail and the reform in education was delayed.

**Recommendations Regarding Basic Education**

1. Provision should be made for free and compulsory primary or basic education for all children between the ages of 6 and 14.
2. The education imparted should be general and emphasis should not be laid on the teaching of 3 R's only.
3. The basic craft to be taught should be suitable to local conditions.

4. Basic Education could not be expected to pay for itself though the sale of articles produced by the pupils.
5. Mother-tongue should be the medium of instruction of Senior and Junior Basic Schools.
6. The course of basic education should be divided into parts: Junior Basic and Senior Basic, the former to be given to all children between the ages 6-11 and the latter to be given to those who could not proceed to high school.
7. The Senior Basic Schools should provide for corporate giving. Physical training, organising of games are essential to supplement the instruction given in the class room.
8. Attendance officers should be appointed to introduce compulsion.
9. The standards of training, recruiting and conditions of service of teachers should be raised.
10. In place of external examinations there should be internal examinations and successful candidates should be awarded certificates.
11. The number of trained women teachers should be increased.
12. English should not be taught in Junior Basic Schools. It can be taught in Senior Basic Schools only when the education Department of the Province gives its decision in its favour.

**Recommeadation Regarding Secondary Education**

The main recommendations regarding Secondary education are given below:

1. Secondary education should be for 6 years for selected students between age 11 and 17.

2. Admission to secondary schools should be made on selective basis and only promising students, about 20% of the children, attending Junior Basic schools should be admitted to High Schools.

3. High schools shall be of two types—Academic High Schools and Technical High Schools.

4. Every child entering a High School remains there till the age of 14 compulsorily. Even after this period steps should be taken to see that children are not withdrawn from the school before the completion of the course.

5. High School leavers should receive an education that will fit them for direct entry into occupations and professions.

6. High School education should not be preliminary to university education and should be complete in itself.

7. Subjects in the Academic High School as well as in the Technical should be common; *for example,* mother-tongue, English, Modern Indian Languages, Indian and World History, Indian and World Geography, Science, Mathematics, Agriculture, Economics, Music, Art and Physical Training. The Technical High Schools should include Science, Wood work, Metal work, Elementary Engineering, Drawing, Book keeping, Type Writing, Short Hand, Accountancy, Commercial, Practice and Domestic Science.

❋❋❋

# 5

# Education in Contemporary India

We need not copy the western models blindly. And thus, consequently suffer the loss of inspiration. Some of the most important individual aims of education are:

**1. The Knowledge Aim.** Knowledge is power. Achievements of all kinds are made possible only through knowledge. An ignorant man can do nothing for himself or for anyone else; and is like an animal. Knowledge is basic for living a rich and happy life. It is for this reason that many educationists consider imparting of knowledge to the people as an important aim. That is why all the schools have graded syllabus for children of different ages and classes. Different subjects are taught in the schools as different aspects of knowledge. In fact acquisition of knowledge is the nucleon around which most of the activities of the schools in the whole world revolve. Most of the teaching strategies developed for teaching aim at imparting knowledge alone. The examination systems in all countries measure, by and large, only knowledge. In fact, education and knowledge giving have become synonymous. Teachers, students and parents all think that good education and good schools are only those which make their children knowledgeable.

There is no doubt that knowledge-giving should be considered an important aim of education. In the past many philosophers like Plato, Aristotle, the Sophists and many others emphasised this aim very much. Comenius said that an ideal school should impart knowledge of all subjects to all men and women. Knowledge and intellectual development go together; and cultivation of intelligence is an importance of education according to Bertrand Russel. Bacon's slogan was "all knowledge for all", knowledge was virtue for Socrates. To Cicero knowledge was a means of mental development. Even the development of other aspects of human personality is dependent largely on acquisition of knowledge. Thus, it is an important aim of education to impart knowledge. But where are we wrong?

We commit a serious error when we accept and say that it is the only aim of education, when we say that nothing else is important. Knowledge alone is not enough and sufficient for living a happy and complete life. Knowledge is a tool which has to be used for achieving many more things. So these many more things should also be brought within the purview of aims of education. Hence, the right way is to say that among many aims of education, knowledge aim is also very important.

**2. Harmonious Development Aim.** It means harmonious development of child's personality. Child's personality is one word but many things. Intellectual and cognitive development is one aspect. Emotional development including emotional control is another. Feelings, attitudes, interests, values etc., also fall within this component of emotional development. Similarly, development of skills, desirable habits and actions constitute still another aspect of personality development. Adjustment to the environment and many social behaviours come under this. Equal development of all these aspects, balanced development of these, is considered an aim of education. If it happens that a person is very knowledgeable, but socially maladjusted, this would mean a lap-sided development of the personality.

**3. Vocational Aim.** This is also known as the 'bread-and-butter" aim of education. Thus, no doubt should be considered an important aim of education. It simply means that education received by an individual should enable him to earn his bread, should enable him to get a job, some work that pays him sufficient money regularly so that the individual is able to buy bread, clothes, house and other things necessary for living a decent and comfortable life. This has led in many countries, to a slogan by the people and educators which is "job-oriented education". Vocationalization of education is another dimension of the same. Gandhiji's basic education concept had this implication. When he said that true education should be, for the boys and girls, a kind of insurance against employment, he meant to emphasize vocational aim of education.

Again, although we all accept that vocational aim is very important, yet we commit a mistake when we say that it is the only aim to which education should cater. We should always think that along with vocational aim there are other aims which are equally important. We should neither ignore or belittle the importance of vocational aim, nor we should consider this only important aim. Nehru struck the balance between vocational and cultural aims of education when he said that cultural and vocational or productive aspects of education both are essential. "Everybody should be a producer as well as a good citizen and not a sponge on another person," said he. Mahatma Gandhi also emphasized the same point when he said that body, mind and spirit all should be developed by education. Although many philosophers from the ancient times to the present day have insisted upon the satisfaction of the soul belittling the importance of vocation in life, yet their view can not be the conscious of opinion. These should be taken as the extreme views and one-sided opinions. The majority of the people in the world feel that education should make individual self-dependent and capable of earning their livelihood.

**4. Aesthetic Aim.** This aim emphasizes that education should develop in the pupil an aesthetic sense which means a taste for good and beautiful things. They feel that excellence of taste and fairness of feeling can form the basis of good character and genuine morality. By developing in the child sensitivity to what is beautiful and excellent ideals may be generated which play an important role in being a moral person. Aesthetic development is, in fact, a part of the education of the whole man. It is a sort of emotional training. In the past the Athenians considered this important. They aimed, through education, to develop a well-rounded individual, one whose physical, moral, intellectual and aesthetic powers were developed. For developing aesthetic sense of the child the educators stressed that while teaching pupils love of beauty and art should be fostered. The students should be presented with a large variety of art forms such as paintings, drawings, beautiful sceneries both real and painted, songs, poetry, etc.

**5. The Moral Aim.** This aim lays stress on the ethical development of the people. Character-formation and learning of social and moral values are the focus of this aim. Gandhiji termed this as "purity of heart". Vivekananda's "man-making" function of education also means the same thing. Dewey said "all education forms character—moral and mental". This, in other words, means emphasizing the moral aim of education. Raymont also considered "cultivation of strength and purity of character" as an important aim of education. Herbart said "the whole work of education could be summed up in the concept of morality." All the idealist philosophers supported the moral aim as an ultimate aim of education. National Policy on Education of 1986 also said that education should be made a "forceful tool for the cultivation of social and moral values".

There can be no gain saying that education should teach morality to children. It is an universally accepted aim of education. But, the difficulty with this aim is how to define character and morality, what are its behavioural components, are these behavioural components acceptable universally, does morality help the individual in actual situations of life, is there any standard way of teaching morality. These questions have no set and unambiguous answers. Morality is good, but very difficult to be taught, particularly in today's materialistic world. Yet, the aim cannot be scored out simply for these difficulties. In a democratic country where the assumption is that the human being is perfect and given the freedom he will make the best use of it in the interest of the society and his own interest, it becomes still more important to teach morality to people.

**6. Complete Living Aim.** This aim means that education should enable the individuals to live a life which is full and complete. In other words it means preparing the individuals for life. Living a full and complete life means exercising and using all capacities and abilities in the interest of one's well-being. Keeping good health, developing a sound mind and using it for the benefit of life's amenities, enjoying life and enriching it culturally, living like a good citizen and gainfully employed may be considered some important features of full or complete living. In other words it is the same as harmonious development of personality. According to this aim education should enable the individual to carry out all necessary activities of life successfully. He should be an enlightened citizen and an efficient man. Herbert Spencer seems to be the advocate of this aim. It is in a way laying an emphasis on liberal education which emphasizes teaching the pupils everything that is needed in life. It may be termed as life-centred education or education for life.

The main difficulty with this aim is how to define "completeness of life". When is life complete? Even it is possible to define completeness of life it becomes more difficult to identify what will make it so.

## GRAVITY OF THE PROBLEM

The attainment of social and national integration as one of the objectives of the national system of education is a challenging problem. For a country like ours, it is difficult to achieve this objective because there is already a wide gulf between the rich and the poor, the urban and the rural, the elite and the masses. Besides, people are bound by local, regional, linguistic, religious and other sectional ties. Old traditions and values are rapidly disappearing. Education is promoting devisive tendencies. The schools for the rich and the poor are segregated. There is a lack of national consciousness everywhere. Communal riots, corruption, strikes, lawlessness, disregard for public property are some of the symptoms of social distingration.

**Steps Suggested.** The Education Commission (1964-66) suggested certain steps to create a strong and united country to make people conscious of what 'India' is and to create an integrated society. This could be done by the introduction of the common school, by making social and national service an integral part of education at all stages, by adopting a proper language policy and by promoting national consciousness.

**1. The Common School System.** The educational system as it exists even today is undemocratic and harmful for national unity and social solidarity. It is undemocratic because under this system good education is not available to all children. The children of the masses are sent to schools managed by the Government or by the local authorities. The schools charge either no fees or normal fees. They provide sub-standard or poor quality education. The children of the privileged class are sent to the private, fee-charging, better schools. The present system of education is harmful for the country not only because 'the identification and development of the total national pool of ability is greatly hampered', but also because it weakens social cohesion.

The common school system of public education has been suggested by the Commission as a powerful instrument for achieving social and national integration, because the schools under this system would be open to 'all children, irrespective of caste, creed, community, religion, economic conditions or social status'. As these schools would maintain adequate standards the rich people will tend to send their children to them and as they will not charge any fees, they would meet the needs of average parents too.

**2. Evolving a Language Policy for National and Social Integration.** The Emotional Integration Committee regarded the use of regional languages from the primary to the college level as media of education, 'a matter of profound importance for national integration'. The National Integration Council (1962) spoke in support of the same view. The Education Commission (1964-66) also agreed with these observations. The Commission recommended that regional languages should be made media of instruction at all levels, that Hindi should be so developed that it becomes the link language of the people in the shortest time possible and English may continue as the link language of the intellectual people or it may function as library language at all stages of education. The language question which had been very 'complex and intractable' so far has been solved by the Commission to the satisfaction of all.

**3. Social and National Service as an Integral Part of Education.** The Commission suggested that programmes of social and national service should be incorporated in the education of children at all stages. The programmes should run together with academic studies in schools and colleges and start from the upper primary stages (V-VII) and continue up to the university. Social service may take the form of participation in community living on the school or college campus or in programmes of community development. Every school and college should try to develop a rich community life for its students and should provide adequate opportunities to them to participate in it; *for example*, much of the work done by hired labour or menial servants can be done by students themselves.

Money so saved may be used for providing amenities to them. Programmes of community service may also be integrated in school and college education. At the higher primary stage students may be encouraged to serve the community in a number of ways. At the secondary stage suitable forms of service to the community may be sought after. At the college level participation in Labour and Social Welfare camps or the N.C.C. may be made obligatory and programmes of community development may be developed agreeing with the available resources, age and competence of students.

Social and national service so organised and made obligatory for all students at all stages would certainly lead to a decrease in the social distance between the educated and the uneducated, the intelligentsia and the masses. It will also help up in evolving a united nation.

**4. Promoting National Consciousness.** The schools under the English regime taught loyalty to the English people by giving instruction to our students in their literature, history and culture. Love for the motherland was never developed before 1937. It was the struggle for Independence between 1900 and 1947 that made people nationally conscious. The development of national consciousness was effected outside the school walls.

After the attainment of Independence in 1947, the people began to forget 'India'. Sectional loyalties grew up. Schools remained sleeping. The unfortunate international conflicts—the Chinese invasion of 1962, the two recent aggressions by Pakistan—did something to unite us. But such happenings could never be regarded as a right solution. Can education be not used as an effective tool for promoting national consciousness? Schools and colleges in other countries have done so.

The Education Commission believed firmly in the efficacy of formal education for promoting national spirit in the educand. It suggested that the Indian youth could be made to understand his cultural heritage by a well-organised instruction in Indian languages, literature, history and philosophy and that he could be helped to instil faith in the future of the nation through a systematic course in civics and politics and political economy.

**Circumstances to Set-up the Education Commission (1964-66)**

**A Need for Social Change after Independence.** Education, all the world over, has been used as a powerful tool of social, economic and political change. The political upheaval that took place in our country in the beginning of the century brought in its train a set of changes in the life of the nation. A need began to be felt to bring about a multiphased revolution within the shortest possible period. The whole Government machinery was set in motion for making an effort at economic growth, social change and cultural advancement. As the Government was convinced that education is the key to national prosperity and welfare, an all-out attempt was made to transform the education system.

**A Need for Evolving a National System of Education.** In spite of much valuable thinking and considerable implementation of educational ideas during the 15 years that followed the attainment of Independence, the nation could not develop a system of education which could meet the needs of the newly born democratic state. The Government of India expressed its grave concern at the state of affairs in 1964 in the following words, "While some advances have been made in (certain) directions, the education system has not generally evolved in accordance with the needs of the times and a wide and distressing gulf continues to persist between thought and action in several sectors of this crucial field of national activity." The views expressed by eminent educationists to evolve a national system of education or the recommendations made by Committees and Commissions (especially appointed ever since the achievement of

Independence) were either ignored or partially implemented. *For example,* the Higher Secondary (three years) pattern was not given a fair trial in most of the states. The scheme of basic education could not achieve desired success. The multipurpose scheme of diversified courses have to meet the same fate.

During the three Plan periods education at all levels had expanded tremendously. Yet people were not happy about a number of educational aspects: *for example,* the nation was not yet able to provide free and compulsory education for all children of 14 + ; nor could it solve the problem of educated unemployment throught diversification of courses nor could it produce an adequate supply of manpower in many sectors of economic life nor could it raise the status of the teaching community. Quantitative expansion of education did take place, but qualitative improvements suffered.

Realising the importance of education in the bringing about of the desired economic and social development, the Government of India in 1964 considered the urgency of surveying and examining the entire field of education. Problems of educational reconstruction had been reviewed by a number of Committees and Commissions which attempted to solve difficulties faced in specific areas only. *For example,* the University Education Commission (1948-49) and the Secondary Education Commission (1952-53) surveyed the fields of university and school education respectively. Towards the end of the Third Five Year Plan, a need began to be felt to make a review of the present education system so comprehensive that it may cover the entire field.

**A Need for Improving Quality of Education.** The need for appointing a fresh Education Commission in 1964 arose out of a grave concern for the improvement of quality of education. The Government wanted an expert advice on the evolution of the much desired national system of education and on the formation of 'general principles and policies for the development of education at all stages and in all aspects.' The Resolution of the Government of India in 1964 said, "It is desirable to survey the entire field of educational development as the various parts of the educational system strongly interact with and influence one another. It is not possible to have progressive and strong universities without efficient secondary school and the quality of these schools is determined by the functioning of elementary schools. What is needed, therefore, is a synoptic survey and an imaginative look at education considered as a whole and not fragmented into parts and stages. In the past several commissions and committees have examined limited sectors and specific aspects of education. It is now proposed to have a comprehensive review of the entire educational system."

## NATIONAL POLICY OF EDUCATION, 1986

On April 20, 1986 a new Educational Policy was placed before the Indian Parliament for consideration and approval. The following objectives of education were particularly emphasized in this policy:

1. Vocationalization of Education. Particularly, at the secondary stage of education the curriculum should be job-oriented.

2. To encourage the Governmental and non-Governmental efforts for wiping out illiteracy and to emphasize the necessity of adult education, formal education, farmers' education and 'open' schools.

3. To awaken the people about the various scientific and technological developments and to make the students at the various stages of education aware of the same in order that they may utilize them in their future life.

Onwards we shall look into some basic details of this new policy:

**1. National Forum of Education.** At least 75 per cent of the curriculum should be identical for all the States. The remaining 25 per cent may be related to the particular local conditions of a State. The purpose of incorporation this basic feature is to acquaint all the citizens of the country with their basic rights and duties, history of the freedom struggle, the common cultural heritage and national identity.

**2. Emphasis on Learning.** The teacher must not harbour the notion that the child learns through his teaching alone. In fact, the child learns many more things by himself. Therefore, the teacher must not emphasize only by teaching procedures in the classroom. Essentially, he should also try to create such an environment in the class and school in general that the children may learn many things through their own creativeness. The prescribed curriculum for children do not contain the latest informations of the concerned subject. Generally, they are four or five years old. So they are not very useful, because they contain incomplete informations. Therefore the teacher must inspire the students to learn things on their own as far as possible. The mental development of children should be so guided that they make understand the utility of knowledge themselves. The Education Policy of 1986 has particularly emphasised this point.

**3. Delinking Degree for any Service.** If the compulsoriness of a degree for securing a job is done away with, many youths will automatically refrain from obtaining higher education. Thus, crowding of aspirants for admissions to colleges and universities will be reduced. In fact, a degree should not be considered as a pre-requisite for a job which has not direct relationship with it. In many foreign developed countries a degree is not considered as a condition for obtaining a job. According to the 1991 Census Report a degree is considered in our country as a requisite for securing a service. At the T.V. centres for the Chaupal or Krishi Darshan Programmes, B.Sc. (Agr.) has been made as compulsory for a person conducting them. Similarly, in our country a degree has been made compulsory for a job. In fact, many students of our colleges and universities have absolutely no interest in their studies.

**4. Education for the Weaker Section of the Society.** The education of scheduled castes, scheduled tribes, handicapped and girls has been greatly emphasised because in the interest of national progress, their development has been considered necessary. Hence, reservation for such persons has been recommended in various types of educational institution.

**5. Emphasis on Reforms in Examination System.** It has been suggested in this new policy that 'grade' should be given in examination in place of 'division'. In the current system of examination the student scoring between 45 to 48 per cent of marks is placed in the second class and those sixty or above are placed in the first class. In this situation the students getting within the range of 44 and 47 and also only 59 think that they have lost their higher division by one mark only. This feature develops a kind of frustration and anguish in them. In order to do away with this situation, this new policy has suggested giving of "grades" and not "class" or "division". According to this new policy those coming within the range of 40 to 50 or of 45 to 55 will be given "B" or "C" grade. A determination of assigning "B" or "C" grade will depend upon the nature of achievements of all the students taking up an examination. Suppose in a certain difficult test no student scores more than 45 per cent, then it is just possible that it may be considered desirable that those scoring 45 per cent or above may be given "A" grade and those getting 40 may be grouped under "B" and those 35 may be assigned "C" grade. Thus, assigning of "grades" will depend upon the nature of a test and how all the students as a whole show performance on the same. Periodical tests have also been recommended in this new policy, because the determination of merit of a student on the basis of only one examination has not been considered as just. Similarly, appointment of external examiners, too, has been considered as undesirable. Thus, the teachers have been made solely responsible for evaluating the merits of his students. It has been felt that this method will increase the importance of teachers and marks of indiscipline in students will also be gradually minimised.

**6. Vocationalization of Education.** Vocationalization of education has been particularly been emphasised in this new education policy. As far as possible, education should be given in a natural environment. The child must acquire some skill in some area of his interest. This is necessary for a happy life in future. With this end in view this new education policy has advocated for inclusion of scientific and technical subjects in the curriculum. It has been specifically stated in the policy that in the tenth class not more than 50 per cent students should opt for literacy subjects and the rest should be encouraged to study vocational courses of various types according to their interests. This kind of vocationalization of education will minimise the unemployment problem, because then the educated person will not depend on some service alone and may utilize his acquired skill for earning his bread.

**7. Ever-Continual Primary School.** According to this new education policy each primary school will have at least a two-room-building with at least two teachers. Of these two teachers, one will be a lady. Each primary school will function throughout the twelve months a year. Thus, all the young children in an area will be receiving primary education.

**. Importance of Moral Values.** The importance of moral values has been recognised by this new policy. The development of healthy moral values in an individual will help him to depend upon his own efforts and not on his self-imposed destiny. Education is a tool for bringing in desirable changes in a society. Therefore, importance of moal values in life should be pointed out wherever possible in teaching. This method of teaching moral values will be more helpful to students.

**9. All India Educational Service.** In order to tone up educational administration, this policy has emphasised the necessity of starting an All India Education Service cadre. Under this scheme any education officer may be transferred any where in the country. It has been felt that this kind of transfer will weaken the undesirable bond of regionalism and will bring dynamism in the educational administration. The policy of transfer will dissuade the education officers from coming into the pressure of politicians in the sphere of their work and as a result they will be more honest in the performance of their duties.

**10. Modernization of Education.** Computerisation has been suggested in this policy. This method will be employed in the expansion of literacy. The utility of correspondence courses, T.V., Radio and Satellite and Video-cassetts has been accepted for education in this policy.

**11. Importance of Sports and Games.** In this new policy importance of sports and games has been recognised because participation in them will maintain the health of children. With this end in view forming of active committees of sports and games has been particularly emphasised. Framing of curriculum of small sports and games has also been suggested.

**12. Right Persons Alone to be Teachers.** This education policy has considered the training of teacher as very important for raising the falling standard of education. Hence, some very useful suggestions have been given for improving the condition of teachers. According to this policy the teachers of a certain cadre should enjoy identical scale of salaries and all of them should be given residential facilitis. The society should be well awakened for giving due respects to teachers. Refresher course for teachers after every five years period has been considered necessary in order to acquaint them with the latest developed teachnique of teaching.

**13. Open University.** In this policy starting of Open Universities has been emphasised. These universities are meant for those persons who have not been able to obain higher education, but are desirous of receiving the same in order to better their prospects. The necessity of open universities has been recognised also for expansion of higher education. In an open university any person may obtain higher education according to his own speed. A certain examination may be passed in parts in an open university.

**14. Establishing Navodaya Schools.** Students in these schools will be admitted to class VI on the basis of an admission test. In the admission process pre-determined ratio for boys and girls of both urban and rural areas will be observed. In admission to these schools no financial criterion will be observed. All these boy and girl students will have to reside in the respective associated hostels after being admitted to the Navodaya schools. Such students will be given free boarding and lodging and free education. Twenty per cent of the students after passing 8th class in a Navodaya school will be transferred for education to other States with a view to promote national integration.

**15. New Educational Institutions.** In the education policy of 1986, it has been recommended that "District Institute of Education and Training" and "District of Education" should be established in the various states of the country. These institutions will survey the educational needs of people of various areas separately and will inform the concerned education officers about the same from time to time. The Constitution of a national institute has also been proposed with a view to raise the standard of education. The main purpose of the new policy has been to prepare such citizens for the coming twenty-first century who may be responsive to their basic duties in consonance with human values and democratic ideals.

**16. Protection of Environment Necessary.** Protection of environment has been emphasised in the new policy of 1986. The students and teachers will be urged to protect rivers, lakes, hills, mountains, forests and pasture lands. They will also see that the existing mills and factories do not pollute the surrounding environments.

**17. Preservation of Own Culture.** There appears to be a wide gulf between the modern formal education and our cultural traditions. This new education policy wants to bridge this gulf, because the scientific and technical developments have to be associated with our proud history and culture. Our system of education should be related with our Fine Arts, Architecture and Oriental Studies. Hence, we shall have to pay particular attention on organization of museums, folk arts and literature. This policy urges us to do the needful in these directions. Modern education has led many of our youths to drug-addiction and it has not taught many of them how to be respectful to teachers and other elders in the society. As a result, deplorable marks of indiscipline in these usually stare at us.

**18. Women Education.** According to this policy the standard of education of women should be raised. In vocational and technical education, women will be assigned their proper place in order to equate them with men as far as possible. An attempt will also be made to minimise the difference existing in the curriculum meant for women and men.

**19. Adult Education.** A literacy programme will be organised for making illiterate persons literate within the age group of 15 and 35. For this purpose Continuing Education Centres will be established in rural areas. It will be a duty of a Project Officer to spread literacy amongst labourers. Distance education will be given through Radio, T.V. and films. These media will be utilized for vocational programmes as well.

**20. Operation Black Board.** In this new policy the term "Operation Black Board" has been used for conveying the ideas that minimum facilities will be provided to a primary school. These minimum facilities will include at least two rooms, some necessary charts and maps, a blackboard, Tatpatti (about one metre wide and 10 metre long pieces of carpet) for seating children and other essential material equipments. In the beginning at least two teachers will be appointed for each primary school. Afterwards more teachers may be appointed as new classes are added. In the "Operation Black Board" the co-operation of voluntary organizations, local bodies and desirous persons will be enlisted. At first-some building will be provided to a primary school if it does not have any.

## Philosophy of New Policy

**1. New Acculturating Role of Education.** One of the most important contributions of New Policy of Education is that it has provided a comprehensive educational philosophy covering the new acculturating role of education by way of refining sensitiveness, building scientific temper and cultivating independence of mind and spirit.

**2. Natural Perspective.** Manpower planning and its educational investment has brought in a national perspective to our development needs. A unifying policy in the development of human resources provides a social dimension to an area of personal perception. The pooling of resources in the area of personnel and research at the national level with the provision for interregional mobility with equal access for every Indian of requisite merit is a most welcome and timely policy statement.

**3. Efficiency.** The policy determination to promote efficiency and effectiveness at all levels (though easier said that done) brings in new dimension in the performance of teachers, students, administrators, Government officials and institutions.

**4. Equalisation.** The special emphasis laid on the removal of disparities and equalization of opportunity by attending to the specific needs of different groups of distressed people including women, scheduled castes, minorities and the handicapped, should enhance the sense of social responsibility and a fair distribution on justice to all concerned.

**5. Universalisation.** The universalisation of education upto a given level with access of education of a comparable quality is another positive aspect of the policy.

**6. Beneficial.** The realisation of education needs to be managed in an atmosphere of ultmost intellectual rigour, seriousness of purposes with adequate freedom for innovation and creativity should bear beneficial fruits.

**7. Cultural Perspective.** Another special feature of the policy is the concept of providing a cultural perspective in the formal system of education.

**8. Value Education.** The focus on value education and work experience as an integral part of the learning process will enable us to uphold human values necessary for raising the quality of life for all. The document speaks about combating certain negative values and promoting positive ones from our heritage. It mentions social, ethical and moral values which have to be cultivated.

## The Essence and Role of Education

The policy envisaged the role of education as follows:

1. Education is fundamental to our all-round development, material and spiritual.
2. Education is the highway to derive the maximum benefit from the areas already created by the economic and technical development and a means to ensure that the funds must reach all sections.
3. Education should be an effective instrument of reducing rural-urban disparities.
4. Education has an acculturating role. It refines sensitivity and perceptions that contribute to national cohesion, a scientific temper and independence of mind and spirit.

5. Education needs to be planned meticulously and developed with great sensitivity so as to make the best use of the human being who is a positive asset and precious national resources.

6. Education should imbibe the coming generations with a strong commitment of human values and to social justice.

7. Education should assist in the realisation of goals of secularism, socialism and professional ethics.

8. Spread of literacy and education among women in the largest single factor in bringing down the growth of population in India.

9. Education must prevent the erosion of long-cherished values.

10. Education should develop the activity of the coming generation to internalize new ideas constantly and creatively.

11. Education develops manpower of different level of the economy.

12. Education is unique investment in the present and the future.

**Features of National System of Education Envisaged by NPE, 1986**

The National Policy on Education, 1986 has envisaged the following main features of the National Systems of Education:

**1. Based on Constitutional Principles.** It derives its inspiration from the ideals and values of democracy, secularism and socialism enshrined in our Constitution.

**2. Access of Education.** It implies that upto a given level all students, irrespective of caste, creed, location, sex, have access to education of a comparable quality. To achieve this, the Government will initiate appropriate funded programmes. Effective measures will be taken in the direction of the Common School recommended in the 1968 policy.

**3. Education for International Understanding.** India has always worked for peace and understanding between nations, treating the whole world as one family. True to this hoary, tradition, education has to strengthen this world view and motivate the younger generations for international co-operation and peaceful co-existence. This aspect cannot be neglected.

**4. Minimum Levels of Learning.** Minimum levels of learning will be laid down for each stage of education. Steps will also be taken to foster students an understanding of the diverse cultural and social systems of the people living in different parts of the country.

**5. National Curricular Framework with a Common Core.** It will be based on a national curricular framework which contains a common core alongwith other components that are flexible. The common core will include the history of India's freedom movement, the constitutional obligations and other contents essential to nurture national identity. These elements cut across subject areas and will be designed to promote values such as India's common cultural heritage, egalitarianism, democracy and secularism, equality of the sexes, protection of the environment, removal of social barriers, observance of the small family norms and inculcation of the scientific temper. All educational programmes will be carried on in strict conformity with secular values.

**. Common Educational Structure.** It envisages of common educational structure. The 10+2+3 structure has now been accepted in all parts of the country. Regarding the further break-up of the first 10 years efforts will be made to move towards an elementary system comprising five years of primary education and three years of upper primary, followed by two years of High School.

**7. Universal Character of Higher Education.** In higher education in general and technical education in particular, steps will be taken to facilitate inter-regional mobility by providing equal access to every Indian of requisite merit, regardless of his origins. The universal character of universities and other institutions of higher education is to be understood.

**8. Priorities in Educational Reform.** The Nation as a whole will assume the responsibility of providing resource support for implementing programmes of educational transformation, reducing disparities, universalisation of elementary education, adult literacy, scientific and technical research, etc.

**9. Promotion of Languages.** Besides the promotion of the link language, programmes will also be launched to increase substantially the translation of books form glossaries. The young will be encouraged to undertake the rediscovery of India each in his own image and perception.

**10. Equality of Opportunity in Education.** To promote equality it will be necessary to provide for equal opportunity to all not only in access, but also in the conditions for success. Besides, awareness of the inherent equality of all will be created through the core curriculum. The purpose is to remove prejudices and complexes transmitted through the social environment and accident of birth.

**11. Strengthening of National Institutions.** National institutions which will be strengthened to play an important role in giving shape to the National System of Education, are the University Grants Commission. The All India Council of Technical Education, the Indian Council of Agricultural Research and the Indian Medical Council. Integrated Planning will be instituted among all these bodies so as to establish functional linkages and reinforce programmes of research and post graduate education. These, together with the National

Council of Education Research and Training, the National Institute of Educational Planning and Administration and the International Institute of Science and Technology Education will be involved in implementing the Education Policy.

**12. Open and Distance Learning.** Life-long education is a cherished goal of the education process. This presupposes universal literacy. Opportunities will be provided to the youth, house-wives, agricultural and industrial workers and professionals to continue the education of the choice and the pace suited to them. The further thrust will be in the direction of open and distance learning.

## EIGHT BOLD STEPS OF NPE, 1986

**1. National System of Education.** National system of education to provide access to education of a comparable quality to all students, to have a common educational structure with national curricular framework containing a common core.

**2. Vocational Targets.** Vocational courses to cover 10 per cent of higher secondary students by 1990 and 25 per cent by 1955.

**3. Navodaya Schools.** Pace setting Navodaya Schools to be started which will be residential and free of charge.

**4. Performance and Accountability.** To ensure that all teachers should teach and all students study.

**5. The Management of Education.** Evolving a strategy of decentralization and the creation of a spirit of autonomy for educational institutions.

**6. Delinking Degree from Jobs.** Beginning to be made in delinking degrees from jobs in selected areas.

**7. Indian Education Service.** Constitution of this Service is likely to bring a national perspective in education.

**8. Raising Resources.** Resources to be raised through:

(*a*) Asking beneficiary communities to maintain school buildings.

(*b*) Raising fees at the higher levels of education.

(*c*) Levying cess or charge on the user agencies.

**Missing Links and Limitations**

**1. Confined to Privileged.** A lion's share of the benefit of education is cornered by about six per cent of students who have been fortunate to join colleges. It is this privileged section which corners 99 per cent of Government jobs. Educational expenditure has become a mechanism of transferring resources from rural sector to urban sector or in other words from poor to the rich.

**2. Neglect of Neighbourhood Concepts.** The New Education Policy has completely ignored the 'neighbourhood' concept of school system advocated by the Kothari Commission. It is interesting to note that the Kothari Commission considered that the 'neighbourhood School' was a step towards eliminating the segregation that now takes place between the schools for the poor and the underprivileged classes and those for the rich and the privileged one.

**3. Need of Basic Education.** The Education Policy does not refer to Basic Education although it has an important place in the ideology of freedom struggle and procedures were finalised as long back as 1937.

**4. Wrong Basics of Reservation.** The New Education Policy should have suggested reservation not on the basics of merit but on the basics of economic conditions.

**5. No Reference to Working Days.** The New Education Policy should have recommended increased number of working days in educational institutions. There should be about 300 working days instead of about 200 at present.

**6. No Check on Nursery Schools.** The New Education Policy has not mentioned concrete steps to curb the mushroom growth of nursery schools charging high fees and meant only for the rich.

**7. No Check on Minority Institutions.** Some suitable checks on the working of the schools run by the minority communities should have been proposed so as to prevent them from exploiting the staff working in these institutions.

**8. Lack of Teachers and Equipments.** The emphasis on teaching and learning through discovery has little meaning as the nation has thousands of schools without adequate teachers and equipment.

**9. No Research Basis.** There is practically no proposal in the documents which is based on authentic research.

**10. No Check on Public Schools.** The New Education Policy has, by and large, evaded the issue of the 'loot' by so-called public schools which take money only and do not give good education.

**11. No Supervision.** The New Education Policy does not include specific measures for supervising and monitoring Government and Central schools properly. There is an urgent need to ensure that, 'All teachers should teach and all students study'.

**12. No Fixed Target.** It is very unfortunate that no target has been fixed in different areas of reforms.

**13. Lack of Funds.** There is very little hope of obtaining community funds for educational purposes as there is a growing tendency on the part of the rich members of the community to contribute liberally to political parties due to obvious reasons. People, in general, are not motivated to donate funds for welfare services.

**14. Multiplication of Authorities.** Setting up State Advisory Boards of Education, District Institutes of Education and District Boards of Education is not likely to serve any useful purpose. Already there is multiplicity of authorities in the field of education.

## Revised Policy Formulations, May 1992

The National Policy of Education (NPE), 1986 is a landmark in educational development of the country. A review of the NPE, 1986 was conducted during 1990-92. The Central Advisory Board of Education (CABE) in its 47th meeting held on May 5-6, 1992 considered the report of the CABE Committee on policy set-up to make an in-depth study of the report of the Committee for review of NPE, 1986. While broadly endorsing the policy, it recommended certain modifications in the light of the developments during the last few years and the experience gained in the implementation of the policy. The revised policy formulations containing these modifications recommended by the CABE were tabled in the Parliament on May 7, 1992.

Following the adoption of the revised policy formulations in May 1992, a revised POA was prepared. The POA 1992 was tabled in the Parliament on August 19, 1992.

Universalisation of elementary education, equalization of educational opportunities, women's education and development, vocationalisation of school education, consolidation of higher education, modernization of technical education, improvement of quality content and process of education at all levels continue to be the themes of national endeavour in the field of education.

## Committee for Girls Education and Public Corporation 1963-65

**Committee for Girls' Education and Public Co-operation (1963-65).** At its meeting held in April, 1963 the National Council for Women's Education endorsed the suggestion made by the Union Education Minister that a small committee be appointed to look into the causes for lack of public support, particularly in rural areas, for girls' education and to enlist public co-operation. The Chairman of the National Council for Women's Education accordingly appointed in May 1963, a Committee with M. Bhaktavatsalam, Chief Minister, Madras as Chairman the Committee in this field. The Committee submitted its report in 1964 and the report was published in 1965.

**Recommendations**

It is only through a willing, educated and informed public that any progress can be made at all. Not only is the need urgent, but the ground is also ready for a comprehensive programme for mobilizing public co-operation to promote girls' education and giving it constructive channels for expression. It is essential that official action and the programme based on public initiative must move forward in close foremen. There has to be a sense of partnership and shared responsibility between official and voluntary agencies. There is also the need for a systematic and sustained programme with an adequate organization for mobilizing community efforts.

**1. Public Co-operation.** Direct co-operation of the public should be encouraged in the following fields :

*(a)* Establishing private schools.

*(b)* Helping in the maintenances of school buildings.

*(c)* Helping in providing suitable accommodation for teachers and students, particularly in the rural areas.

*(d)* Putting up of schools buildings.

*(e)* Contributing volunatary labour for construction of school buildings.

*(f)* Popularising co-education at the primary stage.

*(g)* Creating public opinion in favour of the teaching profession and to give greater respect to the teacher in the community.

(*h*) Setting-up and organizing school betterment committees, improvement conferences.

(*i*) Initiating action and participating in educative propaganda to breakdown traditional prejudices against girls' education.

(*j*) Encouraging married women to take up at least part-time teaching in village schools and to work as school mothers.

(*k*) Undertaking necessary propaganda to make the profession of teaching for women popular.

(*l*) Supplying free text-books and writing materials to needy children.

(*m*) Supplying uniforms to poor and needy children.

(*n*) Supplying mid-day meals.

**2. The State Council for Women's Education.** These are the most suitable agencies for providing the organization and leadership for mobilizing community effort. They should function as a part of the network of which the district Councils at the district level and the Mahila Mandals and similar voluntary bodies at the town and village levels would be strong and active links. These agencies should look upon mobilising of community effort and educating public opinion to promote girls' education as their main and primary responsibility. They should aim at building up in villages and towns' teams of volunary workers, men and women, who are willing to devote themselves to this cause and work actively for its promotion.

**3. State's Responsibility.** The State should educate public opinion in favour of girls' education through:

(*a*) School improvement conferences.

(*b*) Radio talks, audio-visual aids and distribution of informative pamphlets.

*(c)* Seminars.

*(d)* Assisting voluntary, welfare and other organizations, private individuals and associations engaged in the field of education of girls and women.

*(e)* Enrolment drives, generally in June and special additional drives for girls' education during Dussehra.

**4. State Help.** The State should continue to help in an abundant measure in providing necessary schooling facilities in all the areas and in the habitations, however, so that the local population can make use of them.

**5. Reform and Inspection.** The existing functional deficiencies of schools should be remedied by replacing buildings which are totally inadequate to modern educational needs. There should be periodical inspection of school buildings and hostels so as to ensure their structural soundness and suitable sanitary facilities.

**6. Pre-Primary Schools.** It is necessary that in rural areas paricularly, pre-primary schools should be attached to primary schools so that children get accustomed to schooling even at the tender age.

**7. School Improvement Conferences.** These should be arranged widely throughout the State and particularly in the less advanced States in order to encourage people to contribute to educational awakening and advancement.

**8. More Attractive.** School work should be made more attractive and should present education in terms more acceptable to pupils.

**9. Recruitment of Women Teachers.** Concerted efforts have to be made to recruit as many women teachers as possible. Women are by general consent the best teachers forth primary classes in all schools. It should be the aim of all states to appoint women teachers in primary schools and a greater number of women teachers in mixed schools. A school staffed by women will inspire greater confidence in the parents and make them willing to send their children to mixed institutions.

(a) ***Conditions of Recruitment.*** The basis of recruitment of women teachers should be widened and their conditions of work should be made more attractive. Financial incentives like special allowances for hilly, isolated or any other specific backward rural areas should be given to teachers. Each State may specify areas where such allowances would be available.

(b) ***Recruitment Age Limit.*** In order to attract more women teachers the age limit for the unmarried and married women teachers should be relaxed in the case of those working in village schools. The service conditions of such married women who do part-time teaching work should be made more attractive.

(c) ***Married Women Teachers.*** Attempt should be made to bring back to the teaching profession married women who have left it in recent years and to bring women from other occupations to supplement the teaching staff.

(d) ***Training Schools.*** Training schools with hostels need to be located in the rural centres and near 'different' areas where girls from the villages are trained and sent back to work in their own or neighbouring villages.

(e) ***Posting.*** As far as possible women teachers should be posted in or near their own villages.

(f) ***Special Attention.*** Special drives should be organised to as the best form of social service needed for the upliftment of the villages.

(g) ***Condensed Courses.*** Condensed courses should be organised on a large scale foretold, women particularly from rural areas so that they could take up teaching jobs in the villages.

(h) ***Pay Scale.*** The pay scales of all teachers should be improved and the teachers should be paid an economic wage, so that they may be retained in the profession.

(i) ***Sufficient Facilities.*** The training facilities available in each State should be of such a magnitude that the annual output of trained teachers would be equal to the demand for additional teachers.

(j) ***Training.*** During selection of trainees for training schools and colleges, special preference should be given to women from rural areas seeking admission.

(k) ***Hostels.*** The absence of hostel facilities as also the slow progress in the construction of those that have been undertaken, have affected the hostel. The construction of hostels should be included as one of the priority objectives in the Plans of the States and necessary financial assistance for the construction of hostels and maintenance stipends be made available more liberally to local authorities and voluntary organizations working in the field of education of girls and women.

(l) ***Inspection.*** The inspecting staff should be adequate and strong if improvement into be secured and waste reduced. A separate women inspectorate will help to bring in more girls to school.

(m) ***Lodging.*** It is only by providing women teachers with quarters near the schools that we can attract many educated women to the teaching profession.

**10. Social Education.** In the field of social education, a determined effort should be made to increase the number of literacy classes for women in rural areas and to carry out intensive campaigns for the spread of literacy amongst women. Activities in this field should be administered by the education departments of the State Government.

**11. Building and Equipment.** Local bodies should be made responsible for the provision of school buildings, equipments, playing fields and the like and observance of the educational code in the State.

**12. Central Assistance.** Such Central assistance should be:

*(a)* At the elementary stage for:

- *(i)* Preparation and employment of women teachers.
- *(ii)* Grant of free books, writing material and clothing to girls.
- *(iii)* Twin quarters for women teachers.

*(b)* At the secondary stage for:

- *(i)* Provision of separate schools for girls.
- *(ii)* Hostels.
- *(iii)* Grant of free books, writing materials and clothing to girls.
- *(iv)* Preparation and appointment of women teachers in increasing numbers.

**13. Seasonal Adjustment.** Changing of school hours and school holidays to seasonal requirements has been found in some places to be a helpful concession to parents who would otherwise not be in a position to spare the children for attending classes.

**14. Curriculum.** While the curriculum can be the same for both boys and girls at the primary and middle stages, provision should be made for offering of electives comprising subjects which would be of special interest to girls and which would help them later in their fields of activity.

***

6

# Education Under Constitution

A Constitution is a fundamental legal document according to which the Government of a country functions. It is the basic law which defines and delimits the main organs of Government and their jurisdiction as well as the basic rights of the citizens. A Constitution, thus, is superior to all other laws of the country and no law can be enacted which is not in conformity with the Constitution.

A Government looks after law and order in a society. It does so by making laws and maintaining order. But a Government cannot make laws and administer a country according to its own whims and forces. Every Government has to function in conformity with basic law of the land. The Constitution contains those laws which act as the source according to which the rules and regulations of governing a country are framed.

A democratic Government is one in which the citizens participate in the functioning of the Government, directly or indirectly. It is a Government in which the Government's powers are limited and clearly spelt out. Conversely, it is also a Government under which citizen's rights are also given clearly. Now, how are these limits placed on the activity of the Government? This is done by what is called a Constitution.

A Constitution is considered the source of powers and authority of Government. It lays down precisely what the powers of a particular Government agency are, what this it can, or cannot do. The idea is to minimise confusion and conflict of operation between the various organs of the Government. A Constitution is concerned with two aspects—the relation between different organs of Government; and between the Government and the citizens. More than anything else a Constitution is an instrument of controlling the abuse of power by the Government. That is why the Constitution is a very important document.

## INDIAN CONSTITUTION

**Preamble.** "We, the people of India, having solemnly resolved to constitute India into a Sovereign Socialist Secular Democratic Republic and to secure to all its citizens: Justice, Social, Economic and Political; Liberty of thought, expression, belief, faith and worship; Equality of status and of opportunity; and to promote among them all Fraternity assuring the dignity of the individual and unity and integrity of the Nation; in our Constituent Assembly this twenty-sixth day of November, 1949, do hereby adopt, enact and give to ourselves this Constitution".

The Preamble sets out what the objectives of Indian Government the kind of value system the Constitution wishes to set-up in India. It declares India a sovereign state. Sovereignty means absolute independence, a Government which is not controlled by any other power. When India was under British rule, it could not be called a sovereign country. Besides, the Constitution provides for democratic society in India. Here every citizen enjoys equal political rights. The country is governed by the elected representatives of the people. There is no state religion of India. The state does not favour people of any particular religion. The citizens are free to follow and practise the religion of their own choice. The Constitution also declares socialism to be one of the objectives. The ideal of equality remains incomplete if it is restricted only to the political sphere. It must extend to social and economic life too. The Preamble declares India to be a Republic. It means that the head of the state is not a monarch, but a President indirectly elected by the people.

**Secular Government.** The Government under the Indian Constitution has to be secular. This means that the Government must not formulate policies which discriminate between various religious communities which live in India.

**Universal Adult Franchise.** Indian Constitution establishes a system of universal adult franchise. Under this system, every Indian citizen above the age of 18 years has the right to vote and participate in choosing the Government.

**Building a Just Society.** Indian Constitution has one part dealing with the fundamental rights and fundamental duties of the citizens. Another part contains provisions which are called directive principles of the state policy. These are instructions which the Constitution gives to the States (the Government at both the central and the state level) for achieving a just society in India. Indian Constitution, also, has several provisions which seek to protect the interets of those people who have been traditionally poor and socially deprived, the Scheduled Castes and Scheduled Tribes and Other Backward Classes of Citizen (OBCs).

**Emergency Provisions.** Finally, Indian Constitution also foresaw that there could be situations of danger when Government could not be run as in ordinary times. To cope with these difficult times, it lays down some emergency provisions. In case of national emergency fundamental right can be restricted.

**Fundamental Rights.** The Indian Constitution mentions some of the most important rights of the citizens. These are called fundamental rights. These rights, are fundamental in two different ways. *First,* the Constitution gives us these rights and guarantees them because it believes that the rights are necessary if citizens are to act properly and live democratically. *Secondly,* effective procedures for the enforcement of these Fundamental Rights have been guaranteed in the Constitution itself. A citizen has the right to go to the court of law if he/she is denied these rights. The Constitution is their guarantee.

This Constitution guarantees to six fundamental rights. Apart from these rights, the Constitution also mentions some 'Directive Principles of State Policy' and a list of fundamental duties of Indian citizens.

To understand the fundamental rights it is necessary to know about the directive principles and the fundamental duties.

Indian Constitution guarantees to Indian citizens six fundamental rights. These are:

*(a)* Right to equality.

*(b)* Right against exploitation.

*(c)* Right to freedom.

*(d)* Cultural and educational rights.

*(e)* Right to freedom of religion.

*(f)* Right to Constitutional remedies.

**Directive Principles of State Policy**

The name Directive Principles of State Policy, shows that these are actually directions given by the Constitution of the state to adopt policies, which would help to establish a just society in India. The aim of these instructions is to create proper economic and social conditions in which citizens of India can lead a good life. The idea of democracy need not be only a political idea. It can also be extended to the social and economic life of the people. Some of the principles are in the form of social and economic rights, *for example,* the right to work, the right to free and compulsory education of children up to the age of 14, right to equal wages for equal work; or the right to an adequate livelihood. These rights are not fully enjoyed by all Indian citizens today. The Government has to try to provide conditions under which these can become legal rights of citizens. Unlike fundamental rights the rights mentioned in this part are not justiciable. The Constitution, however, tells the state, *i.e.,* whoever runs the Government that it must not forget these long-term aims and it should try to achieve them in reality. If the Government makes a law to enforce any of these principles it cannot be questioned in a court of law on the grounds that it violates any of the guaranteed fundamental rights. Indian Constitution mentions that the state should strive to give the right of work, right to education, right to assistance from the Government in case a citizen is unemployed, sick, retired, or disabled. It should try to give free legal aid to poor people; so that poor people, who suffer greater injustices in society, can also go to courts and defend their rights.

All the Directive Principles, however, are not concerning social and political rights. Some of them are instructions to Government in other matters. For instance, the Constitution says that state should try to prevent concentration of wealth, it should ensure that workers in factories can have a share in decision-making. It instructs the state to promote and look after the interests of Scheduled Castes and Schedule Tribes. The state is asked to promote cottage industries. It is instructed to protect forests, the wild life of the country and ancient monuments.

### Fundamental Rights and Directive Principles

Fundamental Rights are justiciable. They can be enforced by courts. The Government cannot take away these rights. But the provisions of Directive Principles are not ineffaceable by courts of law. If a citizen is out of work, he cannot get a writ from the courts of law. If a citizen is out of work, he cannot get a writ from the courts directing the state to give him work. But if he is jailed by the police without reason, he can go to the courts. And the courts will direct the Government to free him. The Government must obey courts' order.

**Fundamental Duties**

Fundamental Duties have been incorporated by the forty-second Amendment of the Constitution, with the purpose of making citizens patriotic, help them to follow a code of conduct that would strengthen the nation, protect its sovereignty and integrity of India.

*(a)* To promote the common brotherhood of all people in India and renounce any practice derogatory to the dignity of women.

*(b)* To defend the country and render national service when required.

*(c)* To protect and improve natural environment and have compassion for living creatures.

*(d)* To value and preserve the rich heritage of the nation's composite character.

*(e)* To safeguard public property and abjure voilence.

*(f)* To develop scientific temper, humanism and spirit of inquiry.

*(g)* To strive for excellence in all spheres of individual and collective activity.

## DEMOCRATIC EDUCATION

The Education Commission (1964-66), said that the development of values such as a scientific temper of mind, tolerance, respect for the culture of other national groups, etc., will enable us to adopt democracy, not only as a form of Government, but also as a way of life. This clearly shows that in a democratic country like India the first and the foremost goal of education should be development of democratic values. Indian democracy is made by the people who profess different religions, speak different languages, belong to different races, castes, classes and communities. keeping in mind these and several other characteristics of Indian democracy following should be the most appropriate goals of education:

**1. Development of Democratic Values in the People.** These values apart from those given above include a spirit of large-hearted tolerance, of mutual give and take, of the appreciation of the ways in which people differ from one another. No education is worthwhile if an educated man does not translate these values in his behaviour and no democracy in that case can survive for long. Hence, education has to make deliberate and planned effort on development of these values in the people.

**2. National Integration.** It means harmonising religions, language, caste, class and community differences as they exist in India causing social tensions. It is essential that the people of India in spite of these differences live peacefully and co-operatively and utilise their varied talents for the enrichment of the national life as a whole. Education through various programmes and tailored curricula should make efforts to develop in the people such attitudes and values. It is difficult but possible. These changes include realising the importance of knowledge and education, learning various social skills, developing scientific attitude, computer literacy considering science and technology important and so on. The Commission (1964) said that, "The most important tool in the process of modernisation is education based on science and technology." But, the Commission, further said "Modernisation, if it is to a living force must derive its strength from the strength to spirit."

The Secondary Education Commission (1952-53), has formulated three social or national aims of education. These are:

1. Development of democratic citizenship.
2. Development of leadership which means training pupils for discharging their duties efficiently.
3. Improvement of vocational efficiency.

Ishwar Bhai Patel Committee (1977), also reiterated the importance of development of citizenship as a social or national goal of education.

The Adiseshiah Committee Report (1978) formulated the following goals to be achieved through education:

1. Removal of unemployment.
2. Removal of destitution, *i.e.*, poverty.
3. Rural Development.
4. Adult literacy.

All these foregoing aims are social or national objectives to be achieved through education. They are the tasks completion of which is imperative for strengthening the society. These aims have been discussed here with special reference to India. Hence, they may be considered national goals of education or educational aims of national development.

Our schools should develop a strong tradition of striving to generate a sense of national unity and national consciousness, in the pupils. This can be achieved as suggested by the National Commission on Education (1964-66), by *(i)* making pupils understand and revaluate our cultural heritage and *(ii)* by the creation of a strong driving faith in the future towards which we aspire. The first may be promoted by well-organised teaching of the language and literature, philosophy, religion and history of India as well as by introducing the students to Indian architecture, sculpture, painting, music, dance and drama. Faith in future would involve an attempt to bring home to the students the principles of the Constitution, the great human values contained in preamble of the Constitution.

**3. Development of Human Resources** should be considered still more crucial an aim of education in Indian democracy. This aim implies changes in the knowledge, skills, interests and values of the people as a whole. In a democracy the individual is an end in himself and the primary purpose of education should be to provide him with the widest opportunity to develop his potentialities to the full, through social reorganisation and emphasis on social perspectives. Cultivation of essential values in the people, development of dedicated and competent leadership and educated electorate are essential for strengthening democracy. Education, therefore, must develop such human resources needed for the defence of Indian democracy.

**4. Development of Physical Resources** through the modernisation of agriculture and rapid industrialisation should also be an important aim of education in a democracy like India. To achieve this purpose education should be linked with productivity, science should be made a basic component of education, work-experience should be considered important, vocational education should be expanded, scientific and technical education should be improved.

**5. Development of Social, Moral and Spiritual Values.** In a democratic country like India it is inevitable to inculcate social, moral and spiritual values in the people. Knowledge in the absence of essential values may be dangerous. The success of democracy, its strength and stability are contingent upon people's developed sense of social reponsibility and a keener appreciation of moral and spiritual values. Hence, education must make efforts on developing these values in the people. Prime Minister Nehru in his Azad Memorial Lectures (ICCR, 1962) said "Material riches without toleration and compassion and wisdom may well turn to dust and ashes."

## EDUCATION FOR DEMOCRACY IN INDIA

**Democracy in India.** India is not merely a modern democratic state but a country which is traditionally inclined towards democracy. A democratic Constitution was adpoted after independence. In 1938, Jawaharlal Nehru had said, "The Indian Constitution seeks to establish a popular Government in the country on the basis of democratic principles outlined earlier. For this every citizen must participate in the administration, through his right to vote and to be elected. Every individual is guaranteed and given equal status and opportunity, because no one is discriminated against on the basis of religion, race, caste, community, sex, or on any other grounds. The Government is responsible to the people and its elected representatives."

**Provisions in Indian Constitution.** In order to achieve this objective of democracy, education is as necessary in India as anywhere else, a truth which the Indian people have been quick to realise. In the words of F.W. Themes, "Education is no exotic in India. There has been no country where the love of learning had so early an origin or has exercised so lasting and powerful an influence. From the simple poet of the Vedic age to the Bengali philosopher of the present day there has been an uninterrupted succession of teachers and scholars." Not only did the Indian Constitution accept the ideals of democracy, it considered education the prime responsibility of the state. In Article 45 of the Constitution it has been stated that every state must arrange for the provision of free and compulsory education to all children upto the age of 14, within ten years of the date of inception of the Constitution. After the achievement of independence, a new phase began in the history of education. Articles 29 and 30 of the Constitution give fundamental rights to every individual in connection with education and cultural development. According to article 20, every Indian national living in any part of India will have the right to maintain his own specific language, script and his culture. No person can be refused right of admission to any educational institution, established by the state, by reason of religion, race, caste, language or any other similar consideration. According to article 30, every minority community will have the right to establish and maintain educational institutions of its own choice, irrespective of whether the minority is a linguistic or religious one. The state will also not refuse aid to any such institution created by a religious or linguistic minority. Articles 45 and 46 determine the policy for education as part and parcel of the directive principles. According to article 45, the state will make every effort to provide free and compulsory education, within ten years, to every child below the age of 14. According to article 46, the stage will pay special attention to the educational and economic interests of all backward classes, especially the Scheduled Castes and Scheduled Tribes. It also entrusts the state with the duty of protecting such tribes from social injustice and exploitation of every kind. The Indian Constitution laid the foundation for a Federal Government in which the functions of the State Government have some duties with respect to education. It has been realised that there must be co-ordination between the central and state authority on education for a balanced development of the country. The modern Indian state is a welfare state whose objective is the complete development of its people. This welfare can be achieved only through education. Little surprise therefore if all the leaders of the nation stress the importance of education as a first step to improving the future of the nation.

## Views of Secondary Education Commission

The democratic ideals which the existing educational policy is trying to achieve have been outlined most precisely in the Secondary Education Commission's explanation of the objectives of education:

**1. Development of Democratic Citizenship.** The success of democracy depends largely upon the people's awareness of their rights and duties and the extent to which people fulfil their responsibilities. Education aims at developing this ability in the people, because education teaches the man to think and distinguish between right and wrong. He can understand social, economic and political issues and reflect on the possibility of solving such problems. He can decide upon the political party or the leadership which should be entrusted with the task of forming a Government and undertaking administration. He does this after thinking on the problems facing the country and considering the ability of each group or leader to face such problems. He can express his ideas and suggestion through lectures, essays, articles, etc. He can organise new movements or constitute various kinds of committees to solve the problems facing the country. It is the duty of the state to insist upon a syllabus which can be expected to generate such democratic awareness among the children being educated.

**2. Development Vocational Skill.** The Secondary Education Commission has pointed out that another aim of education is to develop some vocational skill in the educand. No nation can progress in the absence of economic progress. The first duty of the state is to provide a system and means of education which imparts some vocational and professional skills to the educands so that they can earn their livelihood at the same time as they contribute to the nation's economic growth. The country urgently needs skilled craftsmen, engineers, doctors, teachers and administrators. For this, specialised colleges are required. Every child should be given the right to choose a profession of his own liking and he should be given the opportunity to acquire the highest training and education in this profession.

**3. Training in Skilful Living.** Democracy can be said to have succeeded only if it translate the democratic ideals to its society. And, for this, socialisation of the individual through education is essential. It is desirable to develop such social qualities as collective feeling, co-operation, discipline, tolerance, sympathy, brotherhood, etc., in the individual. Education must also aim to create faith in social justice and the willingness to rebel against injustice. Education helps people in adjusting to each other and the educated individual is generally tolerant and liberal. Although he may differ from other prople in their opinions, he has the ability to adjust to such people because he can understand their attitudes. Hence, education is the only means of removing the obstacles in the path of democracy and also of achieving some adjustment between people who differ from each other in respect of language, race, caste, religion, sex, etc.

**4. Development of Personality.** The success of a democratic society also depends upon whether mature men and women form the majority or minority in its population. Democracy can succeed only if most of its members have developed mature personalities, because a mature person has gone through physical, mental, social, ethical and spiritual development. Hence, education should aim at the development of all aspects of the educands' personality through various kinds of training. Keeping this in view, most schools and colleges now provide many kinds of extra curricular training, which supplements all that is taught as part of curriculum.

**5. Developing Leadership.** The success of a democracy depends upon the capabilities of the leadership. The democratic Government is a decentralised Government and for that reason it requires skilled leadership at many different levels of administration. The democratic Government is run by the elected representatives of the people, who should be possessed of special qualities. Expert leadership is required for development and progress in every sphere—political, social, economic, artistic, scientific and cultural. Education should aim at evolving such leadership, because without doing this education cannot make any real contribution to democracy, for then it is leaving unfulfilled one of its important responsibilities. The element of leadership can be encouraged through many kinds of curricular and extra curricular activities in schools and colleges.

Apart from these objectives of education laid down specifically by the Secondary Education Commission, it is desirable to reflect upon some other objectives, which have significance in view of the fact that India is a democracy. In fact, the aims of education vary a little bit with the level of education—the primary, secondary and university education—a fact which has been recognised by the different education commissions established from time to time. The aim of education, at the primary level, is to develop the child's mind by presenting the fundamental elements in the various areas of knowledge and also to give him an opportunity to develop all his abilities—physical, mental, moral, motor, creative imagination, etc. At this stage attention should be paid to physical development no less than mental development, but attention must also be paid to the burden such an education places on the child. The education imparted should not become a burden.

At the secondary level, attention should be focused on discovering the interests and abilities of every adolescent and then developing such abilities. Education should be concerned not merely with the general welfare of society but also with the self-realisation and personal development of each individual.

**Recommendations of Indian Universities Commission**

The Indian Universities Commission has laid down the following objectives of university education in the country:

1. Providing leadership in politics, administration, professions, industry and commerce.
2. Causing spiritual development in the educand.
3. Training intellectual leaders of culture and creating inventors.
4. Discovering the inherent qualities of individuals and developing them through training.
5. Protecting the culture and civilisation of the country and instilling the youth with the ideals of this culture.

## IMPACT OF DEMOCRACY ON EDUCATION

It is only in recent times that democratic principles and values have entered the field of education. The credit of this revolutionary change goes to the American educationist Johy Dewey. He emphasised that in a democratic society, educational planning should be done in such a way that each individual member is made capable to shoulder social responsibilities efficiently and discharge them effectively and profitably. According to him, education should inculcate in the individuals the sense to welcome needful changes in the social structure and reoriented one's behaviour smoothly to the ever changing social milieu. The impact of this philosophy has brought about revolutionary changes in the thinking about educational planning and schemes of public education have begun to emphasise the provisions of the education of the masses so that general people become conscious about their rights and duties, about their individual and social responsibilities and about their national and international obligation. As the democratic rule is by the people for the people, they should be made to understand their obligations and to discharge their duties intelligently. Hence, in all democratically ruled countries, more and more emphasis is being laid upon free, compulsory and universal education.

The impact of democratic tendency on education is evident on the working of the following elements:

**1. Provision of Equal Oportunities and Recognition of Individual Differences.** In a democratic set-up, each child is a sacred and valuable entity of society. As such, equal opportunities are made available to one and all for their fullest development. In this connection the principle of individual differences is given proper recognition and therefore, each child receive proper support according to his interests, aptitudes and capacities to develop his individuality to the fullest extent.

**2. Provision of Adult Education.** Under the influence of democratic tendency, in different countries, emphasis is being laid upon adult education, women education and education of the mentally retorted and physically handicapped. Schemes are under operation in our country also for the effective education of the adults who constitute a bulk of our entire population. Night-schools, short-term courses, one day schools and the schemes are being launched to solve this stupendous problem.

**3. Universal and Compulsory Education.** In democracy, the reigns of Government remain in the hands of the people. Hence, common people must be so educated that they develop themselves as responsible and dynamic citizens conscious of their rights and duties, fully conversant with their National and International obligations, well aware with the Government procedures anti-administration processes.

**4. Free Education.** The principle of universal and compulsory education involves free education to all irrespective of their social or monetary status. Hence, education is now regarded as the birth right of each child irrespective of colour, caste, creed and sex. In almost all democratic countries, education has been made free up to a certain standard. In addition, education of the physically and mentally handicapped is also receiving proper and increasingly effective attention.

**5. Methods of Teaching.** Under the impact of democratic tendency, method of teaching are undergoing revolutionary changes. Old, traditional and mass education methods are being gradually replaced by individual attention methods. Nothing is now enforce or thrust in by force. Self-learning devices are encouraged and such methods are promoted which motivate children to pay attention and learn by their own efforts. Such wholesome and welcome environment is created wherein children search for truth, gain knowledge by their own efforts and learn by their own experience.

**6. Social Activities.** Bookish and academic activities are not over-emphasised in schools now-a-days. Proper attention is paid to social, cultural and co-curricular activities, so that children develop in a wholesome way and gain more and more social experience.

**7. Importance of Individual Attention.** As discussed above, each child receives individual attention. His family background, his own interests, likes and dislikes, his needs and capacities are fully taken care off in all plans of educational development, the purpose being to achieve the maximum development of personality.

**8. School Administration.** To inculcate in children the sense of self-discipline and self-administration, their association with school administration is being welcomed. Such schemes are being formulated in various institutions where student participation in actual educational and school administration is a fact.

**9. Child Centred Education.** Democratic way of thinking emphasises the importance of each child as sacred individuality. Hence, educational schemes and plans are so structured that each child receives full attention and full facilities to develop his individuality to the fullest extent.

**10. Student Unions.** Student unions and student welfare associations are formed in institutions to promote student welfare in all spheres with the aim of achieving balanced, dynamic, efficient and socially motivated personalities.

**11. Physical Health of Children.** To promote physical well-being of children, facilities for games and sports, gymnazia, medical tests and medical help are being provided freely and on an increasing scale. Medical check up, advice and medicines are now provided to the needy.

**12. Respect of Teacher's Personality.** Democratic philosophy respects teacher as a very dynamic and effective agency of social change for social progress. Thus, teachers are now made to participate more and more in curriculum construction and educational planning. Side by side, they are allowed to experiment freely in respect to methods, techniques and devices of teaching as well as materials which aid teaching procedures and processes. Not only this, more and more plans are being laid and worked out for increasing the professional competency of teachers.

**13. Intelligence Tests.** Schemes of intelligence tests are under operation in various institutions all over the world to evaluate the mental capacity, growth and achievement of children. Diagnostic tests are proving very useful for this purpose.

**14. School.** School is now regarded as a centre of promoting national consciousness and international understanding. Education for dynamic citizenship is associated with education for national and international understanding, amity and fellow-feeling. Thus, school is now regarded as a miniature of society.

**15. Co-operation between all Agencies of Education.** In a democratic set-up, all the agencies of education co-operate actively for the development of children. Hence, under the influence of democratic tendency, schemes are being formulated now-a-days to establish co-operation between all the agencies of education namely—family, school, community and state.

## SOCIOLOGY OF EDUCATION

Dualism has always been a popular view with the philosophers. It is quite natural also, for we always live in two worlds, namely, the world of things and the world of our own inner experience. Some philosophers have considered the inner world and the individual more important, while a few others have stressed the world outside the individual, *i.e.,* the environment or the society. Rousseau, *for example,* focussed on the individual while Dewey emphasised the social setting in which the individual has to live. Rousseau was the forerunner of psychological tendencies in education. Dewey may be considered a pioneer to shift the emphasis to sociological tendency in education. He maintained that philosophy must be described in terms of the problems with which it deals and which originate in the conflicts and difficulties of social life. He defined the problem of education as "...the harmonising of individual traits with social ends and values." He considered education a difficult process because effective co-ordination of psychological make-up of the individual with the demands of the social environment was, to him, extremely difficult. He lamented that such a co-ordination in the schools of his time was ignored. It was held by him that the process of mental development is essentially a social process. He said that "man is a social being who attains mind and self only when nourished in social experience." By "social" he meant individual's social adjustment to the group or to contemporary social realities. The business of education, as emphasised by Dewey, was "habituation of an individual to social control, sub-ordination of natural powers to social rules." Thus, social efficiency aim of education was emphasised which appealed to many people of his times as it was more in line with democratic thinking of nineteenth century. The great social change emerging from the nineteenth century industrial revolution in Europe may also be considered responsible for the origin and development of sociological tendency in education. The pragmatic philosophy of education also emphasised the social aspect of education for it believed that socially oriented minds alone could forge a better state of society, one in which human wants are fully satisfied.

Thus, the sociological tendency has its origin in the philosophy of Dewey, the pragmatists and the nineteenth century social change resulting from the industrial revolution and acceptance of democracy as a form of Government and a way of life. The tendency emphasised the social aim of education. Its watch words are "education for social service" which means that education should be directed in a broader more elastic way to the good of the community. It emphasises that the individual must be trained to be unselfish, to put the needs and desires of others before his own. Prof. Bagley in America said that, "Social efficiency is the norm against which educational practice must be judged." He, further, emphasised that social efficiency aim of education ought to have the position of primacy in a rational theory of education. The activities of the individual should be valued with reference to his social obligations.

The sociological tendency in education focussed on the interaction between the individual and the social milieu in which he lives. Education, according to this tendency, was defined as reorganisation and reconstruction of this interaction so that the child learns what is socially desirable. Dewey said that education should develop individual's ability to "share in the experiences of others and thus, widen the individual consciousness to that of the race." Emergence of a new branch of knowledge known as sociology in the first half of the nineteenth century contributed significantly to this aspect of the sociological tendency in education. Study of human relations in the schools was emphasised. Scientific study of the process of interaction of persons was considered important. Study of education in relation to social needs and social change was emphasised. Several new trends emerged in the field of education as a result of sociological tendency in education. The relationship between the school and the society, relationship between the school climate and education of the pupils, education as an instrument of social change, influence of various social groups on education, education as related to social mobility of the people in the society, etc., many issues figured for discussion and for being resolved. The aims, content, method and other aspects of education were also affected by this tendency.

## Relationship between Education and Society

Sociological tendency in education made several thinkers in the field of education to discuss and classify the relationships between education and society. Education was considered as a sub-system of the larger society. The character of society and social changes taking place must influence the system of education also. It was emphasised that these social changes and emerging social needs must be rejected in the theory and practice of education also. This point was very mush emphasised by Dewey in his book, *"The School and Society"* wherein he said that while proposing to bring about a change in education the social point of new should always be kept in mind, otherwise it will be considered merely an arbitrary fad. "Education for the society" emerged as the focus of educational thought.

**Education and Politics.** The relationship between education and politics also was emphasised as an aspect of sociological tendency in education. Education for democracy was, particular emphasised. Democratic aims of education, democratic methods of teaching-learning, democratic organisation: of the classroom and the school, democratic discipline, etc., were several new concepts which were extensively discussed.

**Education and Economic Factors.** Sociological tendency in education forced the educational thinkers to analyse and see how economic factors affect education. It was realised that economic factors are important constraints of educational activities. How they affect education and how education affects the economy of the society were some of the themes which emerged for discussion. A new kind of thinking began in the field of education.

**Cultural Aim of Education.** The sociological tendency in education resulted into a greater stress on cultural aim of education. It was emphasised that education help in the transmission of cultural heritage.

**The Curriculum.** Sociological tendency in education resulted into a ranged approach to curriculum construction. These views took the form of sociological principles of curriculum construction. It was emphasised that the curriculum should conform to the conditions, problems and needs of the society. A functional curriculum which could serve the needs of the society was said to be the need of the hour, curriculum for international understanding, curriculum for citizenship, curriculum for vocation, etc., were the ideas about curriculum which gained popularity as a result of sociological tendency in education.

**The Method of Teaching.** In the context of method of teaching, the sociological tendency resulted into considering the classroom and the school as the society-in-miniature.

Hence, it was emphasised that teaching should take help of the principles of group dynamics. Group methods of teaching, group discussions, social interactions, group planning, group activities, project method, etc., were considered important.

Thus, sociological tendency in education tried to approach education, its purposes, methods, content and other aspects from the point of view of the society and sociological forces working within it.

## IMPACT OF DEMOCRACY ON VARIOUS ASPECTS OF EDUCATION

In the following lines we are throwing light on the various aspects of education in a democratic set-up:

### Democracy and Aims of Education

In a democracy, the aims of education are as under:

**1. Development of Democratic Values.** The success of democracy does not depend upon Legislative buildings and massive structures of Parliament houses, but it rests upon the quality of the citizens devoted to democratic values. As such, the prime aim of democratic education is to promote in children a sense of devotion to democratic values. No book teaching can achieve this aim unless children are provided with opportunities to practise democratic norms and standards of behaviour. In fact, a child learns to live democratically by living democratically.

**2. Development of Vocational Efficiency.** For the success of a democratic set-up, economic contentment of citizens is a must. An indigent and poor person can be a victim of all kinds of allurements, inducements and exploitation by the resourceful and the powerful. Hence, the third aim of democratic education is to develop vocational efficiency in children, so that they are able to become self-reliant and serve the nation as much as possible.

**3. Development of Interests in Children.** The third aim of democratic education is to develop useful and worthy interests in children. Interests form character and enrich a child's life. Hence, the famous educationist, Herbart has insisted upon the fullest development of diverse interests. To achieve this aim, children should be provided with various and varied opportunities to participate in diverse activities and programmes in all fields of human life. If a large number of worthy interests are developed in children, they will be happy, well-balanced and efficient as citizens.

**4. Development of Thinking Power.** The fourth aim of democratic education is to develop thinking power of children. In fact, children of today are citizens of tomorrow when they will be confronted with all kinds of problems in political, social and economic fields. Education should develop in children the capacity to think clearly and take decisions confidently.

**5. Development of Social Outlook.** Development of social outlook is the sixth important aim of democratic education. This aim emphasises upon the fact that children should be imbued with the sense that they are the integral parts of society, the welfare of which should be their ideal. Not only this, they should learn to live and die for the nation. Education should develop this sense of service and sacrifice making them learn the sacredness of obligations and duties for the welfare of the nation to which they belong.

**6. Development of Leadership.** The seventh aim of democratic education is to develop leadership qualities in children. For this, education should instil in children the leadership qualities from the very beginning. They are the future citizens who will have to shoulder the multifarious duties and reponsibilities of their nation in all areas. Their character, strength of will, insight, courage of convictions, clarity of thinking and decision-making will be the foundations on which the national edifice will go up and up.

**7. Development of Sound Habits.** The fifth aim of democratic education is to develop sound habits in children. Habits are the sources of good or bad conduct. Hence, education should develop good habits in children from the very beginning to make democracy a successful venture.

**8. Development of National and International Feelings.** For the success of democracy, the ninth aim of democratic education is to develop in children the sense of ardent nationalism and devotion to international brotherhood. It may be noted that the two are not contradictory. On the other hand, they are mutually complementary and supplementary. In fact a nation cannot exist in isolation. All the nations of the world are mutually inter-dependent. Hence, education should foster the sense of inter-dependence, international good-will and fellow-feeling.

**9. Development of Harmonious Personality.** The eighth aim of democratic education is to develop the individuality of a child into balanced and harmonious personality. In the modern world of strife, stress and strain a balance and harmonious personality can only seek and find adjustment with the surroundings. Hence, education should develop character, dynamism and social outlook for this purpose.

**10. Training for Citizenship.** Democratic education should impart of children training in dynamic and healthy citizenship. For this, education should instil in children:

(*a*) Capacity to understand and solve the diverse problems of the country.

(*b*) Economic efficiency.

(*c*) Capacity to distinguish between propaganda and reality.

(*d*) Capacity to think and decide about issues.

(*e*) Consciousness of one's rights and duties.

(*f*) Healthy and dynamic outlook about problems, good behaviour and respect for moral values.

(*g*) Development of human qualities as love, sympathy, fellow feeling, co-operation, sense of nationalism and internationalism.

(*h*) Capacity to shoulder responsibility.

(*i*) Development of diverse interests.

(*j*) Sense of service and sacrifice.

(*k*) Good use of leisure hour.

**Curriculum.** In a democratic country curriculum construction is done with the purpose of realising democratic values. Hence, those subjects, activities and programmes are included in the curriculum which instil and promote healthy attitudes, dynamic habits, insight and understanding so that children are able to lead successful lives as happy citizens. The bases of such a curriculum are as under:

**1. Diversified.** Democratic curriculum is divisively to suit the needs of all children with basic differences of interests and aptitudes. Classroom activities, games, sports and other co-curricular activities bear an imprint of variety to suit various needs of children.

**2. Achievement of Social Aims.** While constructing a democratic curriculum emphasis is laid upon social aims and values. In other words, development of social sense in children is kept in view. As such, student activities, associations, corporate programmes and fellowship programmes are liberally provided.

**3. Emphasis on Local Needs.** Democratic curriculum is constructed on the basis of local needs and available resources. It may be changed according to the needs of time, place and local requirements.

**4. Flexibility.** Democratic curriculum is flexible to accommodate various needs and requirements which are in a state of constant change. A portion of it is made compulsory in the form of co-curriculum and diversified subjects are made optional for children to choose according to their interests and aptitudes.

**5. Place for Leisure Hour Activities.** Democratic curriculum also contains such relevant and useful activities in which an individual can profitable indulge leisure time. Thus, it ensures the total development of personality.

**6. Emphasis of Activity.** Democratic curriculum is laid on the foundation of an important principle known as learning by doing. It is through practical work and activities that development of mind and intelligence is fostered. Instead of enforcing and compelling cut and dried ready-made concepts into the minds of children, they are allowed to search for truth through their own experiments and experiences. This is real learning. It develops confidence, foresight and far-sight, the three important ingredients of wisdom.

**7. Provision of Vocational Needs.** Democratic curriculum very well meets the needs of vocations, professions and economic requirements of a region or the whole country. This explains the country to develop economically.

**Discipline.** Discipline is the corner-stone of democracy. But democratic discipline does not believe in respiration or compulsion. It advocates self-discipline. In schools where democratic set-up is in vogue, the following ideas are emphasised for fostering and developing self-discipline:

1. In democratic schools the headmasters, the teachers and the administrators are not despots or police officers. Instead, they are friends, philosophers and guides. Through their friendly and affectionate behaviour, they mould the behaviour of children

and thus promote self-discipline by creating a congenial and cordial atmosphere.

2. In the administration of a democratic school, children participate actively, discuss problems and decide them freely. They, thus, feel their integral and intimate relationship with the school and feel internal kinship with its progress and development.

3. In democratic schools, such activities and programmes are structured which cater to the interests and needs of children. This develops self-discipline among children.

4. In democratic schools full freedom is given and opportunities provided for each child to develop his individuality to the fullest extent. Hence, no problem of indiscipline arises at any time..

5. In democratic schools, students unions, students parliaments and all kinds of student organisations are encouraged for the benefit and development of children. They learn self-Government, co-operation, fellow-feeling and other human qualities together with qualities of self-discipline and leadership.

6. In democratic schools, the sense of rights and duties is instilled in children. They, thus, learn self-control through social service and social consciousness. Nothing is imposed on them from above. They discuss, decide and carry out the decision with perfect co-operation and cordiality.

**Teacher.** In a democratic set-up a teacher is a friend, philosopher and guide. He often works as a social reformer. Such teachers process the following qualities:

1. The teacher is devoted whole hearted to the ideals and values of democracy. Hence, he tries to impart

the same faith to children through gently persuasion and affectionate rapport.

2. Each teacher is well-versed in knowledge of his subject and has full academic competency to make children develop physically, mentally, morally and spiritually so that they are able to shoulder National and even International responsibilities in times to come.

3. The teacher regards every child as a sacred legacy to society. Hence, believing in the principle of individual differences he allows every child to develop his individuality to the fullest extent according to his interests, aptitudes and capacities.

4. In a democratic set-up, each teacher is fully conscious of his rights and duties towards society. Hence, he tries to instil the same sense of responsibility in children and also to make them capable and intelligent citizens of tomorrow.

5. The teacher tries to solicit maximum co-operation from the guardians, parents and other social agencies for the greatest possible development of children as dynamic and socially oriented citizens of the future.

6. In a democratic set-up, a teacher lays greater stress upon environment rather than on heredity. Hence, he tries to structure such a wholesome environment for the child that fullest development is naturally achieved.

❋❋❋

7

# Women Education in Society

Need for Women's Education. The importance of women's education is certainly great. Women play a very significant role in developing human resources, in improving household affairs, in moulding character of children. The education of women, therefore, is very necessary and more so in the days when we are bent upon checking the growth of over-population. Education among women decreases the fertility rate.

The women not only played an important role in the home, they also played a very, significant role in the last fight for freedom. They rubbed shoulders with men in the past and are doing so even now. They are adopting their own careers and fighting vigorously for eradication of hunger, poverty, ignorance and ill-health.

Once we realise the importance of the roles a woman plays in the home and outside, the urgency of the need for educating her becomes distinctly clear. The role of woman outside the home is becoming an important aspect of the social and economic life of the country. In the coming future that role will assume far greater significance.

**Problems of Women's Education**

In the past no importance was attached to the education of girls. In the beginning of the present century the percentage of literate women was only 0.8. The enrolment in the primary schools was 12 for every 100 boys and that in the secondary schools it was 4 for every 100. The total enrolment in the colleges was 26,474.

The two problems of women's education that attracted the attention of educational commissions were :

(*a*) Backwardness.

(*b*) Slow progress.

As early as 1882 the Hunter Commission said that the female education in the country had been till then in a very backward condition and recommended for an over-all improvement in the condition. It recommended that more grants should be given to girls schools and that moneys should be spent in equitable proportion on girls and boys schools.

To encourage girls education the commission recommended for a liberal scheme of scholarships to girls, a provision of facilities for their professional training and opening of secondary schools.

In spite of valuable recommendations made by commissions and committees on female education, at the beginning of the present century there was hardly any provision for the formal schooling of girls. It was only after 1901 when women came out of homes to shoulder responsibility in the struggle for freedom, that we see a progress in the field of the education of girls.

During the first half of this century much faster progress was made. The education for women expended enormously. Their status in the society got raised. A few aspects of the phenomenal growth in female education are given below:

1. The rate of expansion of female education was higher than that among the boys.
2. The enrolment at the secondary stage increased from 4 for 100 boys in 1901 to 15 for 100 in 1950.

3. The enrolment at the primary stage increased from 12 for 100 boys in 1901 to 39 for 100 in 1950.
4. The education in mixed schools was more in the primary classes than in the secondary classes.
5. The enrolment in the university rose from 264 in 1901 to 40,000 in 1950.

But there was still a very wide gulf between the education for boys and that for the girls. It was specially hinted at by the National Committee on Education of Women under the chairmanship of Smt. Durgabai Deshmukh (1958-59). The Committee pointed out that the Government did not realise even as late as 1958 that the problem of female education was a special one and as such it failed to provide necessary funds for the rapid development of women's education for which a suggestion had been given as early as 1882.

The National Committee on Women Education suggested that the education of women should be regarded as a major programme in education for some years to come and that special schemes should be prepared for this purpose and funds needed to work them out should be provided on a priority basis. The committee also suggested the setting-up of a special machinery at the state as well as at the Central level to look after the education of women.

The problem of wide disparity between the education of boys and girls at all stages and in all sectors of education is really one that claims urgent solution. The Education Commission has stressed the need for solving this problem at an early date. It remarked that had the problem been given due attention right from the beginning the need for special programmes as suggested by the Durgabai Deshmukh Committee would have not arisen at all. We must therefore try to bridge the gulf between the education of boys and girls at all stages primary, secondary and higher and in all sectors of education.

The next Committee for the development of female education was the one which was headed by, Hansa Mehta. The Committee discussed the problem of differentiation of curriculum between boys and girls. The Hunter Commission had recommended in 1882 that curriculum for girls should be different from what it is for boys as the instruction which is useful for a boy may not be useful for a girl. The Committee under the Chairmanship of Hansa Mehta made the following recommendations.

*(a)* There should be no need to differentiate curricula on the basis of sex in a democratic socialistic society.

*(b)* In the transitional period we should accept certain psychological differences between the two sexes and we may build curricula in such a way that these differences are given due importance but care should be exercised not to perpetuate them.

The problem of differentiation of curricula for boys and girls has been already discussed under section 12.9 in detail and hence, need not be repeated here.

There has been appointed one more committee which studied the problem of women's education in 6 states under the chairmanship of Shri. M. Bhaktvatsalam. It had surveyed the education of girls and concluded that the education has been very poorly developed so far.

Three aspects of female education stand out as follows :

*(a)* Problem concerning expansion of women's education.

*(b)* Problem of professional education of girls and married women.

*(b)* Problem of higher education of girls.

The problem concerning expansion has been very carefully examined by the National Committee on Women's

Education (1958-59). So far as the expansion of primary education is concerned, the number of girls enrolled for every 100 boys is about 50 now. At the middle school stage the gap is still wider. The Constitutional Directive could not be fulfilled even by the end of 1980 even we if proceeded at a faster rate in the field of expansion of women's education. We will have to educate public opinion to overcome traditional prejudices against girls education. We will have to encourage girls education by providing free text-books, writing materials and even clothing. We would have to make mixed schools popular at the primary stage and shall have to open separate schools for girls at the middle and secondary school stage wherever they are needed and it is possible to open them. Girls are more useful than boys at home.

Hence, they tend to be withdrawn earlier. Public opinion is still not in favour of extending education among girls to higher stages. Hence, a large portion of girls have to leave school early. For girls who leave the primary stage at about the age 14 and get married, it is proposed that part-time or full-time courses should be organised in homescience or the household industries like tailoring, arts and crafts, poultry and dairying so that they may prepare themselves better for their future life as housewives and mothers.

At the secondary stage, special programmes will have to be initiated for girls who intend to join secondary schools. In 1950-51 the proportion of the enrolment of the girls to that of the boys was about 1:6 in middle and 1:6.5 in higher secondary schools. By 1980 it had been raised to 1:2 in middle schools and 1:3 in higher secondary ones. Special efforts shall have to be still made to achieve targets set. Either more separate schools will have to be opened or where it is not possible to do so, women teachers will have to be kept on the staff. Women's hostels or subsidised transport shall have to be provided. Encouragement shall have to be given in the form of scholarships and free education.

## Problem of Training and Employment

The Indian society is undergoing a change. Woman is adopting her own career. Her age of marriage is rising. Her role outside the home is becoming an important aspect of the social and economic life of the country. The role of woman outside the home will assume still larger significance in time to come. There is a problem of unemployment among educated girls. It is therefore necessary to pay special attention to the problems of training and employment.

The 1961 Census showed that about a million young educated women above the age of 24, though matriculates, were working simply as housewives. The 1971 Census presented even more dismal picture. How horrible is it to lay waste their powers which could be profitably used for national reconstruction and development! There is a need for training and employing them in nation-building activities.

As the marriage age among girls rises, the number of young unmarried women becomes larger. A suitable career has to be singled out for pursuit before a girl gets married. Then again after marriage, when she becomes almost free from home-making activities and when her children reach a school going age, she needs some employment. The time at her disposal before she is married is to be used in some part-time job and the time after marriage when she is free has to be used in full-time work. Teaching, nursing and social service are some of the areas in which part or full-time jobs can be secured for women. Hence, there is a need for training girls for these services.

## Women Polytechnics

In all polytechnics courses of special interest to girls should be developed. A few such courses that have been started for women in 17 polytechnics spread all over the country are courses in:

(*a*) Architecture.

(*b*) Commercial art.

(*c*) Dress making.

(*d*) Electronics and radio technology.

(*e*) Instrument technology.

(*f*) Interior decoration.

(*g*) Library science.

(*h*) Medical laboratory technology.

(*i*) Pharmacy.

(*j*) Secretarial practice.

These courses are being offered at certificate are levels. Efforts should be made to attract into them girls who have just passed the middle or high school examination. More women polytechnics need opening. It is suggested that if guidance services are amply provided to school leavers at the high school stage and if the Principals of women polytechnics associate themselves with the headmistresses and Principals of higher secondary schools more girls may be attracted to these careers.

**Women Polytechnics : Agricultural**

A large number of girls in rural areas may be attracted to supporting services needed by a farmer. There are many trades which are based upon agriculture. At the post-matriculation stage, opportunities for giving vocational education in agriculture may be provided on a sufficiently large scale. Courses of special interest to girls will have to be devised and developed in agricultural polytechnics. *For example;* courses in applied nutrition, dairying, animal husbandry, poultry farming are most suitable for matriculate girls. Besides, there is an urgent need for such courses in the country; for instance, in the present circumstances, we have to change our dietary habits and such courses may help a great deal in meeting food shortage. Women in rural households can safely manage these affairs. A network of agricultural polytechnics may be set up to provide girls vocational education in courses referred to above.

### Higher Education for Women

We do not subscribe to the opinion that it is no longer necessary to give a special attention to higher education of women since they are taking its advantage fully. To begin with, it must be emphasised that there exists an acute shortage of educated women to shoulder directional and organizational responsibilities in many professions and occupations. *For example,* there is a great demand of highly educated women workers in a series of occupational fields, such as nutrition, dietetics, institutional management, etc. Specially vigorous efforts have yet to be made to expand women's education at the university level.

Considering the changing needs of the Indian society and the requirements of national development, a still greater expansion of higher education has become imperative. During the decade 1950-1960 the proportion of women students in colleges and universities to the total enrolment was raised from 13 percent to 21. In the following decade it came about 30 percent: But there is an urgent need to raise it up to 40 percent at least. For the healthy growth of higher education among womenfolk the following programmes have been suggested by the Education Commission:

1. A programme of financial assistance and scholarships to women students in colleges and universities on a liberal scale.
2. A free access to courses in arts, humanities, sciences and technology.

3. A programme of suitable but economical hostel facilities for women on a large scale.

The first two programmes are self-explanatory. The National Council for Women's Education appointed a committee under the chairmanship of Smt. Hansa Mahta. The committee recommended that courses available for women should not be strictly compartmentalised, implying that women should not in any case be compelled to take up a particular course. The Committee gave a warning that if choice is restricted to women it shall be wrong in national interest. The Education Commission also did not like that girls should be forced to take up particular courses only. It suggested that the more academic type of girls with ambitions of pursuing careers of research or teaching at the college or university level or in professions such as medicine and technology should have all the opportunities and incentives for doing so.

The most popular professions for women are nursing and education. Facilities for higher education in these areas have to be strengthened. At the B.Sc. level in some universities Nursing has been introduced with a view to preparing qualified nursing staff. A scientific and professional course needs development so that it may have an academic value besides leading to a higher level of professional training in nursing. Similarly, there is a need to vitalise and upgrade the courses in Education at B.A. level which have been introduced in eleven universities. Women decide earlier whether they would adopt teaching as their profession or not. Hence, it is necessary that either the courses in Education at B.A. level be so prepared that women opting for them may be directly employable in teaching or concurrent integrated courses in general and professional teacher education may be given to them to enable them to join teaching at an earlier age.

Higher education for women must be linked up with avenues of employment because in the absense of employment their education will be wasted away. Hence, specific avenues will have to be searched out where their services may be utilised fruitfully. The services of highly educated women are needed in education, social work and nursing and similar professional fields. Their services are also required in nutrition, dietetics, institutional management and similar occupational areas. Home science has been recognised as an academic discipline in as many as 33 universities. A woman who takes up this subject at the university level should be so equipped that she may be able to work in professional fields of dietetics, food technology, family welfare work, extension work in community development and Welfare Extension Projects. She must be able to take up research work in projects end schemes of I.C.M.R., I.C.A.R. and Council of Child Welfare.

Three or four universities may set-up women wings for giving high level training in business administration and management. A National Institute for Women may be established separately for this purpose.

***

# 8

# Education to Disabled

## Deafness

We use the term 'hearing impaired' but other terms are 'hard of hearing' or 'deafness'. Often we presume that children can hear when in fact they might have difficulties hearing. Children cannot tell us they have problems in hearing because they may not know what it is like to hear properly! Mild hearing losses are much more common in school populations than profound hearing loss (deafness). Remember too, that some hearing problems come and go. If a child is prone to head colds or recurrent ear infections, their hearing can also be affected.

There are some of the common signs of impaired hearing. However, these do not mean that the child has a definite hearing impairment. There may be other reasons for the child's behaviour that you will need to consider. You should also discuss your concerns with parents. They can provide further information that may confirm your suspicions or reassure you that the child has no difficulty in hearing.

1. **Poor Attention :** If a student does not pay attention in class it is possible that he or she cannot hear what is being said or the sounds the child hears may be distorted. Due to these reasons the child either tunes out what the teacher says or does not make an effort to listen or attend. Very rarely a student may

be exceptionally attentive by playing very close attention in an attempt to determine what is being said.

2. **Difficulty in following instructions :** A child who has unusual difficulty in following oral instruction can have a possible hearing impairment.

3. **Poor speech development :** Immature, unusual or distorted speech may be due to hearing loss. Or the child talks in a very loud or soft voice.

4. A child may have difficulty in hearing text read by others or the child may request his peers or teachers to speak louder.

5. The child may respond better to tasks assigned when the teacher is relatively close to him and her, or to written tasks rather than ones that require an oral response.

6. Hearing problems can cause the child to watch what other students are doing before starting his/ her work or looking at classmates or teachers for clues.

7. Children with a hearing loss prefer to work in small groups, sit in a relatively quiet area of the classroom or in the front row.

8. The student may turn or cock head to one side to hear better.

9. Sometimes the child may give an inappropriate answer to a question asked or fail to answer.

10. The student may be shy or withdrawn or appear to be stubborn and disobedient as a reaction to his hearing loss.

11. The student may tend to isolate herself! himself from social activities.

12. The student may have some discharge from the ears.

13. The student may be reluctant to participate in oral activities, may fail to laugh at jokes or understand humour.

14.. The student may complain of frequent earaches, colds, sore throat or recurrent tonsillitis.

15. The student may interpret facial expressions, body movements and contextual information rather than spoken language and thus, sometimes make false conclusions.

**Causes of Deafness**

Some children are born with impaired hearing; others may lose their hearing later on. There are many causes of hearing impairment as this can also alert you to children who may have problems with hearing. The more common causes are:

1. Hereditary (hearing impairment occur in certain families, although the child's parents may not be hearing impaired. This happens more with boys than girls and is more common in affluent countries.)
2. Ear infections, especially long lasting, repeated infections with pus.
3. Lack of iodine in mother's diet Prematurity (baby born early and small).
4. Excessive earwax that blocks the ear canal Meningitis (an infection of the brain).
5. Cerebral malaria and overdoses of medicines used in its treatment.
6. The mother had German measles during early pregnancy.

However, in one out of three cases the cause of the hearing impairment is not known.

**Classroom Adaptations**

1. The child should be seated as close as possible to the teachers (no more than three metres away).
2. Some pupils benefit from seeing both the teacher and their classmates at the same time. They can learn from seeing other pupils responding to the teacher. So position the child in class accordingly or arrange the desks in such a way that it is possible for children to see each other's faces.
3. Try to minimise classroom noises. Use a room that is in a quieter part of the school.
4. Make sure light does not come from behind you, as your face would be in shadow. Work in good light so that the child can see your face, hands or lips.
5. The teachers. must make sure to stand or sit facing the pupil. Do not cover your face with a book when reading; or talk when writing on the chalkboard.

**Teaching Strategies**

1. If a hearing aid has been prescribed for the child make sure it is worn; that it is switched on and that the batteries are good.
2. Use simple words and sentences along with gestures or pictures to help the child understand what you are saying.
3. Speak clearly and loudly but without shouting and exaggerating.
4. Check with the pupil that he or she understands what she is expected to do.

5. Children with hearing impairments learn more from seeing rather than hearing although teachers should use both. Show them what you expect them to do. Use pictorial material or symbol cards.

6. Children with hearing impairments might find group situations more difficult because of all the talking going on at the same time by different people. Teachers can use these times to give face-to-face instruction to a pupil with hearing impairments.

7. Pair the pupil with a hearing student. The partner can help find the correct page; repeat your instructions and so on.

8. If the child's speech is not clear, take time to listen to what the child is trying to tell you. Help him to use the correct words and grammar but praise for their efforts at talking.

9. Encourage the pupil with hearing impairment to watch and listen to other pupils as they answer your questions. If they cannot see other pupils and hear their responses, you may repeat what they said as you face the pupil with the hearing impairment.

With children who are deaf—those with very little hearing—the main means of communication has to be through sign language; lip reading or reading and writing can be used as additional means of communication. All of the above suggestions apply with deaf children but you should also consider the following:

1. Teachers need to take classes in learning the sign language that is used by deaf people in their country. Adult deaf persons, who are trained as sign language instructors, are often the best teachers. Contact your national association of the deaf.

1. Teachers can recap the lesson through signs for their deaf students or alternate spoken and sign language during the lessons.

2. As children's language skills develop, introduce reading as this offers a most important medium of learning for the child and in communicating with others.

3. Young children quickly learn to sign even when their teacher or parents are not very good at it. The more you practice signing the better you become.

4. It may be possible to arrange for an interpreter / teachers of sign language to come regularly to the school. Deaf adults can be used as volunteers in the class to support the deaf child and facilitate communication between the child, the teacher and the classmates.

5. In many countries, special units have been set-up for deaf children in ordinary schools, usually in urban areas. Deaf adults may be employed as teachers and classroom assistants. Here, pupils are taught through sign language and they can use it to communicate easily with one another. Equally they have opportunities to socialise with all other pupils and join them for some classes.

6. Try to ensure that the deaf student receives written copies of lessons from you or her peers. Try to offer books and written material as often as possible.

**Blindness**

Various terms are used to describe differing degrees and types of visual impairment such as low vision, partial sight and blindness. Many children's problems are easily corrected with glasses once the problem is identified but some will have more marked impairments. Some of the warning signs are easily observed but it is possible for other problems to go unnoticed.

**Common Signs**

1. **Physical indictors :** There may be red eyes, crusts on lids among the eye lashes, recurring styes or swollen eyelids, watery eyes or discharge, crossed eye, eyes that do not appear straight, pupils of uneven size, eyes that have excessive and drooping eyelids.
2. The student rubs eyes often or while doing close visual work.
3. The student shuts or covers one eye when he has difficulty seeing with that eye or tilts the head or thrusts the head forward.
4. **Unusual facial behaviours :** A student shows unusual amount of squinting, blinking, frowning, or facial distortion while reading or doing other close work.
5. **Difficulty with rending :** An unusual difficulty with reading or when working that requires bringing the book or object close to the eyes. But he may do very well in oral or spoken directions and tasks.
6. Unable to locate and pick up a small object.
7. **Light sensitivity or difficulty :** A student may show unusual sensitivity to bright light by shutting their eyes or squinting. He may have a difficulty in seeing in dim light or inability to see after dark.
8. The pupil may have difficulty with written work: like not being able to stay on the line or write within the spaces.

9. Difficulty with distance vision may result in the pupil avoiding the playground, or avoiding all gross motor activity. Such a student may prefer reading or other academic activity.

**Causes of Blindness**

The more common causes are:

1. Infectious diseases contracted by the mother during the first few months of pregnancy.
2. Infectious diseases contracted by the child, *e.g.*, measles or chicken pox.
3. Maternal or childhood malnutrition. Eating yellow and green fruits and vegetables helps to protect the eyes.
4. Injuries to the eye.
5. Eye infections.
6. Tumours affecting nerve for sight Brain damage.
7. Xerophtalmia, *i.e.*, nutritional blindness as a result of insufficient Vitamin A in the diet.
8. River blindness caused by bathing in infected water

**Classroom Adaptations**

1. Find out from the child where is the best place for her to see the chalkboard, *for example*, when seated at the front of the class.
2. Ensure the child knows her way around the school and the classroom. Teachers and sighted pupils should lead her by walking in front with the visually impaired pupil slightly behind and to one side; holding on to the guide's elbow. Warn them of obstacles such as steps and narrow doorways.

3. The light should not reflect on the board and you should ensure that the chalk appears clearly on the board.

4. If the child's eyes are sensitive to the light, move him away from the window. Have him wear a peaked hat to shade his eyes or give him a cardboard screen to use for shade when reading and writing.

## Teaching Strategies

1. Use large writing on the chalkboard or visual aids. The use of coloured chalks is recommended. Let the children come close to the board or teaching aids so that they can see more easily.

2. Some children will benefit from using magnifying aids. Two types are available. Ones that enlarge the whole page or line magnifiers, which are a useful aid to reading.

3. Children may have difficulty seeing the lines on writing paper. They can be given paper with thicker lines drawn on it.

4. Encourage the children to use a pointer or their finger when reading. Cover the rest of the page with paper except for the paragraph the child is reading. Use a bookstand to avoid reflection.

5. Use verbal praise or touch to give the child encouragement.

6. Read aloud what is written on the blackboard. Prepare teaching aids that children can read more easily such as large print materials. Other children in the class could help prepare these. Or they can be produced by enlarging images on photocopies or using larger font sizes on computer printouts. This can also help children who have difficulties in reading.

7. Use the name of the pupils during class discussions so that the child knows who is talking.

8. Pair the pupil with a seeing classmate who can assist her to organise their work. The partner can help find the correct page; repeat your instructions and so on

9. Children with poor vision need to learn through touch as well as through hearing. They should be given a chance to handle objects.

10. Make an abacus available to the child in maths lessons.

11. Computers offer particular support to students with vision impairments and blindness. Students can print out a large print copy, read text on the screen using screen enlargement software, listen to the text on a voice synthesiser or convert it into Braille.

12. Lessons can be taped using a cassette recorder for later playback at home or as revision. Students who experience difficulties in writing can also provide information on audiotape. Taped versions of books are sometimes available in libraries.

Blind children have little or no useful vision; they are only able to make out light and dark. Many of the suggestions above apply to these children too but there are others you also need to consider.

1. Blind children should learn Braille. This gives them a means of reading and writing. Perkins Braillers are available across all countries. Braille can be produced directly on a Braille embosser. Also Braille texts can be produced from computer textfile format and printed out using a Braille printer. Details will be available from your national association for the

blind. They will help you to find teachers of Braille. Once children can use Braille they can learn alongside sighted children.

2. Tactile images can be drawn on Braille paper using a special mat and stylus which produces a relief image that can be felt. Similar images can be produced using locally available materials such as string, sand, sticks and seeds. Teachers can enlist the help of sighted children in producing teaching aids. These aids help other children, too.

3. Likewise an abacus will help all children in maths lessons.

4. Daily living skills such as cooking pose particular challenges for blind persons. However children need to acquire these skills in a graded manner, starting with low risk activities before moving on to activities in which there is a risk of burning themselves.

5. Blind children should be encouraged to walk independently around the school using a cane. It should be the same length as the distance from the ground up to halfway between the person's shoulder and waist. A cane that is too short will force the user to bend over when walking. Ideally they should receive training from specialists. Your national association for the blind should be able to advise. Do not remove obstacles all the time, as children have to be trained to move around them. Expect bumps and falls; do not fuss when they occur.

6. Blind children need to learn to orientate their bodies and to move confidently. Physical activities and group games will provide good practice. At first children will need to be moved through the activity in order to understand what they are to do. Teachers should insist on proper posture.

## INTELLECTUAL DISABILITY

Of all the disabilities this is the most common. Other terms are often used to describe this disability; *for example,* developmental disability, mental retardation, mental handicap or severe learning difficulties. This disability affects all aspects of a child's development. They are slower to develop physically, acquire language, learn to look after themselves and in mastering academic skills. However they are not mentally ill. That term is used when healthy people develop an illness that affects their moods, emotions and behaviours. With appropriate treatment they can be cured. With some children their intellectual impairment is obvious at birth, or soon after. But with many others, it will not be identified until the child starts school although the warning signs are often present from a young age. Some children might have very severe disabilities and may have additional impairments such as epilepsy, vision and hearing problems. They are sometimes referred to as profoundly or multiply disabled children.

However, many more children are affected only mildly or moderately—a rough estimate is two in one hundred. With these children there be may no physical reason for their disability. The signs have been grouped into six areas. Children who show signs in all these areas are more likely to have an intellectual disability. Problems that occur in one area but not in another, may be indicative of a specific learning difficulty related to reading, writing or maths, *for example.*

Note that the ages are rough guidelines. The best yardstick is the ages which children in that community usually attain these skills. Even so, the guidelines should be used cautiously as there is much variation in children's development. Some children develop naturally slower than others without having an intellectual disability. Deprivation can cause this kind of slower development. Living in a multilingual community can also slow down child's language development, as she is learning several languages at the same time. Remember too that children may develop intellectual disability later in life having acquired these milestones. This can be the result of a head injury or severe deprivation.

**Talking**

1. Does not say mama (or equivalent) by 18 months of age.
2. Cannot name a few familiar objects/ people by age 2.
3. Cannot repeat simple songs/rhythms by age 3 is not talking in short sentences by age 4.
4. Is not understood by people outside family by age 5.
5. Is talking differently from other children of the same age.

**Behaviour**

Compared to other children of his/her age:

1. The child has short attention span the child has poor memory.
2. The child is apathetic and indifferent.
3. The child is hyperactive, aggressive or disruptive.

**Understanding Language**

1. Does not react to his own name by age 1.
2. Cannot follow simple stories by age 3.
3. Cannot identify parts of face by age 3.
4. Cannot answer simple questions by age 4.
5. Cannot follow instructions in class by age 5.

6. Seems to have difficulty understanding things you are saying, when compared to other children of the same age.

**Moving**

1. Is unable to sit up unsupported by 10 months cannot walk by age 2.
2. Cannot balance on one foot for a short time by age 4.
3. Poor motor co-ordination. Moves very differently from other children of the same age.

**Playing**

1. Does not enjoy playing simple waving games by age 1.
2. Does not play with common objects (*e.g.*, spoon and pot) by age 2.
3. Does not play like other children of the same age.
4. Does not join in games with other children by age 4 (*e.g.*, catch, hide and seek).

**Reading and Writing**

By five years of age or after one year at school, the child

1. Has difficulty copying shapes such as circles and squares.
2. Has difficulty sequencing letters and words on ash cards.
3. Has problems doing simple jigsaws and form boards mixes up letters such as d and b.
4. cannot recall five numbers or words in the correct order immediately after they are spoken.

### Causes of Intellectual Disability

Intellectual disabilities have many different causes. They can be grouped into five types:

1. **Genetic damage :** This is present at conception. Down Syndrome is an example of a genetic fault.
2. **Damage in womb :** Infections in the mother can damage the developing baby. Rubella or German measles is a common example. The HIV virus can also damage growing brains.
3. **Damage at birth or soon after :** Oxygen deprivation, low birth weight and premature births and jaundice can all result in intellectual disabilities.
4. **Social causes :** Children who are extremely deprived of love and affection and stimulation can also experience in extreme cases intellectual disabilities.
5. **Accidents and illnesses :** Damage to the brain from falls or accidents can result in intellectual disabilities as can infections such as cerebral malaria and meningitis, repeated fits and malnutrition.

However, with sizeable numbers of children-upwards of one-third-no cause can be found for their disability. Remember that the same cause can produce very different effects in children. *For example,* a child born with Down Syndrome may grow and develop much like any other child whereas others with the same genetic damage are markedly disabled. Beware of expecting too little from the child because of the label given to their disability. Children need to be offered materials and experiences that will challenge them.

### Classroom Adaptations

Teachers who have experience of teaching children with intellectual disability and learning difficulties in their class recommend:

1. Reduce distractions - keep the desk clear.
2. Try to recruit a volunteer who will come to the class on certain days to provide one-to-one help for the child. You can also ask the volunteer to work with the rest of the class so that you can work with the child. Find time to work with the child on a one-to-one basis even if only for short periods; *for example,* when the other children are occupied with other tasks. During this time, try to reduce the distractions such as noise and remove objects not needed for the lesson.
3. With children who are inclined to run around, seat them by the wall with bigger children beside them. You can also assign them tasks that allow them to move around so that this moving does not become disruptive, such as handing out papers, notebooks and materials.

**Teaching Strategies**

1. Show the child what you want him or her to do rather than simply telling.
2. Use simple words when giving instructions and check that the child has understood.
3. Use real objects that the child can feel and handle rather than doing paper and pencil work. Try to link the lessons to the child's experiences and everyday life.
4. Give plenty of praise and encouragement when the child is successful.
5. Break the task down into small steps or learning objectives. Have the child start with what he or she can do before moving on to a harder step. Go back

to an easier step if the child encounters problems. *For example,* in learning to draw a circle; the child can colour in the shape; then move to joining up dots to make a shape; then copy shapes from a sample and so on.

6. Do one activity at a time and complete it. Make clear when one is finished and a new one is starting.
7. Enlist the help of a family member who will do 'home work' with the child; revising what has been done in class that day
8. Give the children extra practice at doing the task this is sometimes called 'over-learning' but it ensures the child has mastered the skill and increases their confidence. However, be reasonable. Many people with intellectual disabilities remember their school days of being full of doing 'over and over again the same things and never learning new things'.
9. Pair the child with a peer who can help to focus the child's attention and assist with activities given to the class. Pair the child with more-able pupils. When they have finished their work, they can assist the slower child with the task. Assign tasks that they can all contribute to their own level and work out jointly the assigned task. Assign tasks for a whole group in which the other learners are depended on the contribution of the child with intellectual disability. Other pupils can also be asked to assist the child at break times; use of toilets and so on. For individual tasks, have a number of activities that the child enjoys and can manage on his own so that he does not distract the other children.
10. The children need to practice the skill with different materials. For instance, reading words when they

are written on flash cards, on worksheets and reading books. Writing can be practiced on the sand, with finger paint, with crayons and pencil and pen. This is called generalising the child's learning.

11. Ignore undesirable behaviour if the child is doing it to get your attention. Give praise and attention when the child's behaviour is acceptable.

## CEREBRAL PALSY

Cerebral Palsy (CP) literally means paralysis of the brain. Often the parts of the brain which are most affected control movements of the arms, legs or facial muscles, resulting in limbs being either very floppy or, more usually, very tight and tense. Often people with cerebral palsy find it difficult, or are unable, to talk properly due to difficulties in controlling their head movements or facial muscles.

Cerebral palsy is combination of different disabilities. Sometimes when the damage to. the brain is more general intellectual abilities may also be impaired but more often children with cerebral palsy tend to be physically rather than intellectually disabled. Some children may also have difficulties with hearing and/ or seeing. Children may have a mild form of cerebral palsy with minimal loss of function in their limbs or speech defect; to very severe forms when the child is multiply disabled.

### Causes of Cerebral Palsy

There is rarely a single cause for cerebral palsy. It may result from congential malformations, maternal infections during pregnancy, birth difficulties and childhood infections such as meningitis, excessive jaundice, rubella and head injury. There is an increased risk of babies having cerebral palsy with adolescent mothers or those with poor health and living in poverty.

## Teaching Strategies

Many of the suggestions given in earlier sections can be applied to children with cerebral palsy. In particular:

1. If the child's speech is unclear, devise alternative means for communicating, *for example,* through pictures or drawn symbols. These can be placed together on a board and the child points to the picture to convey the message. Computerised versions are also available. When the child touches the picture or symbol, a synthesised voice says the word.

2. Writing will be especially difficult for children if they have problems controlling their hands and arms. They may need extra time to do their writing, or they can be provided with a written copy of the information or another pupil may write for them. Computer keyboards can also be adapted to make it easier for children with cerebral palsy to produce written words.

3. Encourage the child to join in answering questions but leave extra time for them to respond either through speech or via symbol boards. Encourage the peers to interact with the child as children usually find their ways of communication.

## Classroom Adaptations

For children with mild forms of cerebral palsy, very little adaptations may be needed to classroom. However, more severely disabled children may require:

1. Special seating to keep their head and body straight when sitting.

2. Special desks to work at whose height can be adjusted.

3. The use of communication boards (*e.g.*, made up of pictures or symbols) so that the teacher and peers can understand the child.
4. The child may need extra assistance to use the toilet. Sturdy rails around the toilet will help.

**Common Illnesses and Impairments**

There are 13 conditions that can inhibit children's learning. Teachers may hear these terms used by other professionals or they might come across them in books. These conditions affect children differently; some children might have severe difficulties while with others the affect is mild. Some of these conditions directly affect children's learning. Others are health conditions that teachers need to be aware of.

**Aphasia (Specific Language Disorder)**

Some children may have specific difficulties with acquiring language due to some form of brain damage. The children can have difficulty expressing themselves they get words mixed up—or in understanding what is said to them. This disorder is often confused with hearing impairments or intellectual disability. Teaching and therapies that are aimed at helping children to acquire the meaning of words and sentence structures. These can help children overcome their difficulties but it will probably not' cure' them. Aphasia is one form of language disorder. There are others.

**Asthma**

The word means 'panting' or gasping for breath. During an asthma attack, the air passages in the lungs become narrow and children have difficulty breathing out. The lungs become blown up. The causes are not fully understood but it is thought that it is due to allergy to substances such as certain foods, pollen from plants and house dust. Attacks may also be triggered by emotional events such as too much excitement or stress such as school examinations. When an attack occurs, children can take medicines to relax the muscles in the lungs, usually through an inhaler. However, it is important to remain calm and to reassure the child.

**Dyslexia**

Children who experience particular difficulty with reading and spelling may be labelled as being' dyslexic'. (Again some educationalists question thc usefulness of the term.) However, children with dyslexia are of average intelligence and perform well in other aspects of life.

**Autism**

This is a controversial term introduced some 40 year ago but some would dispute that a person (usually a child) can be reliably diagnosed as 'autistic'. The essential feature of the condition is that the child has difficulty in communicating; withdraws from contact with other people and appears to be living in his own world. Sometimes people with autistic disorders display remarkable skills focused on one specific area (*e.g.*, drawing) and some appear to become 'normal'. However, no universally recognised h'eatrnent exists.

**Cleft Palate**

Babies may be born with a deformed mouth and upper lip. They will have difficulty eating and later speaking unless a surgical repair is done to the mouth and lips. They may still have difficulty in speaking clearly but much of the disability results from others' reactions to their facial deformity.

Diabetes is an inherited condition in which the body is unablc to use sugar and starch as energy. When there is too much or not enough sugar in the blood, children will feel ill and may even lose consciousness. Feelings of tiredness, lack of concentration, excessive sweating, difficulty in reading and speaking are all symptoms. The children may to have regular insulin injections and they need to careful with what they eat and the amount of exercise they take.

## Epilepsy

People with this condition experience sudden and uncontrollable 'electrical disturbance' in their brain cells. In severe' fits' or 'seizures', as they are called, the person may lose consciousness and make uncontrollable body movements. Drugs are commonly used to lessen the severity and occurrence of the seizures and many people with epilepsy can lead perfectly normal lives. Epilepsy is prevalent among children with intellectual disabilities (one in eight of these people also have epilepsy) but this does not mean that a person who has epilepsy has an intellectual disability.

## Emotional/Behavioural Difficulties

Some children may experience emotional difficulties. They may be very depressed or anxious; or they may show odd behaviours such as crying and laughing inappropriately. They may be excessively active with a short attention span or they may be indifferent, apathetic or absent-minded. The emotional upsets may result from a recent traumatic experience, the death of a parent *for example,* or they could indicate a more deep-seated, mental health problem. Child psychiatrists may be able to help. Treatments include the use of drugs, counselling and therapy. Teachers can reinforce positive behaviour, or support the child to overcome traumatic experiences, *for example.*

## HIV/AIDS

Women who have the HIV virus have about a 50% chance of giving birth to a baby who will have the virus. A person with the HIV virus may look healthy. The virus can only be passed on to others in very limited ways; through blood or during unprotected sexual intercourse. It is not possible to get the HIV virus from being near or touching those who have the virus. Hugging, kissing, coughing and sneezing will NOT spread the disease. Nor can it be spread by toilet seats, glasses, towels and swimming pools. Children who develop AIDS often die young because they cannot fight off other serious illnesses. However, the virus can remain hidden for a long time and the children can lead a normal life if given the opportunity to do so.

**Muscular Dystrophy**

This is a genetic disorder that leads to the degeneration of muscles as the child gets older. The child may start having difficulties in running and climbing stairs and by the teenage years may have to use a wheelchair. Breathing problems due to chest infections are also common. There is no known cure.

**Spina Bifida**

The child is born with an incomplete development of bones of the spinal column. This may result in a 'sac' of spinal fluid and nerves protruding out of the lower back. Surgical intervention is needed to cover the defect as early as possible to prevent infections. The child usually has muscle weakness and the loss of feeling in the lower limbs. A frequent problem is poor bowel and urine control. Hydrocephalus comes from spina bifida. Spinal fluid collects around the child's brain and gives the child a big head. A valve can be inserted into the child's neck (called a shunt) to help drain away the fluid. However, if this is not done early brain damage can result in intellectual disabilities and visual impairments.

❋❋❋

# 9

# Equalization of Educational Opportunities under New Education Policy

Education Policy provides a sound basis to National Progress. Every ruler in India gave preference to Education according to its need. Present Government declared its National Policy on Education. Following are the main features of National Policy on Education, 1986:

**1. Role of Education.** Education is responsible for the all-round development of the individuals. It is also responsible for cultural assimilation and provide strength to democracy, secularism. Education constructs the nation at every level, creates self-sufficiency and search new areas of development.

**2. National System of Education.** Though Education is a state subject, this policy provides a National System of Education, *i.e.*, 10 + 2 + 3 system.

**3. Women Education.** New Education Policy gave special emphasis to Women Education. This statement owes that women are the keys to nation's progress. Education of illiteracy vocational curriculum, nutrition and child care courses, home management, etc., are given priority.

**4. Equality.** This policy provides equal opportunities to all for education. Navodaya schools have been opened for socially and economically deprived but to talented children. Regional imbalances are also being removed.

**5. Education of Scheduled Castes.** Socially and economically deprived Scheduled Castes are the backbone of our society. They need proper development and place in the society. Scholarships, hostel facilities, adult education programmes are being introduced.

**6. Education for Tribes.** This policy gave main emphasis to the education of tribes. Residential Ashram Schools have been opened for them, scholarships for higher education are given.

**7. Adult Education.** Education Policy gave a programme for adult education to remove the illiteracy from the masses. For this, adult schools, libraries, distance education, T.V. programmes are being introduced.

**8. Education for other Backward Classes.** A large number of backward classes, minority classes have not been given any opportunity for education. These classes have a very crucial situation. They are socially and economically deprived due to their profession, but they usually linked themselves with higher varnas. Thus, upper castes do not give them social sanction. Education is the only way to give them chance to co-operation with the society.

As far as the secondary education is concerned, vocationalisation of it is introduced. At Higher education stage, autonomy will be given to good colleges.

Though, New Policy gave a new direction in the field of education in the light of national unity and development this is the preparation to welcome the 21st century. Life deal, family structure, social organization, national consciousness are influenced by the scientific and technological advancement. Moral, social, ethical and human values need development. This is a felt need of our new policy. Common man is on the cross roads. He does not find his way to destiny. Growing population, expansion of social distances and economic disparities put some questions before the new policy. Those questions are as under:

1. Whether new policy will create class difference?
2. Is this policy competent to shape the socialistic society?
3. What will be the shape of future? This indication is not given by the policy.
4. How will this be helpful to reconstruct the nation?
5. Will it be possible to make free and compulsory education to all the children upto the age of 14.
6. Reservation policy will not give the passage to new policy.
7. Will social justice be possible through it?
8. No equality is possible through it.
9. Language problem is a very big problem before new policy?

Though these questions are before our policy-makers, even then they are much hopeful to build new India. In the word of our deceased Prime Minister Rajeev Gandhi—"We will have to build our society, such a society where education must be honoured. Education does not end after learning school or college. It is a life long process. We cannot progress until our education be honoured and we could not face the challenges in future to save our country."

In the end past is gold, present is full of dust and future is indefinite. New Education Policy is the determination of youth. This will create a faith for future, develop our determination, thus, distance will be dispersed.

## INTEGRATED EDUCATION FOR DISABLED CHILDREN

It has been established scientifically that disabled children with mild handicaps make better progress academically and psychologically if they study with the normal children. To integrate these children with others in common schools, a revised scheme of Integrated Education for Disabled Children was started during 1987-88. Under it, cent per cent financial assistance is given to State Governments / UT administrations / voluntary organizations for creating necessary facilities in schools. Admissible items of expenditure are books and stationery allowance, transport allowance, uniform allowance, readers allowance (for blind children), escort allowance (for orthopaedically handicapped with lower extremity disabilities), equipment allowance and wherever necessary hostel charges. Besides, the scheme also provides, among other things, to meet cost of salary and incentives for teachers, setting up of resource rooms, carrying out assessment of disabled children, training of teachers, removal of architectural barriers in schools, development and production of special instructional material for them. Assistance is also given through the University Grants Commission to the selected universities / institutions to run training courses in special education for teachers of handicapped children. Training facilities are also provided by NCERT and four regional colleges of education. The scheme is at present in operation in Andhra Pradesh, Bihar, Goa, Gujarat, Haryana, Jammu and Kashmir, Himachal Pradesh, Karnataka, Kerala, Madhya Pradesh, Maharashtra, Manipur, Mizoram, Nagaland, Orissa, Punjab, Rajasthan, Tamil Nadu, Uttar Pradesh, Delhi, Andaman and Nicobar Islands and Daman and Diu. By the end of 1993-94 about 40,000 disable children in over 9,000 schools were covered under the scheme.

### Educational Concessions to Children

The Centre and most of the State Governments and Union Territories offer educational concessions to children of the defence personnel and paramilitary forces killed or permanently disabled during Indo-China hostilities in 1962 and Indo-Pakistan operations in 1965 and 1971.

During 1988, these concessions were extended to children of IPKF/CRPF personnel who were killed/disabled during action in Sri Lanka and children of the armed forces personnel killed/disabled in action in 'Operation Meghdoot' in Siachen area.

**Education of SC/ST/OBC**

Pursuant to the National Policy on Education, the following special provisions for SCs and STs have been incorporated in the existing schemes of the Departments of Elementary Education & Literacy and Secondary & Higher Education:

*(a)* Relaxed norms for opening of primary schools.

*(b)* Abolition of tuition fee in all states in Government schools at least up to primary level. Most of the states have abolished tuition fee for SC/ST students up to senior secondary level.

*(c)* A primary school within one km walking distance from habitations of 200 population instead of habitations of 300 population.

*(d)* The major programmes of the Department of Education, *viz*, District Primary Education Programme (DPEP), Lok Jumbish, Shiksha Karmi, Non-Formal Education (NFE) and National Programme for Nutritional Support to Primary Education accord priority to areas of concentration of SCs and STs.

*(e)* Reservation of seats for SCs and STs in Central Government institutions of higher education including IITs, IIMs, Regional Engineering College, Central Universities, Kendriya Vidyalayas and

Navodaya Vidyalayas, etc. Apart from reservation, there is also relaxation in the minimum qualifying cut off stages for admission in universities, colleges and technical institutions. The UGC has established SC/ST cells in 104 universities including Central universities to ensure proper implementation of the reservation policy.

*(f)* Providing incentives like free textbooks, uniforms, stationery, school bags, etc., to these students.

*(g)* To improve academic skills and linguistic proficiency of students in various subjects and raising their level of comprehension, remedial and special coaching is provided for SC/ST students. IITs have a scheme under which SC/ST students who marginally fail in the entrance examination are provided one year preparatory course and those who qualify are then admitted to the First Year of the B. Tech. Course.

*(h)* SC/ST candidates are provided relaxation upto 10 per cent cut-off marks for the Junior Resaerch Fellowship (JRF) test and all the SC and ST candidates qualifying for the JRF are awarded Fellowship.

*(i)* Out of 43,000 scholarships at the secondary stage for talented children from rural areas 13,000 scholarships are exclusively reserved for SC/ST students, seventy scholarships are exclusively reserved for SC/ST students under the National Talent Search Scheme.

*(j)* 50 Junior Fellowships are awarded every year in science and humanities including social sciences to SC/ST candidates who appear in National Eligibility Test (NET) and qualify the eligibility test for lecturership.

*(k)* The Central Institute of Indian Languages, Mysore has a scheme of development of Indian Languages

through research, developing manpower, production of materials in modern Indian Languages including tribal languages. The Institute has worked in more than 75 tribal languages.

*(l)* 146 districts have been identified as low female literacy districts to be given focussed attention by the Centre as well as States / UTs for implementation of programmes / schemes.

The allocation of ₹ 889.98 crore and ₹ 436.54 crore have been made under the Special Component Plan and Tribal Sub-Plan (TSP) for SCs and STs respectively. This accounts for 16.33 per cent and 8.01 per cent of the total outlay.

**Minorities Education**

In pursuance of the revised Programme of Action (POA) 1992, two new Centrally-sponsored schemes, *i.e.*, *(i)* Scheme of Area Intensive Programme for Educationally Backward Minorities and *(ii)* Scheme of Financial Assistance for Modernisation of Madarsa Education were launched during 1993-94.

The objective of scheme of Area Intensive Programme for Educationally Backward Minorities is to provide basic educational infrastructure and facilities in areas of concentration of educationally backward minorities which do not have adequate provision for elementary and secondary schools. Under the scheme cent per cent assistance is given for:

*(a)* Establishment of new primary and upper primary schools, non-formal education centres, wherever necessary.

*(b)* opening of multi-stream residential higher secondary schools for girls belonging to the educationally backward minorities.

(*c*) Strengthening of educational infrastructure and physical facilities in the primary and upper primary schools.

## GROWTH OF DISTANCE EDUCATION IN INDIA

Peter Says, 'Distance education is a method of indirect instruction, implying geographical and emotional separation of teacher and taught whereas, in main stream education, the relationship between a teacher and student in classroom is based upon social norms, in distance education, it is based upon technological rules.' Jack Foks stated the Distance education—'Distance education is a mode of learning with certain characteristics which distinguish it from the campus based mode of learning.'

About 40 years ago, correspondence education in India was started as a pilot project in the University of Delhi. The success of this experiment encouraged other universities to take up instructions through the distance education. By 1985, 31 universities adopted this scheme. About 40000 students at various levels were enrolled by the universities under this scheme. Though the universities are providing education through this media, but there was a great demand for an open university. As a result in 1985, the Government of India decided to set-up Indira Gandhi National Open University. The focal points of this university are as under:

(*a*) To promote open university and distance education system.

(*b*) To allocate and disburse grants to colleges, whether admitted to its privileges or not, or to any other university or institution of higher learning as may be specified by the statutes.

(*c*) To determine the standards of teaching evaluation and research in such system.

Indira Gandhi National Open University is providing Degrees in B.A., B.Sc. and B.Com., Diploma Course in Distance education, Creative writing, Nutrition, Management, Local Self-Government, Library Science, Banking, etc.

Separate Radio and T.V. channels have been started to broadcast and telecast the educational programmes.

As a measure for implementation, the programme of Action has also favoured and recommended Open Universities System to provide higher education through non-formal channel. The main suggestions and recommendations of this Action Programme are given as under:

*(a)* Action Programme suggested the Open University System. This should be cost-effective, flexible and innovative.

*(b)* Non-formal education system should be structured on modular pattern.

*(c)* Indira Gandhi National Open University has been established and is running effectively.

*(d)* Minimum level of learning should be objectively assessed.

*(e)* Separate Radio and Television channels be used for the use of distance education.

*(f)* Network of course be framed.

### Advantages of Distance Education

National Education Policy, 1986 has rightly stressed that distance education will provide many opportunities for education and will lessen the burden of formal education. The advantages of Distance Education are as under:

**1. Reliable.** Distance education is reliable. It has the cost-effective alternative and new means of communication.

**2. Education at Learners' Door.** Distance education is the only way which provide the education to the learner at his door. It provides equal educational opportunities even to those who used to live in remote areas.

**3. Beneficial to Adults.** Distance education provides many benefits to adults. They may up-to-date themselves for the development of skills and knowledge.

**4. Variety of Programme.** Distance education provides variety programmes according to the needs of the learners.

**5. Co-ordination.** Distance education is the co-ordination of various educational factors, *i.e.,* general, basic, professsional, technical, life-long, inservice and expansion.

**6. Learner Centred.** Distance education is learner-centred, therefore, there is no doubt in its success.

**7. Freedom.** This system provides freedom to learner. A learner, learns according to his needs, conditions and facility.

**8. Educational Needs.** Distance education fulfils the need of society through variety of educational programmes.

**9. Minimizing Pressures.** Distance education minimises the educational pressures caused by the explosion of population.

Distance education is still in experimental stage. Even then nobody will disagree that this system will be helpful to solve our educational problems and minimise the pressure of population over the traditional system of education.

## ROLE OF EDUCATION

Before we discuss the role of education in the eradication of pollution let us keep in mind a few things like its impact on health, the radio-active waves, rise in respiratory and eye diseases, the growth in diseases caused by virus, the gastroenteritis diseases, various diseases relating to noise resulting in deafness and other diseases of lungs and heart. The growing adverse effect on all types of vegetation cannot be ignored.

Now it shall be worthwhile to discuss the role of education in the eradication of pollution. Following are the measures if adopted in letter and spirit in the right earnest, may bear fruitful results:

**1.** New ways of looking at the environment so that its value can be reflected in the national accounts, better planning and legislation, more careful and wider use of existing and new environmental technologies, including the all-important environmental impact assessment—a way of appraising the effect of any proposed project on the environment before it is launched.

**2.** There is a section on hazardous industries and environmental disasters. Thus, hazardous industrial pollution is also covered. A hazardous substance is defined as "any substance or preparation which, by reason of its chemical or physio-chemical properties or handling, is liable to cause harm to human beings, other living creatures, plants, micro-organisms, property or the environment."

**3.** There are stringent measures to check hazardous pollution. Section 8 of the Act states clearly: 'No person shall handle or cause to be handled any hazardous substance except in accordance with such procedure and after complying with such safeguards as may be prescribed.' Section 6(f) empowers the Central Government to make rules for 'the procedures and safeguards for the prevention of accidents which may cause environmental pollution and for providing remedial measures for such accidents.' Morevoer, it is now mandatory for a person responsible for the discharge of any hazardous substance in excess of the prescribed norms to immediately inform the concerned authorities and to render all possible assistance. Earlier there was no such responsibility.

**4.** The new Environment (Protection) Act, 1986, is far better in approach than the earlier laws. The Water (Prevention and Control of Pollution) Act, 1974 and the Air (Prevention and Control of Pollution) Act, 1981, were weak and merely regulatory in character.

**5.** However, there are some flaws even in the new Act. One, all power and authority is vested in the hands of the Central Government.

**6.** Vigilant citizens can initiate proceedings against an establishment that is polluting the water supply or otherwise ruining the environment. The penalties for defaulters have been made more stringent. The Water Act provided for a maximum imprisonment of six years and/or a fine upto a total of ₹ 5000; in the Air Act the limits were a maximum imprisonment upto three months and/or fine upto a total of ₹ 5000. The new Act provides for imprisonment of defaulters for upto a total of seven years and/or a fine which may extend upto ₹ 1 lakh.

7. **Strategy Needed.** Having experienced the ill effects of industrial development, it is high time a long-term strategy for environmental protection is evolved. In this respect, the Parthasarathy Commission has strongly pleaded for a Regional Development Strategy and a National Urban Development Policy with a view to contain metropolitan choas, for developing secondary cities and to ensure development of existing small and medium towns as well as establishing new ones, as part of a regional strategy generating employment and promoting decentralised urbanisation. In addition, a clear industrial location policy will ensure setting up of specific large industries at specific locations with a pre-determined time-frame. It will ensure not only systematic industrial growth but also facilitate in taking measures for environmental protection economically and in a coherent manner.

8. **Stress on Ecological Balance.** Addressing the first meeting of the National Land Use and Wastelands Development

Council on February 6, 1986, Prime Minister Rajiv Gandhi called for a nation wide "people movement" to protect the country's ecological balance. He suggested a time-bound land reclamation and afforestation programme. The approach to this problem could not be departmentalised or compartmentalised but had to "respond to the differing needs of every section."

**9.** Apart from increasing the forest wealth, the programme generates additional earnings to the Panchayats, more employment to labour and it provides cheap fuel to the village poor. In Dhanoli, a village in Valsad district of Gujarat, social forestry has achieved remarkable progress. By adopting the scheme of raising village forests in only four hectares of land a net income of over ₹ 43,000 was generated.

**10.** Social forestry not only prevents felling of trees but also tries to distribute the produce of the project directly to the people of the area. The scheme also aims at growing more trees and forests on unused land and promotes research in the science of trees and their varieties.

**11.** All State Governments, semi-Government bodies and municipalities as well as social organizations have been propagating "grow more trees" campaign. To boost the idea of growing more and more trees, the Government has taken up the project of "social forestry" on a large scale. The project aims at planting trees singly or in groups wherever they can be grown.

**12.** Community lands in villages are wasted and used only for grazing village cattle. This unproductive use of land yields the village panchayats hardly ₹ 4,000 to ₹ 5,000. But the same land, if utilised for a cluster of trees for which the Government provides free seedlings, can fetch a much higther income to the Panchayats. The Gujarat Government has decided to give 50 per cent of the net profit realised from the sale of village wood-lot to the Panchayat. Crores of trees are required to strengthen and support agricultural and animal husbandry, to combat pollution and to attract adequate rains and also to stop erosion of fertile soil.

**13. The Ganga Plan.** The Government of India has launched a ₹ 292-crore project to clean up the mighty Ganga, which has been greatly polluted as a result of the inflow of effluents and dirt from various sources. There are about 100 cities situated along the banks of the river, in the States of Uttar Pradesh, Bihar and Bengal. Nearly 4200 small and medium units are responsible for polluting the holy river. The Ganga Project is the largest and most ambitious of all the environment protection plans launched in the country.

**14.** The cleaning up work began at Rishikesh and Hardwar in September, 1985. Cleaning the Ganga is also in progress at Varanasi waterfront, which is heavily polluted. A Central Ganga Authority had been constituted under the chairmanship of the Prime Minister himself.

**15.** In February, 1986 the Supreme Court directed the Union Government to examine the possibility of setting up environment courts. The Court judgement in the Shriram Foods and Fertiliser Industries case may well provide a basis for action by the Government to safeguard the environment in areas where potentially hazardous industies are located. The court has in fact set out a framework for appropriate Governmental action. It has also set-up a monitoring committee to ensure that the expert bodies recommendations are implemented. Even more significant is the suggestion that measures should be taken to educate the workers and provide early warning systems for the public.

**16.** The wanton destruction of natural wealth, including forests and the indiscriminate setting-up of chemical industries endangers the lives of both human beings and animals. The greed for personal gain, the general decline in values, the knowledge that one can flout the laws with a vengeance and get away with it, or at worst to pay a small fine, have cumulatively rendered ineffective the agencies enstrusted with the duty of protecting the environment. There are poachers galore, but it is only rare that legal action is taken against such offenders.

While the increasing awareness and rethinking about the importance of preserving all aspects of the environment, including forests, clean air and wild life is welcome, there is an urgent need for earnest implementation of declared policies. So far, the implementation has been poor and, consequently the environment has been deteriorating; forests, in particular, are disappearing at a disconcerting pace. It is time to recall the farsighted Chanakya's observation in the 4$^{th}$ century B.C. that "the stability of an empire depends on the stability of its environment." Strong and committed machinery is needed and it must have sufficient resources.

Ecology also has some effect on poverty. Undeniably, an ecologically and scientifically sound afforestation programme can provide a solution to the problem of India's poverty, if it is not based on the profit motive alone. More research is undoubtedly needed to evaluate the costs of monoculture based social forestry. Unless afforestation programmes are linked with the basic needs of the rural poor, they will prove economically counter-productive and ecologically disastrous.

Obviously, the plunder of what Nature has built over billions of years has to be stopped. We need a new life-style with environmental ethics as an integral part of it, not only for this generation but also for the future generations to live and enjoy the freedom of this planet and beyond. It is important in this regard to reduce the rate of population growth to one per cent from the present 2.2 per cent, as China has done. Industries generating high pollution should be moved out of the perimeters of cities. Environmental education should be made compulsory at every level of learning.

***

# 10

# Teacher Training Programme in Education

The training and education of teachers in India is of recent origin. Its history can be traced back to 1882. Prior to 1882 we come across evidences of individual states setting up normal schools for the training of teachers. The list of training schools existing before 1882 is given as under :

1. The first Normal School was set-up as Serampur by the Danish missionaries.
2. Educational societies in Bombay, Madras and Calcutta established some centres for the training of teachers in their respective are as.
3. The Government also set-up a few institutions for training teachers at Poona, Surat and Calcutta.
4. Government Normal Schools were also opened at Agra in 1852, Meerut in 1856 and Banaras in 1857.
5. Wood's Despatch recommended the opening of teachers-training schools, but nothing was done in this respect.
6. The Stanley's Despatch of 1859 provided a salary grant to trained teachers only.

By 1882, there were 106 training schools for elementary and two only for secondary schools.

**Indian Education Commission 1882**

The Indian Education Commission gave the following suggestions with regard to teacher education :

1. It urged the establishment of a number of training schools throughout the country.
2. An examination in the theory and practice of teaching was recommended for secondary school teachers.
3. Separate training arrangements for graduate and undergraduate teachers with separate courses of training and Syllabus. Towards the close of the 19th century, there were six training colleges and fifty six training schools for secondary teachers.

**Government Resolution of 1914**

1. Suggested highly qualified and trained teachers on the staff of training colleges.
2. Training colleges should be suitably equipped.
3. A practising school should be attached to a training college.
4. There should be one year's training course for graduates and post-graduates leading to a degree and two years for under-graduates and others leading to teacher's certificate.

On account of these recommendations, there was a great increase in the number of training institutions and better facilities for the trainees began to be offered.

**Calcutta University Commission 1917**

It laid stress on :

1. Creation of a department of education in the universities.

2. Increase in the output of trained teachers.
3. Systematising research work on training in the universities.

**Hartog Committee Report 1929**

It recommended that :

1. The standard of general education of Primary school teachers be raised.
2. Arrangements for refresher courses and in service training be made for the trained teachers.
3. Course of training be sufficiently long.

As a result of above recommendations, teacher training went on benefitting. The standard of training and consequently teaching improved considerably.

**Teacher Education in Free India**

A great change was needed after independence because of the changed social and political conditions. The traditional system of education with its attendant defects did not suit the new conditions. Alongwith the change in the educational pattern teacher's training had to be considered afresh. It is now being based and conducted according to the needs of the pupils and also of the society.

After Independence many types of teacher's training courses were started throughout the country. While in the Punjab there have been two types of teacher-education courses, one Junior Basic Training (now two years duration) meant for elementary school teachers and the other B.T., B.Ed., (one years's duration) for secondary school teachers. At present in Punjab, there is B.Ed. course for secondary school teachers. B.T. has been abolished from 1966. In fact B.T. has merged into B.Ed. and there is a change in the syllabus.

In other states even three years courses have been started for elementary school teachers. There is also M.Ed. of one year after B.T. or B.Ed. in all the provinces. In some universities research in education is being done by post-graduates at the Ph.D. stage.

**In-service Education Programme.** In-service education programme is undertaken these days to enable the teacher to grow professionally. The holding of short-term courses, workshops, seminars and conferences for teachers in service is the responsibility of the State Education Departments. The Ministry of Education, Government of India has set-up a Department of Extension services in a number of training colleges with the financial assistance from the Ford Foundation. The Extension Services Department performs the following activities :

1. Holding of workshops, seminars, group work and conferences.
2. Audio-visual aids service.
3. Publication of literature.
4. Arranging educational exhibitions.
5. Guidance programme.
6. Short and long term courses.

### Importance of Training of Teachers

The importance of teachers in the educational programme of a country is too great. They are the pivot of the system. It is the teachers who interpret the curriculum and aids of instruction. It is they who give an impress of their personality to the children. The teachers have played an important role in the making of a nation. The quality of men in a country are determined by the type of teachers that a country possesses. Teachers work as active agents in ushering forth a new social order and economic policies which in turn affect educational policies.

## Need for Training

Seventy percent of the teachers are trained and the rest are untrained. The percentage of trained women teachers is too low. To cope with this ever increasing demand we need more training schools and colleges because profession training is necessary. There was a belief sometimes ago that teachers are born and not made. Mastery of the subject-matter was all that was expected of a teacher. With the advancement in sciences and humanities, the old belief has changed now. Teaching now is regarded as an expert's job and as such some sort of training is deemed essential. In fact, the whole concept about teachers and teacher education has undergone a great change.

**1. Education has been Psychologised.** A trained teacher understands the child better. Pedagogy demands that the teacher should know the subject as well as the child. What a mighty change in education? Formerly the teacher was required to know the subject matter and not the child.

**2. Education is more than Teaching Learning.** Education is not merely confined to the study of books. It has to consider other co-curricular activities for the wholesome development of the child's personality. An untrained teacher will be at a loss to undertake all these responsibilities properly.

**3. Teaching-Learning Process Needs Motivation.** Before giving knowledge, the children are mentally prepared for it. They have to be active participants in the process. A trained teacher would be adept in using aids and other material for properly motivating them.

**4. Training Equips the Teacher Properly.** It has been realised that there are certain qualities which a teacher acquires through training alone; these are physical, intellectual, social and emotional qualities. Professional efficiency is increased.

**5. Training Essential for Effective Education.** Training of teachers is of great importance to make education effective. Education degenerates into formal instruction in the hands of untrained teachers. Education becomes meaningless and dull under their charge. Training prepares the teacher for his job and makes him competent. He discovers his ability and makes proper use of it. Education, therefore, is rendered more effective at the hands of trained teachers.

**6. Essential for Professional Growth.** For efficient and perfect teaching, professional growth of the teacher is necessary. Training prepares the teachers under training for a new calling in life and gives a purpose to it.

**7. Teaching is a Complex Affair.** Teaching is not as simple as it used to be in the past. It has become more complex. A teacher has to be well-equipped and hence, the need for training. A teacher has to look after the social adjustment and emotional integration of the child.

From the above mentioned points, it is quite obvious that teacher's training is of paramount importance if we wish to raise general standards of teaching and learning. With the diversification of courses, the teacher has to come occupy an important place in the educational system. An untrained teacher cannot fit into it.

## Teacher Training Programme

The training of teachers in India can be classified under several heads. For different kinds of teachers, there are various kinds of teacher training programmes obtaining at different stages/levels.

**1. Primary Training Centres.** Training of teachers for pre-primary students is very important. Unfortunately facilities for pre-primary training are meagre in our country. At present there are nearly 40 training centres for primary class teachers. These different types of centres under this head—Nursery,

Kindergarten, Montessori and the Pre-basic etc. The number of these institutions should be increased.

**2. State Institutes of Education.** These were set-up in each state during the 3rd Plan Period. No regular courses are run by these institutes. These mostly provide in-service courses for teachers, teacher educators and the inspection personnel. These institutions besides organising workshops, seminars and short orientation courses also undertake the publication of literature and solving the problems of primary school teachers. These institutions serve as a guide to all those connected with primary education.

**3. Training Schools for Primary Teachers.** In view of the introduction of the compulsory primary education in practically all the states and the growing consciousness among the people to send their children to schools, there has been a considerable expansion of training schools for primary teachers. The number of such institutions is in the neighbourhood of 1250. These training centres are open to men and women teachers; some are centirely for men while others exclusively for women. Only a few are co-educational. This training is open to Matric pass and the duration of the course is one to two years. It differs from state to state.

**4. Regional College of Education.** These institutions prepare teachers for technological subjects, agriculture, commerce and other practical streams in the various multi-purpose schools. Four regional training colleges exist—one each at Ajmer, Bhopal, Bhubneshwar and Mysore. These colleges are managed by the National Council of Educational Research and Training. These provide one year courses for graduates in technology, commerce, agriculture, home science and science, an integrated four years' course for higher secondary pass candidates for similar subjects, special courses for industrial craft teachers and other short term in-service courses and programmes.

**5. Training Colleges for Secondary Teachers.** There are two types of secondary school teachers—graduates and under-graduates and training exists for both. For the under graduates the duration of the course is one or two years, while for the graduates it is one year. The former are awarded diplomas either by the university or education department and the latter are given a degree by the university. There is some difference in the curriculum of these courses but basic training remains the same. Some differences may be found from one state to another. The graduates and post-graduates receive training in training-colleges whose number is about 250 in the country. These colleges are both owned by the state Governments or private bodies and are mostly co-educational. Some institutions are exclusively for women.

**6. Post Graduate Training Courses.** After the B.T. and B.Ed. Courses, facilities for post-graduate degrees also exist in colleges and universities. These are M.Ed. and Ph.D. Courses. Besides these, there are diploma courses in special areas such as Educational Administration, Guidance and Counselling.

## Existing Programmes of Teacher Education

After achieving independence, there has been a good deal of expansion in training schools and colleges. With expansion, numerous problems have arisen which require our immediate attention. The standards of training have gone down. There is no planned working of training institutions in the country. This problem can be viewed in its two aspects: *(i)* the quantitative and *(ii)* qualitative. As regards the quantitative aspect is concerned, more secondary teachers and primary teachers per year would be required to meet the additional increase in primary and secondary schools. This would obviously mean huge expansion of training facilities and hence, more of institutions.

This expansion if not wisely conducted is bound to lead to further deterioration in training. It is true that our education has remained unchanged even after independence. There is therefore, a great and urgent need not only to offset this deterioration that has taken place but also to strengthen our teacher education programme. Thus, the following points need to be improved :

**(1) Selection.** There cannot be two opinions on the selection of teachers for training. For an important profession such as teaching, proper recruitment would be useful. Selection is a relative term. If the number of applicants is larger, some selection methods would be evolved and if the number of candidates is less, they have all to be admitted. The actual position is that some of the Government Training Colleges and a few good private institutions have selection methods while others have to find out trainees for their institutions.

Right type of students do not come forward for this profession. The intelligent and the superior candidates do not find the profession attractive. The third class students (barring a few exceptions) generally decide to become teachers because there are no other avenues for them.

**Suggestions**

*(a)* The minimum qualification for admission to B.Ed. should be second division in B.A., or B.Sc. degree. This may be relaxed in the case of M.A. and M.Scs.

*(b)* Preference should be given to those who had taken up education as one of their subjects in their degree classes.

*(c)* Marks in the subject of education could be a good indication of interest and success in the profession.

*(d)* Interest, intelligence and aptitude tests should be given to the candidates.

*(e)* Proper interview can also reveal the right type of candidates for the profession.

(*f*) Education should be introduced as an elective subject at the degree stage where there is no such arrangement.

**(2) Integrated Teacher Training.** There is a great need for an integrated programme of teacher education. At present there are a great variety of teacher training institutions in our country preparing teachers for different stages of education. It seems to be a wrong policy to compartmentalise teacher education programmes at different levels. Teacher education ought to be viewed as an integrated whole.

**Suggestions**

(*a*) Training of all types of teachers—elementary, secondary, science, craft, domestic science etc. should be under one roof to enhance the academic atmosphere of training of teachers.

(*b*) If for administrative reasons all the training classes cannot be conducted in one institution, these institutions with separate heads can be placed in one big campus, where they can easily coordinate their efforts.

**(3) Teacher Training Programme.** Our teaching methods have out-grown and hence, training programmes are lifeless. The syllabi and the courses of instruction are completely out-of-date. They have failed to keep pace with modern ideas in education. Thare is no co-ordination between theory and practice. There is a greater emphasis on theory and less on practice teaching.

**Suggestions**

(*a*) Greater stress should be laid on the practical aspect of the training programme.

(*b*) New and practical methods of teaching should be evolved to suit Indian conditions.

(*c*) The teaching practice should be on internship or apprenticeship basis for about three months during which the pupil teachers should be attached to a school as whole time teachers.

(*d*) Trainees should be encouraged to think critically on educational problems.

**(4) Teacher Educators.** Our training institutes are ill staffed and understaffed. Owing to financial stringency they cannot maintain a proper and required student-teacher ratio. The staff members are over-loaded with work. Research work cannot be undertaken.

**Suggestions**

(*a*) There should be adequate staff because seminars, group discussions, paper reading and other jobs cannot be performed. Teaching without these would be useless.

(*b*) There should be at least one with Ph.D. qualification and others should be M.Ed.'s.

**(5) Better in Service Facilities.** It has been observed that newly trained teachers often forget what they have learnt in colleges of education as soon as they join schools. They follow the traditional method, may be for convenience sake or may be that old hands ridicule them. So in-service facilities should be provided to every trained teacher.

**Suggestions**

(*a*) Summer institutes during holidays should be organised.

(*b*) To overcome the difficulty every teacher should be required to attend refresher short-term courses at least once a year. This will brush up his knowledge. A regular programme of in-service education of trained teachers in the field is necessary.

(*c*) The present in-service facilities being inadequate need to be expanded by establishing an Extension Unit in every secondary training college.

**(6) Need for Better Administration.** Teacher education till now had been a neglected subject. At present it has been given some importance and hence, accepted as Professional Education. But it is a pity that there is defect in administration and teacher education and it has not received that recognition which it deserves. The administration needs to be activised.

**Suggestions**

(*a*) The Central Government should assume statutory responsibility for teacher education and establish a National Council for Teacher Education. It should be charged with the Planning work, Co-ordination and Maintenance of Teacher Education standards.

(*b*) Similarly State Councils should be established for each state to pursue the work of Central National Council.

**(7) Need for Better Economic and Social Status.** It is needless to say that the salary scales of our teachers have become a national scandal. A primary teacher in most of the states draws less than a peon of the central Government and the pity is that he is called the nation builder. When teachers are so poorly paid, it is not possible to attract the right type of people to the profession.

**Suggestions**

(*a*) Salary scales should be so revised as to ensured an honourable living.

(*b*) The economic status of teachers should be at least equal to that of equally qualified persons in other comparable professions.

(*c*) Security of service should be guaranteed to them.

**(8) Need for Increasing Research and Publications.** Training institutions should not be merely teaching shops. These are generally knowledge imparting centres. In the absence of good books and professional literature for teachers and teacher educators, the standards of teaching have fallen. Books and journals which deal with the problems of education from Indian point of view are few.

**Suggestions**

(*a*) Selected (efficient) training institutions should be asked to assume the literature production responsibility suited to Indian needs.

(*b*) Research departments be added to really good institutions for research work. Arrangements should be made to publish the research investigations so that teachers may benefit.

**(9) Finance Requirement.** The development of teacher education has suffered for paucity of funds. Most of training institutes are staggering and practically struggling for existence. Some of these do not justify their existence, being without adequate teaching staff, libraries hostel facilities etc.

**Suggestions**

(*a*) Institutions without excellent arrangements should be better closed down than allowed to function in a poor way.

(*b*) Better grant-in-aid should be given to these institutions enabling them to maintain the respectable desired standards.

**(10) Training Wastage.** Considerable amount of wastage is taking place in teacher training programmes. Quite a large number of students fail because of poor instruction. Some of the trained teachers finding their jobs less remunerative, give up the profession altogether. In the case of women teachers, there is still a greater wastage. They give up the profession after marriages or for other reasons like not getting a post at a secure place etc.

**Suggestions**

(*a*) Evaluation techniques should be devised in such a way that minor wastage takes place.

(*n*) Teachers' economic and social status should be raised.

**(11) Status of Training Colleges.** The status accorded to the training colleges is inferior. They are not considered on par with the post graduate institutions. This is obvious that the Government have not realised the importance of teacher training centres. This leads to a doubtful status of the lecturers working in them.

**Suggestions**

Teachers deserve the status of post-graduate teachers because they teach the graduates and prepare them for a degree in education. They should be given all those facilities which teachers in post-graduate institutions enjoy.

**Recommendations of the Education Commission on Teacher Education**

The Education Commission's recommendations on teacher education are of significant importance. It felt that in order to make the professional preparation of teachers effective, teacher education must be brought into the main stream of the academic life of the universities, on the one hand and school life and educational development on the other.

The following suggestions have been given by it :

**1.** (*a*) Schools of education should be established in selected universities to develop programmes in teacher education, studies and research in education.

*(b)* Organization of student practice teaching in active collaboration with selected schools and these schools should receive substantial grants for equipment.

*(c)* Extension work should be reorganised as an essential function of a teacher education institution and Extension Service Department be added to each institution.

*(d)* Recognition of education as an independent academic discipline and its introduction as an elective subject in the B.A., B.Sc., M.A. and M.Sc., degree courses.

*(e)* Establishment of effective alumni associations to bring old students and faculty together to discuss and plan programmes and curricula.

*(f)* Establishing comprehensive colleges of education in each state on a planned basis.

*(g)* Arranging periodic exchange of the staff of the co-operating schools and of the teacher education institutions for the advantage of each category of staff.

**2. Improving Professional Training.** *(a)* Introducing integrated courses of general and professional education in universities.

*(b)* Using methods of study which leave greater scope for self study and discussion and methods of evaluation which include continuous internal assessment of practical and sessional work besides practice-teaching.

*(c)* Improvement of training institutions.

*(d)* Improving practice-teaching and making it a comprehensive programme of internship.

**3. Expansion of Training Facilities.** *(a)* Each State should prepare a plan for the expansion of teacher training facilities in its area to that the output of trained teachers meets the demand for teachers.

*(b)* Supplementary part time facilities should be provided on a large scale.

*(c)* The backlog of untrained teachers should be cleared during of the 4th Plan Period through suitable measures.

**4. Improving Teacher Education Institutions.** *(a)* The staff of secondary training colleges should have a double Master's degree in academic subject and education, a fair proportion should hold doctorate degrees.

*(b)* Qualified specialists in psychology, sociology, science or mathematics may be appointed even if they have no professional training.

*(c)* Summer Institutes should be organised for the in-service training of staff.

*(d)* Attempt should be made to recruit first and good second class students in teacher training institutions and adequate scholarships should be given to them.

*(e)* All tuition fees in secondary teacher training institutions should be abolished and liberal provision made for stipends and loans.

**5.** *(a)* **Duration of the Course.** The duration of the professional courses should be two years for primary teachers who have completed the secondary school course and one year for the graduate students. The number of working days in a year should be increased to 230.

*(b)* **New Professional Courses.** New professional courses should be developed to orientate headmasters, teacher educators, educational administrators, to their special field of work.

*(c)* **Flexible Post-Graduate Course in Education.** The post-graduate courses in education should be flexible and be planned to promote an academic and scientific study of education requiring special knowledge and initiative.

**6. Professional Preparation of Teachers in Higher Education.** *(a)* Some orientation is necessary for teachers in higher education and suitable arrangements should be made.

*(b)* Orientation courses for new staff should be organised in every university and where possible, in college.

*(c)* Newly appointed lecturers should be given some time to adjust themselves to the institutions and should be encouraged to attend lectures of good teachers.

**7. In-service Education.** *(a)* Systematic and co-ordinated programmes of in-service education, in content and method, should be organised by universities.

*(b)* The programme of summer institutes for the in-service training of secondary school teachers should be extended with systematic follow-up.

**8. Standards of Teacher Education.** *(a)* The U.G.C. should take the responsibility at the national level for the maintenance of standards in teacher education.

*(b)* The U.G.C. should set-up a standing committee for teacher education.

*(c)* The U.G.C. should be given substantial funds in the $4^{th}$ Plan for improvement in the teacher education.

❋❋❋

# 11

# National Integration and Education

India is a land of diverse religions, faiths, castes, creeds and communities. There is also diversity of culture. National integration consists in discovering unity in diversity. It is oneness of the nation. It is based on a feeling of oneness, common ideals of life and a common code of behaviour. It is the negation of all differences of castes, creeds, provinces or regions. National integration is a feeling among people to share certain common objectives, purposes and sacrificing personal interest for the interest of the nation. It is the unity of India, taking pride in her past achivements and confidence in her future progress.

## Need for National Integration

India is facing a crisis and a grave danger from the internal conditions. There are different fissiparous tendencies which are disintegrating and pose a threat to national solidarity. These forces have always got the upper hand throughout the Indian history and had brought her downfall. Once again they are very active. It is a fact that the country is surrounded by certain countries which are hostile to it. But it is a reality that external danger or danger, of war is not so great as the internal danger. National and emotional integration is therefore essential to stand united and if there is unity, no nation will dare attack India. National integration is necessary to create throughout the length and breadth of this nation an idealistic concept of the greatness and unity of India, of pride in her past achievements and confidence in her future progress. The beauty lies in welding the people into one strong national unit, maintaining all our wonderful diversity.

A nation is a nation because its people passionately and unanimously believe themselves to be so. In fact, for the fulfilment of our democracy national integration is a must. National integration is possible through emotional integration. According to the Prime Minister, Mrs. Indira Gandhi, national integration is vital for India's survival, especially at a time when the country is under the perpetual threat of foreign aggression as well as the internal centrifugal forces of regionalism, communalism, racialism, etc.

National integration is necessary to stop the country from fragmentations, to bring a sense of unity among the people and to stop history to be repeated or being repeated. It is also essential to create among all the citizens of this country, a spirit of patriotism, a love of one's own people and a realization that destiny lies with the other people of this land. Thus, we can say that national integration is a psychological and educational process involving the development of a feeling of unity, solidarity and cohesion in the hearts of the people, a sense of common citizenship and a feeling of loyalty to the nation.

**Emotional Integration**

Emotional integration is the national integration. It is through training of the mind and heart that a sense of oneness among the people of a country can be inspired. Emotional integration is a feeling among people to share certain common objectives, purposes or ideals and giving them high place over smaller or sensational loyalties. "When the emotions are conditioned by the idea of national loyalty and are directed towards national welfare, the result is national integration." It is thus, very true that complete national integration is impossible without emotional integration or national harmony.

**Education For National Integration**

Education is a panacea to all ills. It is a great weapon against the evil forces which bring the country to the verge of national disintegration. For this it is essential to re-organise the system and devise means to check the forces responsible for national disintegration. The following need a special mention :

(*a*) Communalism.

(*b*) Unemployment.

(*c*) Provincialism.

(*d*) Persistence of inequality.

(*e*) Lack of Vision in Education.

(*f*) Cultural diversity.

(*g*) Linguism.

(*h*) Favouritism and Corruption.

**Objective of Education For National Integration**

The following should be the objectives of education for national integration :

(*a*) To develop attitudes, dispositions, sense of values and spirit of sacrifice and tolerance.

(*b*) To achieve emotional integration and develop emotionally integrated personality.

(*c*) To promote understanding between Communities and States.

(*d*) To provide intimate knowledge of the different aspects of the country to the citizens.

## Programme of Education for National Integration

Indian National Integration Committee has recom-mended the following programme :

(*a*) Promotion of opportunities for minorities in the economic field.

(*b*) Role of Educational Agencies.

(*c*) National outlook in the fields of education and others spheres.

(*d*) Maintenance of Security of Person and Property.

Besides this it is necessary to equip students with an intimate knowledge of the different aspects of this country; encouraging all studies and activities which lead to greater understanding between communities and states and fostering a feeling for national unity. It is also essential to create a feeling that the country and its resources belong to the citizen who thereby acquires certain rights and privileges alongwith corresponding duties and responsibilities. A more concrete programme is given below :

**1. Revision of the Curriculum.** Curriculum needs to be re-designed. A few new subjects, topics, activities ond other necessary features should be included in it. Folk-tales, regions of India, biographies of the national heroes, human geography, a simple account of the heritage of each region in art, industry and literature and a simple account of the social development in India, people, map-reading, scientific and industrial dovelopment in India should be specially emphasised. Indian history, social studies and other social sciences should be a separate curriculum for the separate stages of education. Study of an Indian language other than the regional language should be made a part of the curriculum.

**2. Religious and Moral Education.** A tolerant study of all the religions and religious harmony are the basic things for achieving national and emotional integration. Religious and moral education should support moral character, train emotions and help in the cultivation of social and spiritual values. Since India is a secular democratic country, it is therefore very essential to have a secular, democratic and dispassionate religious policy and programme for religious education in the schools and colleges. The ideals of secularism should be properly interpreted.

**3. To have a National System of Education.** For this, Kothari Education has rightly emphasised the need for a national system of education. It is suggested that various recommendations of the commission must be implemented as a whole throughout the country.

**4. Co-curricular Activities.** Activities like daily assemblies, talks, loyalty, open air dramas, exchange of students, tours, variety programmes, film, folk festivals, celebration of important days of national significance, birth anniversaries of great men of the country, N.S.S., N.C.C. Camps, Scout and girl-guide camps, social service should be organised whole-heartedly. Singing of National Anthem, Jai-Hind as the mark of greeting, organising various projects, religious ceremonies etc., are a few more activities to be included in the programme.

Much has been said about tbe need and importance of national integration. The country must explore and mobilise its resources to evolve a concrete national programme. In this programme co-operation of parents, society, teachers and people as a whole must be secured. This reminds us the famous words of Dr. S. Radha Krishnan, who said, "National Integration cannot be built by brick and mortar or with chisel and hammer. It has to grow silently in the minds and education." Thus, it is the collective responsibility of all citizens--politicians, educationists, artists, writers, teachers, parents and students, intellectuals, businessmen and trade union leaders. Let us live for our nation and establish cordial relations with others Nations as well. We must follow the footprints of our great leaders and make our nation strong and great.

## Educational Programme For Securing National Integration

Education can play an important role in strengthening the bonds which make us Indians first and Indians last whatever our religion, language, caste or political affiliations. Our educational system should be geared to bring about national consciousness among our people. Schools and Colleges must be made centres for the realisation of national ideal. The students must be made to feel that they belong to a worthy national community which had a brilliant past and present full of hopes ultimately merging into a glorious future. Education must make the youngmen realise that they are very closely bound to the nation and its destiny and that in the welfare of the nation lies their welfare. They must be mentally prepared to share its joys and sorrows. Education can foster a feeling of oneness and nationalism, a spirit of sacrifice and tolerance. These will further help them to submerge their narrow group of personal interests in the large interests of the country.

## What can Education do in This Direction?

**1. Evolving a National System of Education.** Since 1947, we have been trying to evolve a common system of education for the country and the more we are trying, the more we are drifting away from it. The Central and State Government do not pull together in the matter. There should be proper co-ordination between the Centre and the States. The Central Government should first confer with the States before taking decisions and once agreed up, must enforce those decisions with all the power at their command. The recommendation of the Education Commission (1964-66) are important in this respect. This samework suggested by it should be accepted by all the States. They may differ only in their subjects and curriculum. Other things should remain the same. Educational patterns and standards should be uniform all over the country.

**2. Improvement in Textbooks.** Textbooks should be improved and reoriented. Proper care should be taken in the preparation of history textbooks and textbooks for the primary class. Facts should not be distorted or mis-represented or exaggerated lest they should create prejudices.

**3. Co-curricular Activities.** Co-curricular activities occupy a very important place in education. These are sports, scouting, N.C.C., A.C.C., Girl Guiding, camps, debates, symposia, dramatics, youth festivals and tours etc. These activities help in the growth of a well-balanced and well adjusted personality. They develop a spirit of comradeship and fellow feeling among students.

**4. Adapting Education to Economic and Social Needs.** If education is not planned for the development of aptitudes and abilities of students and for the economic and social progress of the country, there will be inecreasing wastage of human talent and material resources, resulting in bitterness and frustration which are obstacles to national integration, therefore education should suit the aptitudes and abilities of the students. It should meet the economic and social needs of the country.

There should be more terminal stages where the students could branch off and enter different walks of life and at each terminal stage there should be provision for vocational and semi-vocational training. Admission to Universities should be restricted to only those who are likely to benefit from such education.

**5. Re-orientation of the Curriculum.** It has been realised by an the educationist that the curriculum at the secondary and college levels should be so reoriented so as to suit the need of our young men.

**6. Uniform for Students.** Each school and college should prescribe uniforms for their students. This will bring about uniformity and the poor and the rich students will look similar. There will be no unnecessary showing off the rich children in beautiful clothes.

**7. Reverence for the National Flag, National Days and National Anthem.** Students should be told the history of the National Flag and asked to respect it. Stories of heroes who laid down their lives for the honour of their flag, should be told to them. National days should be celebrated with enthusiasm. The importance of National Anthem and its meaning should be told to them. They should be taught to sing it in unison and behave in a disciplined manner when it is sung.

**8. Tours.** Travelling if an education by itself Rousseau recommended travels for Emile as he thought that her education without it would remain incomplete. Through tours of the country one learns history, geography and sociology in practice. These will bring the people closer. At present a Madrasi may not have a thorough knowledge about the Punjab is and their state and *vice versa*. Tours will improve the knowledge of the students and a spirit of oneness would be created. If Youth Hostels are set-up at important places in the entire country, it will help the tourists.

**9. Exchange of Teachers.** Teachers should be deputed periodically to other states so that a large range of students can benefit from their experience. This can be tried at the University level as well.

**10. School Projects.** Several projects can be conducted by the schools in order to improve the general knowledge of the students. Information of the country's resources, man-power, production projects, architectural monuments and dams etc., can be given through projects.

**11. Scholarship Facilities.** Democracy provides everyone with equal opportunities. Poor talented students need help to enable them to prosecute higher studies. Selection for higher education should be made purely on the basis of economic conditions and merit. Greater assistance should be provided to students from backward communities and areas. None should suffer because of social and economic disabilities. Poor intelligent students should be provided adequate scholarship so that the country benefits from them fully.

**12. Exchange of Educationists.** A reserve pool of educationists should be created in the centre and there should be a free exchange of them between states. This will lead to better inter-state understanding, ultimately resulting in national integration. Students who come into contact with these educationists will realise that knowledge knows no regional distinctions.

**13. Change in School Education.** A change in the school educational system is badly needed. Better education can be instrumental to national integration. The school education objectives should be so restated so as to develop emotional integration *e.g.*, practice of healthy living and self-confidence, participation in cultural and creative activities, developing patriotism and inculating a spirit of universal brotherhood in children.

**14. Study Tours.** Study tours to important educational centres in the country are sure to exercise a profound effect in enlarging human sympathy and understanding. It is true that with change of place, we change our ideas, our opinions and feelings. Life-transforming experiences are gained through personal face to face contact and group discussions.

**15. University Education.** The universities should maintain uniformly high standards through a better system of admissions, prescription of good textbooks and syllabi and good teaching personnel. Universities should fight against casteism and communalism in all their manifestations. The Universities can foster mutual respect of all religions.

**16. Through a Common Link Language.** A common language should be evolved so that the people are drawn closer. The use of Indian languages as the medium of instruction from the lowest to the highest stage of education helps national integration.

**17. Importance of Literature.** Importance of literature towards national integration can hardly be disputed. Pt. Nehru said, "Art and literature often give greater insight into a nation's soul than the superficial activities of the multitudes." Literature is the expression of a nation's mind in writing. Literature depicting the customs and traditions, patriots and heroes of the country can be prepared. Its study will enable the students have a clear idea of one's country.

**18. All India Youth Organization.** An All India Youth organization should be set-up to coordinate all the youth programmes that the central and State Governments can undertake.

### Factors which Determine Unity and Integration

India is a vast country with great diversity of culture, religion, language and caste etc. The main factors responsible for national disunity are described below :

**1. Cultural Diversity.** The people of each state have different culture. Even people in the urban and the rural areas have different habits. Customs of marriage, food habits and occupations also differ from place to place. These difference impede the work of national integration.

**2. Religious Diversity.** There are fanatics among all communities and they cause communal disharmoney. They exploit the ignorant masses in the name of religion. Religious fanaticism is, perhaps the greatest disintegration force in our country. Religious madness has plaimed many precious lives. It was communal frenzy which led to the cartition of this sacred land of ours. As a matter of fact, religious considerations should not inflluence the administration of justice and other state policies. Religious discrimination should be avoided.

**3. Lack of Idealism.** There is complete absence of idealism in our public activities. We should tap the spring of idealism to inspire a person to identify himself with something higher and bigger.

**4. Regionalism.** The feeling of regionalism also impedes integration.

**5. Provincialism.** One does not feel at home in another province because of the mounting spirit of provincialism which breeds hatred.

For instance people of Rajasthan may find difficult to live honourably in Calcutta. Bengalis' provincialism may deter others to settle down in Bengal. Similarly a Behari may feel awkward in Punjab. So provincialism is prejudicial to national integration.

**6. Geographical Diversity.** India being a big country, has diverse geographical features. Obviously the people of this country speak different languages and have different customs and traditions. Some of the people live in intractable hilly areas like, Assam and are cut off from the national main stream and take part in anti-national activities.

**7. Problem of Language.** A common nationality generally presupposes a common language. We have many languages and that is why there is no common link between the people of states. As a matter of fact, multiplicity of languages should be in reality no bar to a common nationhood. In England there are many languages, English, Welsh, Gaelic etc., but they have English as the link language. In Russia again there are dozens of languages but yet they enjoy national solidarity.

Similarly in India we can develop and study different languages and maintain one language, Hindi as the lingua franca. Unity of language is one of the most marked features of nationality. Unity through language is one of the strongest bonds that unite different communities in a country.

**8. Unemployment.** There is unemployment on an alarming scale in India both among the educated and the uneducated. Unemployed feel frustrated and become easy victims of anti-social and antinational activities employment opportunities to these young men will improve and help in national integration.

**9. Caste.** It is a great disruptive tendency. It is a great check on progress. People are very much caste-ridden. It widens the gulf between the people of the different castes and prevents their coming closer. This system causes irritation and heart-burning among people. It prevents the people of low castes to improve their condition. Caste system has resulted in sub-dividing the people. Castes which enjoy traditional economic and ritual dominance exploit the economically underpriviledged.

There is no doubt that with the diversities mentioned above it would be a very hard problem to build by national outlook and through it to achieve national integration. It is also true that the religious, linguistic and communal conflicts tend to disunite us. But in spite of all these things we can make a strong national unity by eschewing narrowness of all kinds, maintaining at the same time all our wonderful diversity. If we wish to live well, we have to submerge narrow group interest in the larger interests of the country. Our Government is trying her best to achieve national integration through educational programmes. For this the Ministry of Education of the Government of India appointed the Committee of Educational Integration under the chairmanship of Dr. Sampurnanand May 1961, which suggested ways and means to achieve this end.

The Education Commission of 1964-66 recommends the following for national integration :

*(a)* Adoption of a common school system of public education as the national goal.

*(b)* Development of community life in every educational institution.

*(c)* Organization of social and national service programmes concurrently with academic studies in schools and colleges and to make them obligatory for all students at all stages.

*(d)* Promotion of national consciousness through the promotion of understanding and reevaluation of our cultural heritage and the creation of a strong driving faith in the future towards which we aspire.

*(e)* Participation of the students in programmes of community development and national reconstruction at all stages of education.

❋❋❋

# Index

**E**



**F**



**G**



**H**



**I**



**J**



**K**



**L**

Other Books on

# TEXT BOOKS

Unit No. 220, Second Floor, 4735/22,
Prakash Deep Building, Ansari Road, Darya Ganj,
New Delhi - 110002, Ph.: 32903912, 23280047, 09811594448
E-mail: lotus_press@sify.com, www.lotuspress.co.in